SEXISM AND THE FEMALE OFFENDER

CAMBRIDGE STUDIES IN CRIMINOLOGY

Sexism and the Female Offender

An organizational analysis

Loraine Gelsthorpe
Series Editor: A.E. Bottoms

Gower

Aldershot · Brookfield USA · Hong Kong · Singapore · Sydney

Published by
Gower Publishing Company Limited
Gower House
Croft Road
Aldershot
Hants GU11 3HR
England

Gower Publishing Company
Old Post Road
Brookfield
Vermont 05036
USA

British Library Cataloguing in Publication Data
Gelsthorpe, Loraine
  Sexism and the female offender: an
  organisational analysis - (Cambridge
  criminology series)
  1. Women offenders. Imprisonment
  I. Title   II. Series
  364.3'74

ISBN 0 566 05443 4

Printed in Great Britain by
Billing & Sons Ltd, Worcester

HV
6046
G45
1989

Contents

List of tables and figures

Foreword

It is now some twenty years since the *Cambridge Studies in Criminology* first included within its list a study which focused solely on female offenders (Cowie, Cowie & Slater, *Delinquency in Girls*, 1968, vol. XXIII). That book has subsequently been the subject of critical comment, but it was very important at the time because issues relating to women and girls within criminological theory and within the criminal justice system were then largely hidden issues, neglected by criminologists, practitioners and politicians alike.

This study by Loraine Gelsthorpe moves on from descriptive, empirical accounts of female offenders; and importantly not only exposes some of the misconceptions and exaggerations in some early research studies, but also records the critical enterprises, mostly feminist, of the 1970s and early 1980s. Such critical enterprises have undoubtedly been important in focusing on the misrepresentation of female offenders in conventional criminological literature, in developing a critique of the 'accumulated wisdom' about female offenders, and in presenting exposés of discriminatory practices. Indeed, a whole generation of feminist researchers has sought out and exposed the sexism which exists within the criminal justice system.

The special contribution of this book is that it makes an evaluation of the feminist contributions in this sphere through a close and detailed account of how 'sexism' works in practice. Dr. Gelsthorpe's work probes beneath the descriptive accounts of institutionalized sexism and beneath the theoretical assertions about sexist ideology to explore how far feminist critiques in themselves help explain the internal life of the criminal justice system, and of other agencies which deal with women and girls.

Sexism and the Female Offender contributes to a growing body of sophisticated and subtle approaches and analyses of the law and social institutions in relation to women and girls. I am very pleased that we have been able to publish it in the *Cambridge Studies in Criminology* as a modern successor to *Delinquency in Girls*.

A.E. Bottoms

Preface and acknowledgements

This book is based on a Ph.D. thesis submitted to the University of Cambridge in 1984. Since that time my work has moved on and so too has the work of many to whom I refer. In retrospect, my methodology might have been different and new perspectives in the sociology of law more closely studied. Nevertheless, I think this study is still of value both for its substantive content and as an illustration of how people actually go about doing research.

Translating the thesis into a book has been a very different enterprise to writing the thesis. Accordingly, my debts of gratitude are now to those who have created the time for me to do it, and who have encouraged me to continue with it amidst mounting pressures and responsibilities.

My sincere thanks are offered to Pam Paige and Joanna Beamish who patiently and uncomplainingly dealt with the manuscript. I have received from them both practical support and friendship. My thanks are also offered to Jane Morris. I have benefited greatly from her critical comments and from her generous care and support.

The study on which this book is based could not have been undertaken without access to the three agencies which form the cornerstone of the research. I should like to thank the staff in all the agencies, their managing authorities and the young people I spoke with. My gratitude is not a whit less sincere because they remain unnamed.

Introduction

Many of those who have recently turned their attention to the study of women and crime have lamented the fact that the picture of women's crime is distorted and incomplete. Moreover, it has frequently been argued that the subject area is grossly neglected. It is undoubtedly surprising that the sex difference in crime has not been more frequently or more ardently pursued, and Barbara Wootton's early plea for more research into the sex differences in crime has oft been repeated:

> One of the few established features of criminology and one which is repeated right round the world is the fact that at all ages many more males than females are convicted. In scale and constancy, the sex difference far outweighs any other factor which we have yet been able to associate with delinquent behaviour. No one seems to have any idea why; but hardly anyone seems to have thought it worthwhile to try to find out. (Wootton, 1959: 318)[1]

But female offenders have always been thought of in different ways from male offenders, as less delinquent, less dangerous, and less involved in criminal subcultures and as a consequence they have less frequently provided a focus for criminological theory. Male offenders have been described both as inherently more criminally inclined and as rational, adventurous beings who sometimes stray beyond the confines of the criminal law to fulfil their own needs and desires, and theories about their offending are legion.

Explanations for the different level of interest in male and female offenders have rested upon the comparative rarity of the female offender, as if the female is 'good' or even 'morally superior' until she becomes the victim of adverse physiological, psychological and environmental influences. Indeed, for students of the 'women and crime' debate it has now become almost 'received wisdom' that women who commit crimes have largely been ignored or have been depicted in terms of stereotypes based on their supposed biological or psychological nature. In other words, because there are fewer female than male offenders dealt with by the criminal justice system, there has been a tendency to view female criminality in terms of individual characteristics and only peripherally in terms of social forces and influences.

Much discussion has been generated within criminological literature in recent years about the reasons for the neglect of women and girls and the use of biological positivism to explain their crimes. Many writers (who may be loosely defined as feminist) have suggested that both the relative neglect and the theories which exist express 'sexism', and that our knowledge about female offenders has been systematically distorted either by males alone or by male domination in a capitalist society. This is, of course, a dubious claim. First, the issue of women and crime is not the only 'blind spot' in criminology. This subject has traditionally focused on the young rather than the old, the poor rather than the rich, and so on. True, criminologists have also, at times, 'discovered' hitherto concealed criminalities, through self-report studies or through 'radical exposé' criminology which has looked, for instance, at corporate crime and the crimes of the powerful. However, one can still easily observe the 'selective' nature of criminological study, and its whole history may be described as erratic.[2] Secondly, in their writing about 'sexism' commentators tend to draw upon other people's texts and examples and they do not test out to any great degree whether or not the stereotypical images which they denigrate are held by modern-day practitioners in the various agencies which make up the criminal justice system. This means that claims about 'sexist' theories and practices tend to be pitched at a level of analysis which is not immediately accessible at the level of everyday activities of practitioners at work. Indeed, whilst there are numerous descriptive accounts of sexism and much emphasis on ideological elements of 'sexism', there has been little attempt to explore the nature of sexism as seen in the routine activities of practitioners who respond to female offenders.

The main aim of this book is to reveal how practitioners working in the criminal justice system and allied agencies view the young female offenders who pass through their hands, and to reveal how complicated the notion of sexism becomes once it is placed in an administrative and organizational context.

In the first chapter, therefore, I refer briefly to images of the female offender in theory, policy and practice. Such images and theories provide an important basis for current misunderstandings of female offenders. A main part of this chapter is a critique of common images and theories, concentrating on the contribution of writers who have claimed that the criminal justice system and allied agencies are imbued with sexism. There follows in Chapter 2 a description of the methodology employed and an exploration of images of girl delinquents in practice.

Chapters 3, 4 and 5 represent fieldwork in three different agencies (an observation and assessment centre for boys and girls, a regional 'secure' assessment and remand centre for girls and a police juvenile liaison office). These agencies carry out crucial 'gatekeeping' practices in relation to central parts of the criminal justice system (the courts and institutions), and therefore study of them is very significant in terms of measuring discriminatory of 'sexist' treatment.

I describe typical day-to-day considerations and beliefs which form the basis of practitioners' accounts of girls' delinquency or 'problem behaviour' and comment on some of the ways in which the conduct of girls is perceived and responded to as a distinct social problem. Initially, I look at the context of professional policy and commitments of the agencies' staff and then at the themes which emerge from their comments about girls and from their interpretations of girls' behaviour.

In the sixth chapter I address the issue of how images of girl offenders are shaped in practice and discuss how complicated the notion of sexism becomes once it is placed in an administrative and organizational context. Finally, I explore the implications of my fieldwork findings for wider feminist theories. When it is found that images of female offenders are mediated by a whole host of factors which cannot be directly linked to the notion of sexism, attempts to theorise the wider 'subjection' of women and girls remain at the level of rhetoric. Indeed, as a consequence of this finding, our acceptance of feminist theories about sexism and the discriminatory treatment of women and girls is shaken. This does not mean, however, that feminist arguments should be dismissed *in toto*. It means that they have to be modified, and the wide claims and assumptions about sexism more closely tied with the everyday activities of practitioners at work. Following this, the study of images of female offenders and discriminatory practices against them has to be more comprehensive than hitherto carried out.

I want to include two important caveats which may assist the reader in her/his reading of the book. It is clear from the literature that theorists and commentators have rarely conceived of female delinquency as a distinctive phase in females' lives, unlike male delinquency which is often viewed as a normal part of adolescence (West, 1967; West and Farrington, 1977; Heidensohn, 1970). Commentators more typically describe female delinquency in terms of a gender perspective than an age perspective (Hudson, 1981 and 1984). I also found this to be an accurate assessment of the ways in which female offending was perceived during my pilot work (see Appendix A). For this reason, my general comments about females apply to both girls and women. Similarly, my description of responses to girls should be taken to signify a number of themes which apply to females in general.

It is also important, perhaps, to explain why my research was carried out with the police and other agencies allied to the criminal justice system. The choice of a police agency requires less explanation than the assessment centres since it is widely considered to be a key route into the criminal justice and other control systems. The choice of the assessment centres was based on empirical evidence that there is often overlap (in terms of personal characteristics and life histories) between those who end up in the criminal and the care systems. There is also evidence to suggest that girls are more likely to end up in care, as opposed to the criminal justice system, even when they have committed offences (Casburn, 1979).

Thus I would argue that it is misleading to separate offence and care categories, both on empirical and theoretical grounds. The empirical objection is because those in need of care when they are, for example, in 'moral danger', 'beyond parental control' or not receiving education 'of the appropriate kind', are dealt with by the same people and in the same place as those charged with offending. Moreover, they are liable to some of the same dispositions as those appearing in court on criminal charges. The theoretical objection rests on the argument that the dichotomy between punishment and welfare, characteristic of many debates about juvenile justice, is a false one, and that the emphasis on welfare as opposed to penalty is rather an extension and transformation of judicial power (Donzelot, 1980; Hudson, 1983).

Notes
1. Wootton (1959).
2. Both Rock (1977) and Bottomley (1979) have made such observations regarding the nature of criminological research.

1 Images of girl offenders in theory and policy: institutional responses to girls

> Of all the vulgar modes of escaping from the consideration of the effect of social and moral influences on the human mind, the most vulgar is that of attributing the diversities of conduct and character to inherent natural differences.
>
> J. S. Mill, *Principles of Political Economy*, 1848

Responses to female offenders present a confusing patchwork of images. On the one hand, a female offender or delinquent is seen as 'weak', 'submissive' and 'dependent', and, therefore, in need of protection. On the other hand, her offending is associated with 'uncontrollable sexuality' or with the rejection of prescribed feminine roles (e.g., through aggressive behaviour) and therefore, she is an object of condemnation and contempt. In both cases, however, there is perhaps a further tendency to perceive the female as a creature of impulse, easily swayed by emotion and, in the extreme cases, incapable of fully intending her own actions (Henry, 1963). This frequently leads to the interpretation of her behaviour as mentally abnormal or unstable. Moreover, there is ample evidence that females are assumed to be less 'criminally inclined' than males, less recidivist, and so on. When they do offend, their actions are, for the most part, perceived as being symptomatic of a 'cry for help' requiring individualized help and understanding; actions resulting from a stressful home situation, for instance, are met with renewed concentration on 'coping at home' and with domestic life.

These themes abound in early theories about female criminality and in penal responses to women and girls. But the themes have been well rehearsed in recent texts.[1] In this chapter I shall concentrate on the responses to girl delinquents and restrict my critique of the trajectory of theories to a dimension of the general critique of early theories and writings about female offenders which is often neglected: the politics of sex differences.

Girls are different from boys, or so it is assumed by those professionals and practitioners (for example police, probation officers, educational welfare officers, social workers, teachers and magistrates) who deal with them. It is argued that girls need a different kind of handling from boys within the criminal justice system and allied agencies. This claim is not a new one. From the eighteenth century onwards there is considerable

1

evidence of both public and governmental concern about the 'irregularities in the moral behaviour' of girls.[2] There were numerous missions to 'save the souls of girls' (see for example, the White Cross Army, 1883). At the same time there were frequent and vociferous claims that delinquent girls, like their older sisters, were worse than boys. Carpenter (1853) quotes a number of writers on this topic. Mr Thompson, for instance, interested in children in the industrial schools, had this to say about girls:

> A poor half-starved outcast girl, trained up in ignorance and filth and sin, is even more painful and a more degrading sight than a boy of the same description. She seems to have fallen or to have been forced, into a state farther below her right place in the world than the boy. (Carpenter, 1853: 83)

Another of Carpenter's working associates, relating details of work in his own institutions stated:

> We find that though a wild boy, conscious of his own strength, may resist for a time, he soon yields to constraint, and probably before long, acknowledge thankfully the benefits bestowed on him in the form of compulsion; or he obeys from fear of a power which he feels to be superior; while the brutalised girl says decidedly, 'I will not', and abides by it; or furiously gnashes her teeth, clenches her fist, and stamps with her foot, in vain attempts to give vent to her rage. (Wichern, 1835, quoted ibid.: 84)

Carpenter herself was clearly in agreement with these statements:

> Let us, then, admit it to be a fact that young girls when low and degraded are worse than boys in similar circumstances. (Ibid.: 85)

And she notes, too, that girls were 'more refractory under imprisonment than boys', a comment which echoes those who wrote about the pains of imprisonment for women (Ibid.: 107–8).

Clearly, these practitioners found it more difficult to retain a hold over the girls and to make an impression on them, and a strange duel image of the girls persists. Girls are more vulnerable than boys and need a lot of care, but, at the same time, they can be more wicked. None the less, despite these observations and claims that girls were more difficult to 'rescue' than boys the main aim of the missions and societies to help girls was not to punish them *per se*, but to instil good virtues in them, to 'rouse a consciousness in them'. Mary Carpenter, inveterate critic of the penal system adopted for juvenile deliquents, argued all the more strongly that the existing system (whereby many juveniles were imprisoned) was iniquitous when it was used for girls:

> the present system adopted towards female juvenile deliquents is even more certain to prove their ruin than that of boys. (Ibid.: 83)

Indeed, the system which was needed to reclaim them was a 'wise and kind system'. (Ibid.: 83).

The establishment of reformatory and industrial schools for juveniles is described in detail elsewhere;[3] there was increasing provision for juveniles to be kept out of prison through this system during the latter half of the century. In so far as there was any special provision for juvenile girls one need look no further than the content of training programmes to realize that one of the prime objects of such a system was to teach boys and girls their respective occupational and domestic duties. Girls were to become home-makers and mothers, and steps towards these roles were indeed perceived to be steps towards redemption.[4]

The Prevention of Crime Act of 1908[5] set up borstal institutions for young men and women, to which they might be sent for not less than one year nor more than three. The first such institution for girls was established in a wing of Aylesbury Convict Prison.[6] Until the 1920s girls in this system shared the penal discipline of the Convict Prison with occupational activities of needlework, laundry work, general housework, cooking and gardening. Some attempts were made by individual governors in the years leading up to the war to make the regime more progressive, but it was not until the 1940s that further borstal facilities were set up in Holloway, Durham and Exeter.[7] The borstal system was thought to be a considerable success then and in post-war years; more facilities were introduced (mostly in existing prisons) though there were major developments, too, in setting up new institutions. Bullwood Hall in Essex was acquired in 1957 as a closed borstal (girls pregnant on admission were transferred to the borstal wing at Exeter Prison), and it opened in 1962. The first (and only) detention centre for girls was opened in 1962 in the grounds of Moor Court open prison. However, this did not survive long.[8]

Turning to approved schools, there was equal attention paid to the 'special needs' of girls. In a report of the Association of Headmasters, Headmistresses and Matrons of Approved Schools (1954) it is made clear that girls' admission to approved schools was primarily due to prostitution and sex offences.[9] Their 'needs' were, as a consequence, for medical treatment (in many cases) and for an emotional security which would divert their attention from sexual activities. In designing schools and school policy it was desirable to take note of the fact that 'girls appreciate the value of a homely atmosphere' (1954: 10) for instance. Also, girls were seen to be 'less gregarious than boys' and the report continues: 'delinquent girls are particularly individualistic' (1954: 10). As for special management problems within such a school, the report argued that there were recurring periods of emotional strain of a kind and an intensity that is rarely experienced in approved schools for boys. The reason was seen to be that:

Sex problems cause a great deal of worry and the hysterical, truculent or destructive girl tends to behave in a dramatic manner. Girls are more prone to form loyalties to individual members of staff and are less influenced by the intrinsic interest or absorption in the activities which the school can offer. (1954: 10)

Continuing these themes, Anneliese Walker (1962), for instance, clearly saw girls as 'less criminally inclined' than boys, as 'vulnerable' and 'at risk' of contamination from the more hardened delinquent boys. She viewed girls' behaviour as 'wayward' more than 'observably delinquent' as in the case of boys, and regretted that the two met in the arena of the juvenile court:[10]

> There is ample evidence that delinquent girls meet their boys for the first time in the precincts of a juvenile court or after they have become known as having been in trouble.
>
> ... one has to face the fact that once a girl has entered a juvenile court she is introduced to the world of delinquency. From that moment onward what matters to the girl most is to be accepted in her new group.... It is, therefore, not surprising that we find a considerable number of girls, who though in no way criminals themselves, become the affectionate, protective, wholly supporting though unstable partners of seriously delinquent youths and men. (Walker, 1962: 270)

Further, she argued that it was predominantly interpersonal conflicts which characterized and precipitated girls' entrance to the criminal justice system and that therefore relationship-building ought to feature in the response to girls.[11] For example she wrote:

> The greater need of girls (as distinct from boys) for personal contact with the head of an institution is now widely recognised. The way this relationship is used is in fact the most important therapeutic factor: it has been seen over and over again that the relationship between a girl and the headmistress remains in the girls' memory years after all the other things about the institution have been forgotten. (Walker, 1961: 276)

Indeed, researchers Parker, Casburn and Turnbull (1981) have reiterated the theme of girls' interpersonal relationship problems more recently in their summary of discussions with working-class adolescents who had attended juvenile courts. Their social workers and probation officers described:

> For girls... family conflicts ... and tensions proved a focal concern: for them, it seems, adolescence is not a time of youthful freedom, but of persistent attempts to struggle and bluff their way out of family restrictions. (Parker *et al.*, 1981: 18)

Nigel Walker, writing in 1965, described methods of dealing with the girls as extremely difficult:

> The senior girls' schools (approved schools), like borstals must be among the

most difficult establishments in the country to manage. Since most of the girls have already freed themselves from parental control such – as it was – they resent attempts to reimpose it, especially if they regard the staff as lacking in experience of 'life'. Moreover, many realise that had they been a year or so older they would have been exempt from this interference with their freedom. They abscond more than the boys do, and are in many ways more difficult to manage. (Walker, 1965: 306)

Of the hundred or so girls who were committed to borstal each year at that time, he said:

Most of them have histories of theft, 'breaking and entering' and other delinquencies, interspersed with stays in remand homes and approved schools; and they present some of the most difficult psychological and social problems with which the penal system has to deal today. (Ibid.: 306)[12]

Interestingly, the Advisory Council on the Penal System stressed the psychological problems of girls in their 1968 recommendation to the government that the only existing detention centre for girls should be closed without replacement. They concluded

We are sure that the detention centre concerned is not appropriate for girls. (Home Office, 1968: 1)

and argued that

The needs of delinquent boys and girls are so dissimilar that there is no reason why disposals open to the courts should be the same for both sexes. (Ibid.: 2)

Girls in trouble, it was said, are

usually unhappy and disturbed, often sexually promiscuous and often rejected by their families. They are usually in great need of help and understanding however reluctant to accept sympathy and affection they may appear to be. Frequently they need protection while they are given a chance to sort out their problems. (Home Office, 1968: 1)

Some of the psychological and behavioural problems of females within institutions are described in Hoghughi's study of disturbed juvenile deliquents. In 'Troubled and Troublesome' he noted that:

the girls emerge as substantially the more abnormal group in comparison with both extreme and ordinary boys. Fewer girls seem clinically as impulsive and extroverted with a delinquent self-image but more are emotionally and socially immature, aggressive, deficient in self-control, stubborn and emotionally unstable. (Hoghughi, 1978: 57)[13]

Hoghughi continued:

The girls have the greatest trouble in coming to terms with clear boundaries (i.e. structured environment). (Ibid.: 88)

Kozuba-Kozubska and Turrell (1978), however, take issue with some of these claims about highly disturbed adolescent populations. Referring to their own institution, the Bullwood Hall borstal, they argue:

> staff are expected to deal with girls within a nineteenth-century system which is designed to be operated by men for men and boys. The resulting difficulties, therefore, are often called problems peculiar to girls. Consequently we would go so far as to suggest that girls do not create any greater problems than boys: it is our inadequate response to their disturbed and perhaps different behaviour which gives rise to special problems. (Kozuba-Kozubska and Turrell, 1978: 4)

Nevertheless, within this critique lies an assumption that girls require different responses and handling from boys in such institutions.

Much of the evidence of mental instability amongst women has been derived from institutionalized samples. Numerous studies (e.g., Cowie, Cowie and Slater, 1968; Richardson, 1969; Goodman *et al.*, 1976) have noted rather high rates of 'psychiatric disorder' – rates which were higher than in other samples of male delinquents. For example, Goodman *et al.* (1976), in their eight year follow-up study of borstal girls, found that about one-fifth had been admitted to a psychiatric hospital at some time.

The main themes to emerge in this characterization of institutional responses to girls are that unhappiness, sexual promiscuity and familial rejection are all seen as features of the girls' problematic behaviour. In girls, we are told, appearances may be deceptive. In contrast to boys they are seen as relatively pathetic and helpless, in need of protection and help.[14]

Both Ackland's 1982 study of girls in care and Petrie's more recent research (1986) on girls in residential care, reported in *The Nowhere Girls*, confirm this claim. The school which *The Nowhere Girls* attended was based on a 'social care model'. The causes of committal to the institution were found to be mainly 'status conditions' (being out of control of the parent, being in moral danger, potential or actual sexual abuse, absconding from a place of safety and so on; Petrie,1986: 295).

It is significant that the Criminal Justice Act 1982, and the rearrangement and renaming of resources which it entailed, did not change the disparities in custodial provisions for males and females. The Act did not reintroduce detention centres for girls, and this is somewhat surprising, given the apparent increases in girls' crime at the time and the 'law and order' emphasis in the Act designed to meet public concerns about crime. Presumably the detention centre concept, with its primary emphasis on control and on providing a 'short, sharp shock' for miscreants, is still thought by policy makers and legislators to be inappropriate for girls.[15]

The 'case-work' response to girls

There is relatively little work on the possibility of a differential response to males and females within the context of social work supervision, probation orders, intermediate treatment, group work and so on. The work that does exist, however, is none the less informative in expressing what is thought to be appropriate. From 1948 to 1967[16] it appears that women and girls had to be supervised by women probation officers only, although these officers could supervise young boys. Walker (1965) has suggested that this was partly to protect women against abuse and partly on the assumption that their behaviour is better understood by other women rather than by men.[17] This 'case' work' approach to female offenders suggests that consideration of their supposed psychological needs and motivations tended to be uppermost in the minds of practitioners and policy makers (as well as magistrates). Thus their behaviour is interpreted in the light of these considerations. Gibbens (1959), for example, when attempting to measure the effectiveness of probation and supervision orders upon girls, spoke of their delinquency in terms of 'disturbed behaviour'. In his words,

> it is characteristic of girls that they nurse their grievances in silence until they burst out into disturbed behaviour in adolescence. (Gibbens, 1959: 102)

A further example is provided by Shacklady Smith (1975) who was repeatedly told by probation officers that there was no such thing as female delinquency:[18]

> Most female cases that came to their attention were those under care, protection and control orders and these girls were seen as not sophisticated delinquents, but rather deprived and sensitive adolescents, and extreme caution would have to be taken not to upset them in any way. (Shacklady Smith, 1975: 6)

Priestley *et al.* demonstrate that sex differences, or perceptions of sex differences, feature prominently in practitioners' views of boys and girls who are found guilty. The responses of the interviewees in their study, which included probation officers, police officers, social workers and juvenile court chairmen and women, indicated that:

> Boys were seen as aggressive, adventurous, active, gang-oriented creatures seeking outlets for their energy and their exhibitionist tendencies through criminal activity. Girls were thought of as domesticated, solitary, more mature and possibly cleverer than boys, who express their deviance via sexual misconduct or disturbed behaviour which does not break the law. (Priestly *et al.*, 1977: 46)

These views are reflected in the observations of Bambridge (1979) in an intermediate treatment centre. Practitioners in this field, she noted, did not view the general absence of girls from the centre as problematical (only two were referred in the first four years of the centre's operation). Their explanations were that, first, girls were not so likely to be involved in delinquent activities or 'gangs' and, secondly, that female offenders were bound to be treated more leniently by the police and were more likely to be cautioned rather than anything else. But significantly those who were referred were apparently 'more psychologically disturbed' and were seen, therefore, to be in need of 'more specialised help'.[19]

Further, Bambridge noted that, whereas the boys' intermediate treatment groups tended to be 'activity orientated', those formed for girls had a 'problem solving orientation'. Again, it was thought appropriate for the girls to be supervised by women who could, perhaps, offer greater understanding and intimacy, whereas the boys' groups were led by both males and females. The content of the intermediate treatment programmes for girls, she argued, despite the feminist framework within which they were set, contributed to the 'personal problem' syndrome which appears to be intrinsic to any conventional responses to females. The stated aims of one girls' IT group were

A.   to develop a positive self-image of themselves and of girls in general;

B.   to develop self-confidence to overcome passivity to become more assertive and more aware of their own needs and how they could best be met;

C.   to raise the possibility and discuss alternatives to traditional roles of wife and mother.

Bottoms and Pratt (1985) in a more recent study on intermediate treatment also note that most of the available literature on girls' intermediate treatment groups indicates that the sexuality problematic (the idea that girls are subjected to a range of discriminatory and unfair assumptions about themselves solely on account of their sex) is a prominent theme in these groups. They also suggest that what may be an attempt to treat perceived ideas about female sexuality as the problem, ultimately focuses on the supposed sexual problems of girls. This is a theme which I continue to address in the next section.

Sentencing patterns

Information about the 'perceived needs' of girls and views about their 'just desserts' can also be usefully gleaned from statistical analysis of sentencing disposal patterns. Statistics show, for instance, that females are more likely than males to be cautioned by the police rather than proceeded against. And figures on sentencing reveal a greater tendency to deal with girls by the way of conditional discharges, fines and super-

Table 1.1 Offenders cautioned for indictable offence: as % of persons found guilty or cautioned by sex and age (1982, 1983, 1984, 1985 and 1986)

| | Males | | | | | Females | | | | |
	1982	1983	1984	1985	1986	1982	1983	1984	1985	1986
10–14	70	74	75	79	81	88	90	91	93	94
14–17	38	42	45	51	55	65	68	71	78	80
17 and over	4	4	5	7	10	11	12	14	18	24
All ages	17	18	20	23	24	34	34	35	41	44

Source: Home Office, Criminal Statistics.

Table 1.2 Percentage of persons aged 10 and under 14 sentenced for indictable offences who received various sentences by sex and type of sentence or order in England and Wales

Sex and year	Percentage of total persons sentenced						
	Absolute or conditional discharge	Supervision Order	Fine	Attendance Centre Order	Care Order	Otherwise dealt with	Total
Males							
1971	26	28	20	12	12	–	100
1981	33	21	20	19	8	–	100
1984	39	18	17	20	5	1	100
1985	39	18	16	22	4	1	100
1986	42	17	15	21	4	1	100
Females							
1971	32	31	24	*	10	–	100
1981	39	26	24	2	8	–	100
1984	46	24	21	4	4	1	100
1985	55	18	18	5	3	–	100
1986	57	20	17	3	3	–	100

Source: Home Office Criminal Statistics, 1971, 1981, 1984, 1985, 1986.
* Not applicable – less than $^1/_2$ per cent.

Table 1.3 *Percentage of persons aged 14 and under 17 sentenced for indictable offences who received various sentences by sex and type of offence or order in England and Wales*

Sex and year	Absolute or conditional discharge	Super-vision Order	Fine	Comm-unity Service Order	Atten-dance Centre Order	Detention Centre Order	Care Order	Borstal training/ Youth Custody	Otherwise dealt with	Total
	Percentage of total persons sentenced									
Males										
1971	17	19	40	*	7	4	8	2	2	100
1981	19	17	32	*	16	10	3	3	1	100
1984	22	17	27	3	16	8	2	4	1	100
1985	22	17	25	4	16	8	2	4	1	100
1986	24	18	24	4	15	8	2	4	1	100
Females										
1971	26	27	34	*	*	*	9	1	3	100
1981	31	25	32	*	5	*	6	1	1	100
1984	37	21	28	1	7	*	3	2	1	100
1985	39	20	28	1	7	*	3	2	1	100
1986	42	19	26	2	7	*	2	2	1	100

Source: Home Office Statistics, 1971, 1981, 1984, 1985, 1986.
* not applicable – less than ¹/₂ per cent.

vision.[20]

Whilst these overall figures need to be related to offence seriousness, previous record and so on, there is some evidence to suggest that preconceptions about girls' delinquency do produce discriminatory responses. Harris and Webb (1987), having analyzed some 13.4 per cent of all supervision orders made in England and Wales during 1978, concluded that 'girls are proportionately significantly more likely than boys to be placed on supervision for offences'. Indeed, their data point to a more rapid deployment of a supervisory sanction for girl delinquents than for boys (Harris and Webb, 1987: 146).[21]

Many commentators have identified 'difficult' family relationships as being a cause of female offending and particularly 'sexual delinquency' or 'sexual acting out' (Pollak and Friedman, 1969). Indeed, psychoanalysts, sociologists, psychologists, criminologists and practitioners alike have viewed female delinquency as mostly 'sexual delinquency' stemming from relational problems.[22] As West commented:

> Whereas the wayward boy usually takes to stealing and breaking in, and only exceptionally to sex offences, the wayward girl more often takes to sexual misconduct. The promiscuity of wayward girls serves as an effectively upsetting form of protest against the attitudes and restrictions of older relatives. Often, it also seems a way of searching for affection which was wanting in an unhappy parental home.... Girl thieves are often, but not always, sexual rebels. (West, 1967: 198)

Sexual delinquency

It is this very tendency to opt for 'supervisory sanctions' when dealing with girls that has led some commentators to suggest that girls' delinquency is currently defined or interpreted in a different way to boys' delinquency and in a way which leads them into a network of children's homes, assessment centres, special schools, secure units and so on, rather than into the criminal justice system (Procek, 1981; Campbell, 1981; Gelsthorpe and Morris, 1987). But we know, too, that paternalistic concerns about girls' moral welfare have sometimes led to them being dealt with more severely than boys, in the sense that they are judged not only for what they have done in terms of criminal offences, but for who they are and how they behave in general. When dealing with girls there is a tendency to measure their needs (Casburn, 1979). By this I mean that assumptions about what a typical girl delinquent is like or needs have sometimes led practitioners, magistrates and judges to focus on girls' social and sexual behaviour instead of, or at least as much as, their offences.

David May's study of decision-making by a Scottish panel showed that girls were more likely to be placed under supervision or in an institution and less likely to be fined than boys even though actual offences against the law were similar (May, 1977). Cohn's (1970) study in New York found that girls deemed to be 'sexually delinquent' were three times more likely to be institutionalized than were boys, and typically on a probation officer's recommendation. In the words of Cowie, Cowie and Slater, the prevailing understanding of girls' delinquency is that

> The effective motivational factors are connected, much more than with boys, with the intimate family and with the girls' personal relations with their parents. (Cowie, Cowie and Slater, 1968: 144)

The most common explanation of promiscuous sexual behaviour relates to the Oedipal syndrome and the repression of early sexual love for the parent.[23] Freud argued that because the early attachment to parents is frustrated by the incest taboo, subsequent sexual partners become mere surrogates because with the promiscuous person the sex instinct remains attached to its first love object. Further, because sexual partners are mere surrogates, complete satisfaction is unobtainable; and so remaining unsatisfied, the individual continually searches for new partners. The promiscuous person is usually thought to have remained within childhood in a sense, when the love object is the parent.[24]

Much of the writing on this topic, however, upholds the myth of the asexuality of the 'respectable' woman, a theory which was propounded in the Victorian era.[25] Moreover, it depends on evidence which is the product of differential surveillance and consideration, and of the application of a 'double standard' of behaviour.[26] What this means is that staying out late in the company of boys and actual or suspected sexual promiscuity are taken more seriously in girls, partly because of the risk of pregnancy, partly because it is considered particularly unseemly – reflecting myths about female asexuality and assumptions that it leads to loss of 'femininity' and to prostitution (West, 1967). It has been argued that women's sexuality is suppressed by men or suppressed in the interests of patriarchy (Daly, 1979).[27] McIntosh has depicted this understanding of events in the following way:

> Women are kept on leading strings by father, husband, Church and State, so that the extent and range of their sexual expectations and opportunities is limited and they are prevented from realising their full potential. (McIntosh, 1978: 64)

There is, of course, the further point that 'sexual behaviour' is shaped and controlled by socialization patterns and available social and sexual 'scripts'. Failing to conform with stereotypical behaviour in this area and to prescribed 'scripts' generates some of the concern here.[28]

In addition to the fact that the weight of psychoanalytical and biological theory may have created an understanding that much female delinquency is 'sexual' in origin, it is also possible that other kinds of activity may be actively given a sexual connotation or may be used as a basis for 'searching out' sexual 'delinquency'. Chesney-Lind (1973), for instance, argues that law enforcement agencies positively 'sexualize' female delinquency; for example, through specific kinds of questioning and by the administration of medical examinations to determine virginity and possible infections. There is no similar study in this country, but support for this thesis is found in Shacklady Smith's (1975) account of police interactions with girls and in Wilson's account of events in a juvenile court.[29] As Wilson comments:

> it was often doubtful whether supervision orders made on some girls, were imposed on them as a result of the offence which had been committed, as in the case with boys, or whether the orders were made because of deviations from the expected form of feminine behaviour. It was certainly not unusual for questions to be asked by the magistrate concerning the moral welfare of female offenders, and the few orders for 'care and protection' and for being 'beyond control' were all concerned with sexual activities or rather the suspicion of sexual activity. The posing of questions of this kind can only be understood by realising that female delinquency is generally assumed to be synonymous with sexual delinquency. In contrast the sexual behaviour of delinquent boys is generally considered to be immaterial by the courts. (Wilson. 1978: 72)[30]

However, the argument is not as clear cut as it may seem. Whilst there is some evidence to suggest that girls' behaviour is interpreted differently from boys', and is responded to differently and in a way which may lead them to agencies allied to the juvenile justice system, there are actually fewer girls than boys in the care of local authorities. From the preconceptions of girls' delinquency outlined here we might expect to see proportionately more girls than boys in care for a range of reasons, many of which perhaps conceal the 'sexualization' of their behaviour or situation. The imbalance – in the direction of boys– is noticeable in infancy and increases with age (see DHSS statistics, 1984; and Lawson and Lockhart, 1985: 179). This imbalance holds in all categories both of care orders and receptions into care except where the moral danger criterion is used.[31] The predominance of girls in this category, however, is significant and it does support the research evidence that the sexual activity of females is more closely regulated than that of males and is punished more severely, and that sexual meanings are given to other kinds of conduct. The perception of females who are sexually active as 'sexual delinquents', however, is obviously a phenomenon which pervades all areas of social interaction, and indeed, characterizes it (Sumner, 1980; Kress, 1979), and is not one generated solely by criminal justice systems and allied agencies of control. The 'policing of femininity' as a corollary of this is an area which has also been closely examined (e.g., Hudson, 1982; Cowie and Lees, 1981; McRobbie and McCabe, 1981; Griffin, 1985).

The general themes about female offenders in the literature may be summarized in the following way: (a) that 'criminality' is alien to their 'natural disposition' because essential biological and psychological traits suggest a tendency towards docility and passivity; (b) that offending behaviour on the part of females is a reflection of some biological and psychological disturbance; and (c) that such disturbance often manifests itself in sexual delinquency (Smart, 1976; Heidensohn, 1985).

Traditional critiques of these themes generally lead to a conclusion that our knowledge about female offenders is 'distorted'. They do so by following a route through the criminal statistics to a 'rogues gallery' of writers who have propounded biological and psychological arguments to explain female offending, to social role theories, and to the notion of women's liberation as an explanation for changes in the nature and patterns of female offending (Smart, 1976). Such critiques have been critical in evaluating the 'received wisdom' about female offenders. In sum, they teach us that it is inappropriate to rely upon criminal statistics for a picture of women's and girls' crime; there is the problem of the 'dark figure' to contend with and, importantly, it may be that female behaviour is 'policed' or 'defined' in different ways from male behaviour making females less susceptible to control via the criminal justice system.[32] Indeed, 'criminality' itself may be differentially constituted for males and females. There is a suggestion, for example, that female deviancy is likely to be classified as 'mental illness' of one sort of another, though there is little evidence to validate the 'equalization theory' proffered by some writers. Neither is there evidence to substantiate claims made about the 'sexual' nature of female deviance. Much depends on the differential application of control in this area of activity. Beliefs about the lower crime rate of females and about their committing different crimes from males remain open to debate (Morris, 1987).

Many of the theories about women's and girls' crime clearly confuse 'sex' and 'gender'; anatomical differences are held responsible for personality and behavioural characteristics when these attributes must be seen as shaped in historically specific cultural situations.[33] Instead of looking at the combined effects of environmental influences, cultural traditions and physiological and psychological factors, some theorists see criminality solely as the product of hereditary characteristics. Neither can psychological differences between men and women, when considered in isolation from other factors, provide an adequate explanation for differences in behaviour. Not only are there fewer differences than is often assumed, but it is important to note that socialization plays a part in the development of sexual identity and appropriate sex role behaviour both by direct prescription and by implicit expectation.

Sex role theory, too, has proved inadequate to the task of accounting for women's and girls' crime. It has, for instance, been used in an inappropriate way – to search out causes for crime in such terms as 'undersocialization' and' role frustration', when there is no reason to suppose that the reasons why women commit crimes are different from those of men. Sex role theory is clearly limited; its contribution is that it helps to explain how behaviour is shaped but it does not actually explain it. Indeed, the theory concentrates on the female's role in society without exploring the underlying historical and cultural legacy (see Smart, 1976).

As for the idea that the Women's Liberation Movement has precipitated an increase in the amount of crime committed by females,[34] we learn that there are not only statistical problems with the correspondences which are drawn (Box and Hale, 1983), but there may be good reasons why women could be more involved in crime than previously; for example, unemployment, low wages, families to support on their own, and so on (Morris and Gelsthorpe, 1981). This leaves aside the whole question of whether or not the Women's Liberation Movement may be more powerful in rhetoric than in reality.

I intend to concentrate on two facets of the critique at this juncture: on an historical perspective and then on a more recent perspective which takes up some of the writings and commentaries of feminists.

Accounting for the theories: an historical perspective
From descriptions of the trajectory of theories regarding the criminal behaviour of males and females it is clear that the tradition of biological positivism has tended to prevail in relation to female offending, whereas theories relating to male offending have returned to a sociological base.[35] Discussion must now turn, therefore, to a consideration of the special significance of this positivistic approach in relation to females, to explain why these theories survived the union of the political and psychological is the focus of this part of the critique of images of female offenders. First, a general comment on the dominance of positivism will help to explain how theories about offenders and delinquents gain popularity.

The dominance of positivism
The search for a single theory of criminal behaviour has long since been castigated as a vain one. Indeed, Walker has likened the situation to mediaeval alchemy, by referring to it as the search for the 'criminologists' stone' (1966). More recently, Walker has referred to single-factor theories as 'monoliths' of a criminological 'Stonehenge Era' (1974). The concern here is not to advance the case for a multiplicity of causes, however, but to comment on the erection of particular monoliths at particular points in

history and to offer an explanation. Commenting on the trajectory of criminological theory, Levin and Lindesmith noted that the 'progress of science is often portrayed as a majestic and inevitable evolution of ideas in a logical sequence of successfully closer approximations to the truth' (1937: 671). This is clearly a misconception (Young, 1977). Indeed, to search for some Olympian platform supposedly detached from values is illusory: one has to explore the relevance of the historical aggregation of value choices to explanations for criminal behaviour, as to law and social policy, for instance.[36] Thus, the aim should be to explain why theories gain support. They have to be placed in social context to be re-examined. Taylor *et al.* have put the matter more succinctly. Seeking to describe the appeal of positivism, they comment:

> We wish to remove ourselves from that comfortable school of thought which believes that theories compete with each other in some scholarly limbo, heuristic facility being the only test of survival. We need to explain why certain theories, despite their manifest inability to come to terms with their subject matter, survive. (Taylor *et al.*, 1973: 31)

Consequently, we have to look at the ideological import of theories and the benefits which might accrue to society, or certain factions of it, in their adoption. We have to examine how theories might serve to protect interests inherent in the *status quo*. As Taylor *et al.* argue, what is necessary is to explain why a particular mode of thought is taken up and 'how the interests of the politician and practitioner are meshed together'. (Ibid;32)

Three ideological strengths have been identified regarding the adoption of the positivistic approach to explain criminal behaviour; *consensus, determinism* and *scientism* (ibid.). A *consensus* view of the world might be construed as a convenient way of ruling out any discussion or recognition of conflict in society:

> In one stroke, ethical questions concerning the present order and the reaction against the deviant are removed, for the humanitarian task of the expert becomes that of bringing the miscreant back into the consensual fold. (Ibid.: 31)

Within a *deterministic* view of human behaviour, deviant realities are effectively defused. Moreover, any intervention to stem 'objectionable' behaviour is seen as justified, as rational and humane. *Scientism* refers to the process of invoking a natural body of knowledge such as in the natural sciences. As Taylor *et al.* remark, this would serve to grant the positivist the gift of objectivity, 'it bestows on his pronouncements the mantle of truth' (ibid.: 32). Thus the basic premise is that delinquent behaviour has antecedent causes which explain it and that these causes are observable and have a regularity. In essence, the positivistic approach is one which deals in single causes; there is discussion only at one level of ontology. The subjective meaning of the behaviour for the actors is ignored and so too are their experiences and contribution to the shape and form of behaviour. Moreover, the approach is a conservative one, justifying the 'fashions' of reformation. There is an assumption that delinquents or deviants share pathological conditions which make them fundamentally different from the law-abiding.

The ideological strengths contained within this approach have been discussed at length (see, for example, Bottomley, 1979; Chevalier, 1973; Radzinowicz, 1966; Levin and Lindesmith, 1937). One example of the ideological import of the approach has been the discussion of the 'criminalizing' of the lower classes in late Victorian society. It is argued that the social and political unpalatability of early criminological surveys, which identified poverty and social environment as key ingredients for crime, encouraged the development of the themes of the moral depravity and biological 'atavism' of the criminal classes (and the poor) which dominated the second half of the century.

Thus, a simple analysis would be that despite the extensive statistical and sociological studies of crime that had been carried out in England and France in the nineteenth century (e.g., Guerry, 1963; Mayhew, 1862; Bonger, 1916)[38] which provided a firm foundation for the establishment of a respectable, sociologically based criminology, the demise of their approach can be explained in terms of society seizing theories which would, in effect, 'let it off the hook'.

This 'marriage of convenience', however, between the ideas of positivists and the need to reduce society's responsibility towards the poor and criminals, the deprived and the depraved (on economic grounds, at least), was not one that was arranged in a direct way. The adoption of the positivistic approach as a solution to the problem of the 'dangerous classes' has to be viewed alongside Darwinian ideas and the need to substitute a new ethical code in place of religious justification.

That the Victorian period was characterized by an unprecedented number of transitions is undeniable. These transitions affected not only city and industrial life, but are thought to have had corresponding effects in the human mind. Indeed, it was an age of science, new knowledge, searching criticism – yet also of multiple doubts and shaken beliefs.[39] Logically, one has to look at the possibility that criminological theory derived in part from these unprecedented social changes and from a religious crisis of the time. The quest for 'moral earnestness', for instance, which evolved out of the uncertainty, may have contributed to the idea of there being a 'moral stratum' in society. But this is merely speculation. It is obviously not possible within the confines of this book and its main considerations to relate in detail the religious dilemmas and their impact on Victorian life and thought. Nevertheless, it is possible that criminological theories were influenced in this way.

It seems that the Victorian mind was, in general, committed to the concept of absolute law (although admittedly there are always hierarchies of ideas). Politics, history, economics, art and education were all believed to be governed by universal laws and principles true for all times and places. Moral predicates were thought to derive from the metaphysical world. Previous consideration of the long tradition of natural law in philosophy and mediaeval theology explains this inheritance (Houghton, 1957). If the Bible was believed to contain the eternal laws of morality it seems plausible that ignorance or defiance of those laws would become a potent cause (though not the only cause) of Victorian dogmatism. Furthermore, in an age of wavering faith, the wish to believe led perhaps to a rather more demonstrative attitude of belief than people had thought necessary at a period when their personal conviction was more complete. Moral ideas may, in part, have been born out of this attitude, in the sense that positiveness is often a telling clue to underlying insecurity. To be earnest morally was, perhaps, to recognize that human existence was not a short interlude between life and death in which to satisfy hedonistic pleasures, but a spiritual pilgrimage to eternity in which man (sic) was called upon to struggle with all his power against the forces of evil, in his own soul and in society. The prophets of earnestness and the 'Evangelical' discipline[40] set about this task by imposing on society its creed of puritanism. Young depicted it thus:

> Evangelism has imposed on society... its code of Sabbath observance, responsibility, and philanthropy; of discipline in the home, regularity in affairs, it has created a most effective technique of agitation of private persuasion and social persecution. (Young, 1960: 5)

Thus the Victorians' exalted conception of human nature derived much from this ethnic of purity and also from a belief in their own ability to achieve such an end. It follows that movements to remove the 'scum' and the 'slum' in Victorian life accompanied this moral reform. It is within this context that the maxim 'cleanliness is next to godliness' may be used to parody the approach; it was a case of 'rational means to moral ends'. Man's journey of progress was not to be hindered.

What we should abstract from the above, in relation to the development of criminological theories, is the simple point that with this same rationality that had conquered the economic and industrial world, the Victorians sought to conquer their own destiny. This aim brought with it a harsh deterrent nature to mirror the ideals of Victorian society, and the need to separate and segregate the poor and the 'bad'.[41]

An obvious and simple way to accomplish this drawing of distinctions

...y intervention was to withdraw the view that all behaviour ...al (as in the Classicist view) and to assume that criminal motivation was irrational, unrelated to social and economic conditions and dominating power structures. Victorian society had to justify the pressing need to modify an individual's ability to exercise free will (because of increasing crime rates, for example) and at the same time choose a method of dealing with this problem which would necessitate no major structural changes. Crook (1970) has made the point that biological explanations may provide a substitute for the ethical code, lost when religious beliefs are no longer followed. Although he refers to present society, and to the appeal of biological positivist theories amidst conflicting standards and norms of social behaviour, this seems particularly applicable to Victorian society.

The dominance of biological positivism

The coincidental nature of Darwin's discoveries and the newly established principles of scientific method are entirely relevant here. For the premises and instruments used in the physical world of science were soon to seem of equal validity and promise in the study of men and society. What appeared to be so logical and 'natural' in the scientific world was readily and easily applied to the human world. The notion of the 'born criminal' seemed obvious, dealing as it did with visible, physical manifestations of the cause of delinquency and affording the opportunity to predict and classify. Moreover, this positivistic approach reflected the philosophy of reductionism, a simple and seemingly logical philosophy which facilitated an understanding of the causes of crime and delinquency. Reductionist philosophy involves the arrangement of sciences in a hierarchical order, from 'higher' level disciplines, such as sociology and anthropology, down to psychology, biology, chemistry and physics at the base. It claims that higher level sciences can be explained in terms of those at the lower level (Rose and Rose, 1973); that is, that psychological phenomena such as 'motivation' can be explained at a 'lower' (biological) level.

Some observers of the transition from sociological theories to biological theories have stressed the importance of the growth of the medical profession as a contributing factor. Levin and Lindesmith, for example, account for the Lombrosian myth in this way:

> basically, not so much in terms of the acceptance or rejection of theories or methods of research as in terms of a changing personnel... the Lombrosian myth arose, therefore, as a result of the 'seizure of power' so to speak by the medical profession. Medical men compiled bibliographies and traced the history of criminology as a branch of medicine through the works of Gall, Lavater, Pinel, Morel, Esquirol, Maudsley etc., ignoring the voluminous

sociological literature. (Levin and Lindesmith, 1937: 669)

Thus a distortion of knowledge takes place to bolster the professional's institutional role in society.[42] Indeed, it is argued that the positivist's epistemological split between facts and values corresponds to this institutional role in society. As Young points out:

The [experts] must explain what is perceived as unusual in terms of the values associated by their audience as usual. In this process, utilising the theoretical ploys listed, they circumscribe and negate the reality of values different from their own. They do not explain, they merely explain away. They are well trained men, but the rigour of their training has enabled them to view the world only from the narrow-blinkered perspective of their own discipline. ...As a result such experts can, from the vantage of their cloistered chauvinism, scarcely grasp the totality of the social world even in terms of their own values let alone take a critical stance outside of these values. (Young, 1971:72–3)

Clearly, the 'expert' becomes blinkered from receiving information at odds with this world view, and the practitioner is also a politician who has to rationalize his or her own position, using 'popular' theories to support it.

It is indubitable that the appeal of biological positivism is related to all these issues. It may be that the theory of the born criminal offered a convenient rationalization of the failure of preventive effort and an escape from the implications of the doctrine that crime was essentially a product of social organization, but this suggests a theme of conspiracy for what may also be described as a latent function of events. A more discursive analysis sets the 'superior' ideological efficacy of biological positivism alongside the related factors discussed above.

The impact of the medical discourse

The point I want to argue here is that major theoretical elements in nineteenth century medical discourse have had far-reaching implications regarding the view held of women and girls, simply because that discourse was closely bound to notions of a 'natural order'. Put very generally, conceptions of women's social position were integrated with naturalistic descriptions of disease types and determinist explanatory schemes. It was relatively easy to objectify women as part of physical nature. Further, this facility was present within both medical discourse and law thought systems, creating, very significantly, the possibility of some medico-legal consensus.

Recent feminist orientations have involved the rethinking of a great deal of medical history. There are new studies of the establishment of male medical dominance over midwifery and gynaecology, medical antagonism to the increase in birth control during the nineteenth century, and opposition to medical education for women (Ehrenreich and English, 1979; Lipschitz, 1978; Procek, 1981; Sachs and Wilson, 1978). In addition, there is new interest in women's diseases and in the medical element of family relationships as microcosms of society (Laing and Esterson, 1964; Cooper, 1972; Gordon, 1976).

Some of this work, however, argues that scientific knowledge was misused to support the repression of women, when clearly the case for suggesting that 'women' and 'nature' were terms with a degree of interchangeability in their meaning is stronger. Again, just as I rejected a 'mechanistic' view of the dominance of positivism as a solution to the problem of the 'dangerous classes', I reject the idea of a 'mechanistic' relationship between the rise of the (predominantly male) medical profession and the social control or 'repression' of women.

It is relevant here to extract one general point from the recent and extensive literature: the network of correspondence between 'women', 'nature', 'passivity', 'emotion' and 'irresponsibility'. These correspondences did not exist in themselves but in a socially contingent contrast to men: 'culture', 'activity', 'intellect' and 'responsibility' (see Jordanova, 1981).[43] Much nineteenth-century medical writing, however, discussed such polarities in terms of autonomous existence. In particular, medical men identified women as natural objects and therefore described them with all the objective standing associated with science. Put another way, nineteenth-century medical statements of woman's passive nature abounded (see, for example, Edwards, 1981; Woodward and Richards, 1977). Such statements also implied woman's intellectual, cultural and economic dependence on man. Natural passivity and cultural dependence were not separately definable, however; cultural values entered into the accounts of woman's nature and were then taken to define cultural possibility (Haraway, 1978; Young, 1977). Thus, medical accounts of femaleness were, in themselves, a cultural product; they merely restated the terms of woman's existing position.

In summary, much of the medical discourse in the nineteenth century was founded upon the principle of the conservation of energy.[44] There was an assumption that physiology both contained a fixed level of energy in activity and in physiological functions. Thus reproduction was central to any analysis of the female physiology. Consequently, the social and biological function of reproduction was considered both the strength and weakness of femaleness. Women gave life, but at the cost of menstruation, emotional dependency, nervous weakness, and a world view restricted to the family.[45] This principle of the conservation of energy was subsequently used to exclude women from educational and intellectual pursuits and areas of public life (McWilliams-Tulberg, 1977; L'Espérance,

1977; Sachs and Wilson, 1978). Doctors agitated vociferously against the dangers of female education, R.R. Coleman MD, for instance, thundered this warning:

> Women beware. You are on the brink of destruction. You have hitherto been engaged in crushing your waists; now you are attempting to cultivate your mind. You have been merely dancing all night in the foul air of the ballroom; now you are beginning to spend your mornings in study. You have been incessantly stimulating your emotions with concerts and operas, with French plays, and French novels; now you are exerting your understanding to learn Greek, and solve propositions in Euclid. Beware! Science pronounces that the woman who studies is lost. (Quoted in Haller and Haller, 1974: 39)

Several writers proclaimed that education for women was a disastrous error since girls between twelve and twenty could not stand the strain of higher education, largely because of the physiological strains which puberty and ovulation put upon them. Clarke, for instance, held that:

> to digest one's dinner, it was necessary to temper exercise and brain work; likewise, during the growth of the female reproductive system, brain work must be avoided. (Clarke, 1984: 40)

He proceeded to demonstrate, at least to his own satisfaction, that higher education (presumably referring to the education of young middle-class ladies in academies and universities) left a great number of its female adherents in poor health for life. He said:

> It will have to be considered whether women can scorn delights and live laborious days of intellectual exercise and production, without injury to their functions as conceivers, mothers, and nurses of children. For it would be an ill thing, if it should so happen that we got the advantage of female intellectual work at the price of a puny, enfeebled, and sickly race. (Ibid., 1874: 156)

Other writers listed illnesses produced in females by 'brain work' or argued that by being 'bookish', women lapsed into male manners and fashions. They declined from their 'orbit' and obscured their 'original divinity'.[46] Even having the vote would apparently prove far too taxing for female physiological (and thus emotional) resources.[47]

But these strengths and weaknesses were ethical as well as biological: through the family women transmitted moral feelings and improvement. Medical practitioners, rationalizing their professional status and seeking to establish an expert body of knowledge, shared this evaluative view of nature. Indeed, for reasons which essentially relate to the emergence of professions, medical discourse had to be a tenable one and correspond to popular ideas. Thus medical practitioners perceived an inseparable scientific and social duty to inform and guide their professional position at the heart (literally and metaphysically) of the social order. The description of female biology, character, diseases and care made medicine a central resource in the political mediation between the individual and society. Medical men clearly become deeply engaged in exploring the mutual responsibilities of women and society. They were society's delegates in this task.

Ehrenreich and English have described the rise and influences of the new profession in this way;

> as the Old Order faded into the past, and the 'rising middle class' became the new ruling class, science made its peace with the social order. The science which arose to the defence of sexual romanticism was a pale, and not wholly legitimate, descendant of the science which had once challenged the authority of kings and popes. The scientific experts, who committed themselves to the defence of sexual romanticism – professional physicians, psychologists, domestic scientists, parent educators, etc. – each claimed a specialised body of scientific knowledge. Their careers rested on this claim. Without connection to science, they have no legitimacy, no audience for their ideas or market for their skills. (Ehrenreich and English, 1979: 25)

Clearly, this description of some of the influences upon the development of views in which women are depicted as generally 'enfeebled', and so on, contains some important lessons for any examination of criminological theory and the way in which women and girls are depicted within it. More recent commentaries on depictions of female offenders within criminological theories, however, have adopted an alternative perspective on the source of theoretical positionings and it is to an examination of these which I now turn.

Recent commentaries

Over the last fifteen years many contributions to the debate about women and crime in Britain and the United States have characterized criminological theories and penal responses to women and girls as 'sexist'. Klein (1973); Rasch (1974); Smart (1976); Pollock (1978); and Campbell (1981) have all contributed to discussion in this way.[48] Smart, for instance, states:

> ideologically informed studies have become 'leading' works by default.... The main thrust of theories of female criminality, even more than those concerned with male criminality, support and justify the prevailing methods of treatment and the ideology of social control adhered to by the administrators of legal and penal policy. (Smart, 1976: 4)

And as Pollock describes in her review of the literature:

> In general, women were believed to be very different from men and almost always inferior. Whether they regarded women as infantile, amoral children or as pampered slaves, early sociologists were guilty of gross sexism. (Pollock, 1978: 25)

Clearly, it is important to establish whether or not these kinds of commentary and their concerns from any kind of collective. Some writers have claimed that such commentaries and their new perspective may be termed 'feminist criminology', but there are obvious problems inherent in the use of this term. There is some difficulty in identifying who the feminist criminologists are.

This same issue was the object of the much quoted polemic between Smart (1981) and Greenwood (1981). Victoria Greenwood defined a feminist criminology as a collection of recent research, predominantly inspired and affected by the influence of the women's movement, which illuminated the institutionalized sexism of the criminal justice process. Smart argued that neither the existence of feminist criminologists (self-appointed) nor studies of women and crime constituted a 'feminist criminology', for whilst some authors conducted research from one theoretical position, others adopted an entirely different approach. Indeed, we have to be able to distinguish between 'women studying criminology', the 'criminology of women' and 'feminist women studying criminology' to achieve this task of identification. Moreover, not only are there, at a theoretical level, numerous criminological perspectives, but there are also many forms of feminism; for example, socialist, radical and bourgeois (see Oakley, 1981; Bouchier, 1978, 1983; Evans, 1977).

Perhaps the major difference between recent contributions and orthodox criminologies (which have been individualistic, positivistic and ahistorical), however, is that they are concerned essentially with a triadic study of the relationship between traditional notions of crime, women and their place in the social and economic structure.[49] Feminists commonly address themselves to gender relations, particularly the notion of male supremacy and the oppression of women, though they may differ on what forms that oppression takes. In the main, it is Greenwood's group of writers with whom I am concerned here, and reference to them as 'feminist writers' (although perhaps inappropriate in some cases) is convenient and justifiable to distinguish them from orthodox writers.

Within criminology itself sexism has assumed many different guises. Early attempts to consider the question of women in relation to crime and deviance, for instance, were concerned about the 'amnesia' of criminologists in neglecting women.[50] Thus, despite the defences offered by Rock (1977) and Bottomley (1979) which emphasize the erratic nature of criminology, some writers assumed that a remedy could be sought by appropriating existing criminological theories and 'inserting' women; for example, by discovering girl gangs (Velimesis, 1975)[51] and considering females in relation to subcultural theory (McRobbie, 1980; Shacklady Smith, 1978). Shacklady Smith, for instance, commented that:

It is my firm belief that a labelling approach far from being irrelevant to female delinquency studies is absolutely necessary in understanding their pattern of delinquent activities. (Shacklady Smith, 1978: 85)[52]

While Michael Hindelang argued:

Sociologists ... should incorporate the sex variable into existing emerging theories. (Hindlelang, 1979: 154)

Heidensohn had early on suggested that more research was necessary to remedy the problem of missing data about females:

What seems to be needed in the study of female deviance is a crash programme of research which telescopes decades of comparable studies of males. (Heidensohn, 1968: 171)

And Rafter and Natalizia presented the message in a different way:

If the vacuum of crucial information is to be filled, another key need is for more 'women only' studies – research that focusses on women without necessarily including comparative data on men ...(Rafter and Natalizia, 1981: 86)

with the additional suggestion that 'women only' studies should strive to produce a body of information as extensive as that which exists for men.[53]

The assumptions were essentially that women were simply hidden within the trajectory of theory relating to male delinquents. Indeed, Kuhn and Wolpe have noted that this tendency to 'add to rather than transform' work was not confined to criminology; rather, it took place in a variety of areas – 'in the social sciences, in psychology, history, and art history in particular' (1978: 2).

This approach, however, is particularly myopic. It ignores the fact that, although male crime has been the subject of a tremendous amount of research, the positivistic approach adopted has failed to further our understanding. Indeed, to call for more research is a familiar cry in criminology. What has to be addressed is what form this should take.

Kress has, rather cryptically, characterized such attempts to bring women to the fore as 'speaking bitterness'. She states:

In recent years the legal apparatus, like most major institutions in this country, has been intensely criticised by the women's movement for its endemic sexist attitudes and practice.... Within criminology, this has meant a radical departure from the biologically psychologically determinist literature that has dominated the field for more than half a century. In effect, some women – in criminology and in the social sciences in general – have spoken bitterness and have broken through a long history of silence and misconception. (Kress, 1979: 44–5).

Moving on from some of these critiques there have been more sophisticated approaches. Smart (1976), for example, expressed particular concern to 'cite accounts of female criminality within social relations.[55] For instance, when talking about the validity of role theory as an explanation for differential crime rates, this approach would entail locating the concept of role within a theory which, first, can account for the existence of specifically differentiated roles as well as other features of human activity (like criminality); and secondly, treats both as the outcome of socioeconomic, political and historical factors, rather than treating one (crime) as the outcome of the other (role).

The major contribution to our understanding, however, has been through a concentration on institutionalized 'sexism' within the criminal justice system and criminological theory. Chesney-Lind (1978), for example, argues that 'sexist ideology pervades all instruments of the criminal justice system and the family and the law'. Whilst Klein and Kress claim:

> the special oppression of women by that system [the criminal justice system] is not isolated or arbitrary, but rather is rooted in systematic sexist practices and ideologies which can only be fully understood by analysing the position of women in capitalist society. (Klein and Kress, 1976: 45)

Rafter and Natalizia's view is:

> Sexism is not merely the prejudice of individuals: it is embedded in the very economic, legal and social framework of life.... The criminal justice system, as one part of that institutional framework, reflects the same sexist under-pinning that is evidenced throughout capitalist society. (Rafter and Natalizia, 1981: 81)

Additionally, Sachs and Wilson (1978) assume in their writing that the law has a material or economic base, so that women have been excluded from larger areas of public life in men's interests.[56] Kress, however, refines this perspective in her comment that:

> It is not a mystical ahistorical sexism that permeates the criminal justice system apparatus, or for that matter all capitalist institutions. Nor is it men who are the primary enemy. Sexist ideology and practice is rooted in bourgeois morality which defines and controls women – as well as working class men – in ways that mystify the real relations of production, that divide the working class, that defuse class consciousness, that perpetuate the petty bourgeoisie as the upholders and expressers of morality, and that provide a rationale for the victimisation of women inside and outside the criminal justice system. (Kress, 1979: 48)

The issues are clearly complicated, however, not least by our interpretation of the term 'sexist ideology' itself.[57] Joseph Schumpeter has epitomized some of the difficulties here:

> The temptation is great to avail oneself of the opportunity to dispose at one stroke of a whole body of propositions one does not like, by the simple device

of calling it an ideology. This device is no doubt very effective, as effective as are attacks upon an opponent's personal motives. But logically it is inadmissible-explanation, however, correct, of the reasons why a man says what he says tells us nothing about whether it is true or false. Similarly, statements that proceed from an ideological background are open to suspicion, but they may still be perfectly valid. (Schumpeter, 1955: 36)

Similarly, Jorge Larrain, writing of the difficulties in dealing with the concept, pronounced:

Ideology is perhaps one of the most equivocal and elusive concepts one can find in the social sciences; not only because of the variety of theoretical approaches which assign different meanings and functions to it, but also because it is a concept heavily charged with political connotations and widely used in everyday life with the most diverse significations. (Larrain, 1979: 13)

However, I shall not attempt to explore fully the different usage of the terms at this juncture for that would occupy a whole book, my concept of it, from much of the writing I look at here, is that ideology refers to the *ideological,* this being understood as the capability of dominant groups or classes to make their own sectional interests appear to others as universal ones.[58] More recent writings has used 'ideology' to mean the body of ideas which express individuals' lived relationships within the world, which 'makes sense' of their everyday living (Althusser, 1972; Mepham, 1972; Williams, 1973).[59] In this writing it is not used in a political sense to imply conscious manipulation, partiality or falsehood; it is not a conscious conspiracy by any section of society to distort reality and produce a 'false consciousness' in the minds of individuals in other sections of society (see Taylor, Walton and Young, 1975: 81).

But this is not the place to describe the disputes about whether or not there can be a direct relationship between the world as experienced and scientific knowledge of the underlying structures and conditions of existence that give rise to that experience.[60] I leave aside the more critical analyses at this point to concentrate on the usage of the term within feminist analyses as the distortion of knowledge and as a vehicle through which certain ideas about women are transmitted, inculcated and reproduced. Before engaging in theoretical discussion, however, I address the issue that, despite numerous claims and assertions about sexist ideology and sexist practices, we know very little about the form which 'sexism' is alleged to take in everyday practice. We do not know, for instance, the extent of sexism within criminal justice agencies; whether it is found only in certain sections of the system or whether there are sexist views and practices consistently maintained throughout the relevant agencies. Chapters 3, 4 and 5 thus concentrate on revealing 'modern images' of female offenders and attempt to discern elements of practice which might be viewed as 'sexist'.

Notes

1. It is not my purpose in this chapter to refer to the 'rogues gallery' of writers who have written about female offenders. For a critique of early writers see Smart (1976), Heidensohn (1985), Leonard (1982), Campbell (1981) and Morris (1987). See Gelsthorpe (1984) for an historical account of the institutional response to women and girls in the British Criminal Justice System. See also Smith (1962). See Morris (1987) and Home Office annual Criminal Statistics for analysis of the sex differences in crime rates.

2. See, for example, 'A plan for the establishment of Charity Homes for exposed or deserted women and girls and for penitent prostitutes', by Joseph Massie (1758); the work of the Society for Organizing Charitable Relief (1888) and Ellice Hopkins's efforts to save girls described in *Preventative Work* (1881), or *The care of our girls* (1881). Material on this subject is far too extensive to enumerate here, but the British Library contains many documents and reports which reflect this concern.

3. See Carlebach (1970), for example.

4. See the annual reports of the Reformatory and Refuge Union, for instance, and particularly the report entitled 'Fifty Years' Record of Child Saving and Reformatory Work 1856–1906' (being the Jubilee Report of the Reformatory and Refuge Union) and the Reports of the National Association of Certified Reformatory and Industrial Schools, 1901.

5. 8 Edw. 7c. 59.

6. See Cecily McCall (1938) for a description of the regime. The minimum period for training was raised to two years in 1914. 4 & 5 Geo. 5c. 58.

7. See Smith, (1962) for a description of these changes. For a description of training in these institutions see the Reports of the Prison Commissioners, especially 1956: 100, 1957: 79, 1960: 56.

8. The characteristics of girls within such institutions as borstals and detention centres have been described by Goodman and Price (1967).

9. This theme is reiterated throughout the literature, but see especially Ball and Logan (1960); Warren (1961); Richardson (1969); Hart (1977).

10. Gibbens (1959) and Richardson (1969) make similar observations.

11. See also Reige (1972) and McRobbie (1978).

12. The Inspector's Panel of Girls' Approved Schools, in a Working Party Report (1967), made similar observations. Having been set up in response to Approved School requests to study ways of dealing with an increased number of disturbed and difficult girls, members of the Working Party recommended the use of separate rooms, intensive care units and central secure units in response to these problems. Ackland (1982), in recording staffs' perceptions of girls in a CHE, notes a high incidence of such problems.

13. See also Warren (1961).

14. Though some practitioners have recorded changes in the behaviour of girls who reach such institutions. Tom Hart, for example, claimed that:

> Girls are learning early on in life that violence pays and that most people will give into them because they are afraid of violence. They find they can obtain money and cigarettes through threats of violence. With the arrival of Women's Lib. they don't see themselves as criminal decoys, they are joining in the actual robbery. Indeed, often the teenage girls I have met are more sophisticated and brighter than their male counterparts, and are the prime instigators. (Hart, *Evening Standard,* 20 December 1977)

Such claims have been reiterated in the media, see Morris and Gelsthorpe (1981).

15. It is significant, too, that there is a widespread assumption that corporal punishment is suited only to males. Since the nineteenth century corporal punishment has gradually been seen less and less appropriate for girls, though this view is increasingly adopted with regard to boys.

16. See Criminal Justice Act 1948 and Criminal Justice Act 1967.

17. Worrall (1981) notes this assumption in her study of probation work. See discussion of Parsloe (1972).

18. Hudson (1981) observes that social workers tend to describe the delinquent activities of girls as 'problematic behaviour' rather than 'delinquent behaviour'.

19. See Donohue and Todd (1981) for further illustration of this view.

20. That there are inherent problems with the use of official statistics is a point well documented. The chief problem here relates to the 'dark figure' of crime and those social acts prohibited by criminal law but which are not reported to the police or recorded by them and thus do not appear in statistics. It is now well recognised that official statistics may be an index of crime categories and their enforcement, but cannot be regarded in an unproblematic way as an index of levels of offending or of who commits crime. See Box (1981); Wiles (1971); and Kitsuse and Cicourel (1963).

21. See also Webb (1984).

22. See, in particular, A.K. Cohen (1955); Blos (1957); Gibbens (1957); Eysenck (1964); Morris (1964); Konopka (1966); Terry (1970); Cowie, Cowie and Slater (1968); and Richardson (1969). See Schofield (1965) for detailed discussion regarding girls' sexual problems. Some of these studies unproblematically accepted that the primary reason for girls being in institutions was sexual delinquency (e.g., Ball and Logan (1960); Richardson (1969)) and that this reflected a greater amount of sexual delinquency in girls (Terry (1970)), although some studies have attacked the vagueness of categories like 'moral danger' and 'incorrigibility' and have emphasised the importance of notions of 'morality' being included in discussions here (see e.g., Tappan (1969)).

23. Early writers such as Lombroso and Ferrero (1895) and Gibbens (1957) tend to equate a perceived interest in sexual matters by women with a debasement, as if they are in some way 'oversexed'.

24. See Deutsch (1944) for detailed exposition of this. The Freudian perspective has also influenced the work of Rolph (1955), Gibbens (1957) and Greenwald (1958) who have all addressed the topics of prostitution and promiscuity. Vedder and Somerville (1970) and Herskowitz (1969) who have written about girl delinquents in the United States also incorporate Freudian perspectives in their work. One criticism which might be applied to these writers is that they sometimes use the term 'sexual delinquency' to refer to promiscuity (which is surely as prevalent in male as female delinquents), sometimes to prostitution (which is seen to be commoner among females). Writers of this genre do not adequately address the issue of whether the higher incidence of prostitution is to be explained by socioeconomic or biological factors.

25. See Edwards (1981). See also Houghton (1957) for commentary on the ethic of purity in Victorian society.

26. See Eichler (1980) for an explanation and history of this concept.

27. See also Figes (1978), Shulamith Firestone (1979) and de Beauvoir (1979). The concept of 'patriarchy' is explored in the concluding chapter.

28. See Sharpe (1976). Script theory is described by Harris (1977). He suggests that 'type-scripts' are less rigid than 'roles' and refer in a general way to the type of behaviour we might expect to see given a particular background. He describes 'homologous legal, educational and occupational structures ... provide powerful expectancies by which actors come to assign themselves and others to limited classes of behaviour according to social "type". Such expectancies – which specify broad behavioural sequences as well as type to role images – are referred to as typescripts.'

29. See also Canburn (1979) on this point, and Parker, Cashmun and Turnbull (1981).

30. See Datesman and Scarpitti who came to the conclusion that girls who are sexually active have a much greater probability of being officially handled as delinquent than their male counterparts (1980: 50).

31. Children and Young Persons Act, 1969, s. 1(2)(c). See also Pat Cawson (1987).

32. See Hutter and Williams (1981) *Controlling Women*, whose contributors elaborate upon this point and illustrate different ways in which women's and girls' behaviour is 'boundaried' and controlled.

33. And consider some of the physical descriptions of girls in penal institutions and care homes for a moment – 'oversized, lumpish, uncouth and graceless' (Cowie, Cowie and Slater (1968: 166–7). The real issue here is whether or not these characteristics are the inherent property of the girls or a resultant effect of institutional regimes.

34. See Adler (1975 and 1977), Simon (1975) and Austin (1981).

35. See discussion in Smart (1976) and Campbell (1981), cf. Farrington (1984) who argues that this is not always appropriate.

36. For debates on the possibility of a value free social science, see Cotgrove (1972).

37. Bottomley (1979) has reiterated this concern to give attention to the symbiotic relationship between the origins and popularity of particular theories and the wider climate of opinion in society about deviance and the appropriate social response.

38. For a review of these writings, see Morris (1957).

39. John Stuart Mill wrote upon this theme in 1831, see von Hayek (1942) *The Spirit of the Age.*

40. The Evangelists were a religious group who emphasised salvation by faith and, in particular, the authority of the scriptures.

41. Kai Erikson's (1966) notion of the concepts of crime and 'deviance' bringing together 'upright consciences' seems relevant here in that the drawing of clear distinctions between the 'good' and the 'bad' may have served to justify the 'moral status'.

42. C. Wright Mills (1943) has reiterated this line of thinking in his description of the translation of public issues into private issues through the development of professional ideologies. See also Pearson (1975) on this issue.

43. For discussion regarding place of women in nature – culture polarity, see 'Natural Facts: an historical perspective on science and sexuality', by MacCormack and Strathern (1980).

44. See Havelock Ellis (1894) for an exposition which embodies this theme.

45. For detailed discussion see Sayers (1982), Edwards (1981), and Banks and Banks (1964).

46. See Vicinus (1977); Delamont and Duffin (1978); Sachs and Wilson (1978); Wolpe (1974); Atkinson (1978); and Dyhouse (1981) who describe opposition to women's education.

47. See, for example, *The Unexpurgated Case Against Woman Suffrage*, Wright

(1913), and Karslake (1867).

48. See also contributions to Bowker (1978) *Women, Crime and the Criminal Justice System*; Shacklady Smith (1978); and Casburn (1979). Other commentators have approached the 'knowledge' or images of female offenders that we have by directly contrasting theories about male and female offenders and by pointing out where the trajectories of theories differ; see Campbell (1981), and Leonard (1982), for example.

49. 'Feminist criminology' might be considered akin to the 'new criminology' with its emphasis on political conceptions of crime and deviance, especially since there is concern to discuss notions of power and power relationships as they affect these conceptions.

50. The lack of interest or research in this area has also been attributed to the statistically small numbers of female offenders. See Heidensohn (1968), and Walker (1973).

51. See Bowker (1978), ch. 5 for a brief summary of research on girl gangs.

52. See Datesman, *et al.* (1975) who similarly seek to apply to females (or at least to test the utility in applying) theories of delinquency previously limited to males.

53. See also the earlier comment of Chetwynd (1975) that it is imperative to include women in current studies to correct 'imbalances and injustices' in our knowledge. Stanley (1981) calls this the 'women and ... syndrome'.

54. Moreover, the concept of 'criminality' itself needs to be examined. The approach does not question the acceptance of 'criminology' as a field of study, but rather protects conventional analyses. See Cousins (1980), for example.

55. This is akin to the demand of Taylor *et al.* (1973) for a 'fully social theory of deviance' and, incidentally suffers some of the same problems, by not specifying what kind of social theory we are to use, for example.

56. See Figes (1977), and Sachs and Wilson (1978) for further references here.

57. For a history of the concept of ideology see, for example, Lichtheim (1967) and Larrain (1979).

58. Another way of depicting what is meant would be to refer to 'discourse' theory (Foucault (1972); see also Hudson (1982)). The term 'manipulation' too is relevant in referring to the production of ideas by dominant groups transmitted via the cultural institutions of education, the mass media and so forth. Marcuse (1965), for instance, in his writing tends to identify the conditions under which people live and think, and which thereby determine what they think, with 'the prevailing indoctrination' by the media, advertisements and so on to which 'they are exposed.

59. For further discussion on the different usages of the term see 'Ideology and Consciousness', Giddens (1979), and Abercrombie *et al.* (1980).

60. Amongst writers on this more sophisticated theme, tying the concept of ideology to epistemological issues, there is Coward and Ellis (1977); Larrain (1979); and Sumner (1979).

2 The research methodology

The preceding comments combine to suggest that there are many 'biases' and distortions in our knowledge about female offenders. The images of females which form a criminological legacy may be false. We do not know with any certainty, for instance, the relative influences of 'nature' and 'nurture' upon the behaviour of females, nor whether sex differences have been exaggerated out of proportion. Some of those recently engaging in research in this area have readily and pointedly turned to an examination of 'sexist' ideology within theories about female offenders. But they have been content to examine past and present theories about female crime to stimulate discussion on the apparent sexism within the criminal justice system.

Often, writers have referred to sentencing patterns to make us aware of the sexism, as if this procedure alone reflects sexist ideology, in that female offenders may be dealt with on the basis of their sex more than on the basis of the usual factors of current offence, previous offences and so on.[1] This viewpoint and analysis is limited. Sentencing is more complex than this since it is the culmination of numerous processes. Where reports are submitted, for instance, they reflect the beliefs and assumptions of practitioners who contribute to the court's understanding of the offence committed by 'shaping' explanations for the crime.[2] Moreover, sentencing reflects the provision of disposals for offenders in the criminal justice system.[3] The main import of my critique of the feminist analysis of criminological theories and the criminal justice system as sexist is that it concentrates on the ideological focus and direction of the 'distortion' without acknowledging the practical influences which may affect it. Attempts to theorize 'sexism' remain at a level which is not accessible to any analysis grounded in practice.

In the following section of the book I provide examples of 'sexism' in practice, and on this empirical level it will be shown that the evidence cannot be read as a simple endorsement of claims about sexism.

My aim to illustrate sexism in operation entailed the consideration of practices in three different agencies: a mixed (male and female) assessment centre (Agency One), a girls' assessment centre (Agency Two), and a police juvenile liaison office (Agency Three). The intention was to gain a sense of the typical day-to-day routine considerations and beliefs which form the basis of practitioners' accounts of girls' delinquency or 'problem behaviour', and to gain some idea of the ways in which the conduct of girls is perceived and responded to as a distinct social problem. Some of the questions within the research were formulated thus: What are typical explanations for female offences proffered by practitioners? How do girls become labelled as a 'problem' group of offenders, and which girls pose the most problems for practitioners? Another question related to the prevalence of the notion of the 'disturbed' female. My aim here was to question how frequently and in what ways are female crimes said to be due to the 'abnormal psychology' of the offender.

In sum, these questions both relate to traditional images and understanding of female offenders which I have previously outlined, and are concerned with the extent to which 'femininity' is being 'policed' through the organizations. In other words, how far does action on the part of the practitioner correspond to traditional notions of 'the gentle sex', and to what extent does this constitute 'sexism'?

The research task
My aim was to gain information from professionals currently engaged in practice and to see these professionals *in situ* so as to be able to observe the interplay between the professionals' personal views, professional ideologies and organizational constraints.

Whilst it may be argued that qualitative methodology has little of the social prestige attached to quantitative research and is not always recognized as a legitimate source of either data collection or theory construction, this was an obvious choice of method. Indeed, qualitative methodology is an approach that is so constructed as to yield verifiable knowledge about the empirical social world. As Filstead describes it, 'qualitative methodology allows the researcher to "get close to the data"'. (1970: 6)[4]

Setting out the theoretical orientation: towards interactionism
Interactionists, phenomenologists and ethnomethodologists in considering how to study organizations treat as problematic all meanings which both individuals and groups have in the world in which they exist.[5] As Blumer (1969) notes, 'rules, roles and attitudes have no meaning outside the actors' perspectives and, for this reason, the actors rather than the institutions within which they are located and their roles become the primary focus of attention.[6] Indeed, the actors' perspective is seen as the important key to understanding the everyday world of the organization or agency. Following the definition of Becker *et al.,* the actors' 'perspective' is taken to be a set of ideas and actions used by a group in solving collective problems. The content of a group's perspective involves a definition of the environment and the problems it presents as seen by group members, an expression of what members expect to derive from the environment and the ideas and actions group members employ in dealing with the problem situation (Becker *et al.*, 1960: 280).[7] Thus the 'real

world' of the actors can be seen by the reader, and the actors' accounts and actions can be analyzed in terms of their contribution to the members' everyday world within the organization.[8]

Indeed, interactionists have provided an alternative perspective for the study of organizations. The structural-functionalists' assumptions that organizations can best be understood through an analysis of their stated and unstated goals, their decision-making structure and the various roles which participants are expected to fulfil[9] have given way to the more fundamental question of how the actions of everyday life are constructed into legitimate organizational behaviour (Silverman, 1970). Thus the 'normative idealizations' of Weberian bureaucracy and Etzonian 'goal models' have been put aside in favour of attempts to appreciate the construction of rational conduct.[10] In this perspective, therefore, duties, rules, goals and decisions are treated as problematic and are identified as structural features of organizations only by virtue of their recognition and definition as such by the actors involved (Cicourel, 1976: 44–53; Silverman, 1970 and 1974).

The interactionist perspective has been used most notably in relation to the sociology of deviance. Indeed, a statement which encapsulates the approach adopted by interactionists in their investigations of everyday life is that of Volkart, and this has been well applied to the concept of crime:

> Facts do not have a uniform existence apart from the persons who observe and interpret them. Rather the 'real' facts are the ways in which different people come to define situations. (Volkart, 1951: 30)

Becker has summarized the perspective in the following way:

> Deviance is not a quality of the act the person commits, but rather a consequence of the application by others of rules and sanctions to an 'offender'. (Becker, 1963: 9)

Certainly, in the study of juvenile delinquency the focus of attention has generally shifted from the search for pathological features of crime causation towards an appreciation of what the act defined as deviant means for both the youth concerned and the definer. Thus activities labelled as deviant have been located in their social setting.[11] In their work the interactionists have clearly called into question the presuppositions upon which the criminal justice systems and its agencies operate. Further, by critically analyzing the institutions and agencies of the criminal justice system, the interactionists have opened a field of enquiry which previous epistemologies either ignored or treated as non-problematic.

Cicourel (1976), for instance, considers the everyday workings of the police, probation departments, courts and schools, and demonstrates how these agencies all contribute to various kinds of transformations of the original events that led to the law enforcement contact. Coupled with these organizational factors are those relating to the establishment of 'character' from family background and future potential (Sachs, 1972: Emerson, 1969). In this way, Cicourel argues, the agencies appear to generate delinquency by their routine encounters with juveniles.

Pearson includes the interactionist approach as a variant of 'misfit sociology' and makes the pertinent comment that:

> The critical appraisal of deviance, morality, order and deviance-correction which misfit sociology provides points through the professional routine, taken-for-granted world to a world of moral and political uncertainty. Dereification shows up the professional's capacity in creating the problems which he solves. The dissolution of the metaphysics of hierarchy gives the underdog misfit a voice in what consensus welfare had imagined was an already settled debate. (Pearson, 1975: 74)

In the sociology of education, too, there have been parallel developments; the use of interactionist precepts has made a major contribution to the understanding of the process of schooling. Seminal contributions have been made by Young (1971), Hargreaves (1967, 1972 and 1978), and Lacey (1970), for instance. All have attempted to explore the ways in which the education system defines certain types of knowledge and certain cultural styles as more valid and worthwhile than others.[12]

Whilst there are certain deficiencies in my own work which make it difficult to label my approach as purely 'interactionist',[13] it is the perspective with which I tended to identify most closely. The deficiencies relate mainly to the fact that in the agencies my formal representations were to the staff and not to the 'clients' or 'residents'. I did, of course, engage in conversation with the juveniles involved but my attention was primarily focused upon the staff.[14] However, since my interest was not so much in the interaction between these groups but on the *processing* of juveniles and on how staff developed views of girls, this was done with some justification. Clearly, it would have been important to include the juveniles' perspectives had my intention been to complete an analysis of a total institution (along the lines of Goffman, 1961) where an inmate culture is likely to develop and where 'inmates' make a significant contribution to institutional life. But in the agencies or organizations which formed the focus of my study the juveniles were a transient population.

It might be suggested in criticism that I accept, wholesale, the view that staff definitions of events are simply imposed on the subordinate group (the clients) by virtue of staff control over the use of coercion, scarce resources, time and space, for instance. This is not the case. I am aware that organizational reality is very much the result of negotiation and that subordinate groups in effect modify the dominant group's attempt to impose its own sectional meaning on others. Nevertheless, despite this complexity it is perhaps possible to say that negotiation nearly always *favours* the dominant group. This is true in the sense that staff have more power in shaping the norms of everyday life than subordinate groups, thus negotiation, response and possible modification of those forms takes place within the already established framework (Gouldner, 1968; Gill, 1974; Bramham, 1981).[15] Since my fieldwork was concerned with the development of practitioners' ideas through daily practice and events (partly in an attempt to counter some of the wider claims and assertions of radical theorists who consider levels of distortion), concentration on 'overdog' as opposed to 'underdog' views[16] seems important in the sense that they 'shape the world in which the juveniles move' (see Gouldner, 1968). This is not to say, however, that whilst staff may control events, they are not influenced by various factors relating to the agencies in which they work and it is some of these influences which I describe.

In addition to my awareness of these deficiencies, however, there are more serious criticisms of the approach which subsequently had a major impact on my work. One criticism is that interactionism is empiricist. It is obviously important to note that interactionism is not a monolithic tradition, nor is it clearly marked off from other forms of sociology. Despite distinctions made between phenomenological labelling and ethnomethodological approaches and much talk about these competing paradigms, the discipline, it may be argued, is not so much composed of a set of mutually exclusive, internally coherent approaches, as a number of loosely defined, overlapping and, in important respects, internally inconsistent frameworks.

There are other limitations, too, which refer to the fact that interactionists' studies tend to be partisan (Huber, 1973) and to the fact that the world of the subjects being studied is rarely contextualized. The partisanship, however, is not denied by interactionists. Becker, for example, unashamedly concludes that the researcher 'can never avoid taking sides'; he argues that any search for a 'balanced picture' is fallacious and illusory (1960). The failure to contextualize micro-sociological studies, Taylor *et al.* (1973) suggest, leads to paradoxical determinism. So whilst at one level the interactionists allow their actors free will to chose the activities in which they engage and the definition to which they ascribe, at another level the actions are seen as channelled into a set pattern of interactions which shape and sustain their social world and the definitions which others put on it. For instance, teachers (Hargreaves, 1972), policemen (Piliavin and Briar, 1964) and psychiatric workers (Strauss *et al.,* 1964) are rarely described in their interactions with those who shape, sustain or restrict their perspectives.

A serious criticism relates to the fact that interactionists have consistently ignored the historical and political pressures which have created the social structures within which the events they are investigating are played out. Kantner (1972), Smith (1973), Gouldner (1968 and 1971) and Taylor *et al.* (1979), for instance, all offer pertinent criticism here.[17] The basic tenet of their criticism relates to the absence of a critical conception of ideology and power. Interactionists have repeatedly ignored the way in which ideology is developed and employed by the powerful to create social institutions. As Gouldner describes, this is partly derived from the identification with the 'underdog' which is prevalent in interactionism. Moreover, in everyday life, reference to power differentials is rarely expressed directly by members involved, though as Gouldner argues:

> Legitimacy and 'authority' never eliminate power, they merely defocalise it, make it latent. (Gouldner, 1971: 292)

Taylor, Walton and Young present it this way:

> In so far as it is legitimate to view deviance as a challenge to authority at either the instrumental or oppositional level, it must also be viewed as ultimately predetermined by structural inequalities and ideologically enforced consensus, *no matter how complex the mediatory variables*. From this viewpoint, structured inequalities, preserved and protected by the powerful, act as causal forces prevented the realisation of actors' interests by means other than deviant ones. [Their emphasis] (Taylor, Walton and Young, 1975: 169)

Thus the deviant's version of events becomes a kind of reproduction of that of the master institutions, whose definition of reality with all embracing power has never been stamped upon him or her.

The Marxist critique focuses on the tendency of the interactionists to neglect macro-level theory (see Taylor, Walton and Young, 1975). Their argument is not simply that there is a gap which needs to be filled, but that there is an inherent defect in the approach which renders comprehensive analysis unattainable. The argument is often presented along the lines that interactionists' work focuses on appearances and neglects the underlying forms which produce those forms. Further, this formulation is sometimes faced with the claim that these appearances are ideological, and that any study which restricts itself to them is itself ideological.

In some versions of this argument the criticism is put more forcibly, and interactionism is not simply charged with accidental neglect but lambasted because it is *unable* to theorize the larger social system. In other words, criticism rests on the view that the interactionist approach is unable to recognize the way in which events in a setting are produced by features of that larger system. This inability essentially derives, it is argued, from a presupposition that actors are free to define and construct the world in any way they wish. Allied to this is the failure to go beyond recounting the views of participants to questioning how these views are generated and what consequences they, and the actions deriving from them, have.

In defence, however, and with equanimity, a number of things must be said about these criticisms. The first is that the appearance/reality dichotomy is only really drawn in rhetoric, useful for assigning priority to one set of phenomena over another. Secondly, it may be argued that criticisms which extend beyond this dichotomy may still only apply to interactionist rhetoric rather than to practice. Thus, for example, it is difficult to find an interactionist study which deals with the actor as if s/he is completely autonomous.

Although aware of some of the problems associated with the interactionist approach, I proceeded with the understanding that noting elements of this methodology could, in fact, contribute to my attempt to 'paint in' some of the subtleties involved in analyses of the distortion of knowledge about female offenders. It would help to modify early insistence that any bias in our knowledge is direct and explicit.

The experience of previous studies (e.g., Hargreaves, 1967 and 1975) would seem to indicate that despite some limitations, participant observation is a method which can elicit a considerable amount of information of this type and ideally this would have been the chosen method. Professional boundaries and ethics made this impossible. None the less, simple observation seemed to have distinct advantages over other kinds of approaches and it was the method I adopted.[18]

Why observe?

First, I aimed to use this method to avoid the 'cold interview' situation of simply meeting practitioners on one or two occasions and expecting them to talk freely; my premise was that familiarity would be conducive to the giving of information. Indeed, to meet the worker or practitioner in his or her work rather than in the interview room is a situation in which the worker is more confident than the researcher and consequently one which is likely to induce the giving of information. Moreover, by 'being around' and observing, the researcher has access to remarks and conversations, clues and insights, which cannot be obtained otherwise. Secondly, my intention was to examine the disparity which sometimes occurs between thought, or belief, and action.

The research process

Wiseman has usefully outlined the various steps involved for the researcher entering the actor's world. Comparing the researcher's approach to 'what any social actor does in order to conduct himself as properly as possible in a foreign setting and thus avoiding sanctions' (1970: 270), she describes the sequential steps in the following way:

1. He [the researcher] observes everyday action and attempts to reconstruct the definition of the situation on which 'natives' appear to base their

activities.

2. He asks questions of 'the natives' to find out 'what is going on' and what sort of action is expected to ensue as a result.

3. He finds special informants. These are people who, by virtue of some official capacity in the world under study, or because of some marginal status that makes them unusually sensitive to everyday expectations, can give the researcher a great deal of insight (the real 'low down') about some society.[19]

4. He *tests* both the answers received to direct questions and the interpretation he makes of the action observed to see if, in the context they were made, the perspective he is developing 'works'. That is, he sees if his analysis would enable a person to participate intelligently in the setting and to reasonably understand and predict the reactions of others. (Original emphasis) (Wiseman, 1970: 270)

Some of the initial material in the agencies took the form of taped interviews with staff whom I identified as 'key workers'. These tended to be the senior staff (management), the team leaders, senior supervisors or senior officers as well as the 'experts' on hand – the psychiatrists, educational psychologists, school co-ordinator, those who had 'been around' for a lengthy period of time, and others who, because of their strategic position within the staff organization, were seemingly well-placed to give insights into the work.[20] Indeed, I chose these individuals because they were able to crystallize the current social scene, describe the various perspectives of the staff and identify characters and events which might elucidate these features.[21] This is not to imply that their assessment of events was always unimpeachable. However, as Blum comments when writing of the use of 'informants':

A word of caution should be added in regard to data thus obtained. They should not be accepted at face value but must be carefully screened in the light of the nature of the researcher's relationship to the people and the motives which prompt certain people to give him information and others not to do so. (Blum, 1970: 85)

From observation in Agencies One and Two particularly, I learned that there was, in fact, a seeming paradox in that those who wrote the most about the girls tended to have the least to do with them in day-to-day activity. It was a constant complaint from supervisors that the credibility of the seniors' view about the girls was dubious, simply because they had the least knowledge about them. The seniors reported to me that they not only caught glimpses of their 'charges' and sometimes talked to them, but that they relied to some extent on 'picking up' information from supervisors, both from their reports on the girls' behaviour and from informal chatting.

Nevertheless, because during the early period of observation a proportion of the incidents and interaction lay beyond my powers of interpretation, a reliance on 'key informants' helped to 'escalate' insight. For example, I could record an interaction between a residential social worker[22] and a girl (or boy) in Agency One, but very little added up to produce a clear idea of the responses to them, thus discussion with 'informants' initially helped to place events in perspective.[23]

Additionally, much information was gained from casual conversation with staff; comments about girls were followed up with questions as to why a particular view was held, or why a certain action relating to a girl was thought to be necessary. Information was also collected by attending meetings (group meetings, reviews, case conferences), and I had open access to all files and reports.

As a general note on my approach, I should record that I experienced what Colin Lacey (1976) has termed the 'it is all happening somewhere else' syndrome in these first stages too. The feeling developed very vividly at times in all the agencies that the real action, the real social drama was going on somewhere else. Whilst I was in the group room there were perhaps important discussions in the assistant superintendent's office; whilst I was observing one confrontation, a really critical commentary on the girls was being provided by the consultant psychiatrist to another audience. The root of this feeling lay in the nature of the task, however, and I had to learn to record as accurately as possible selected aspects of everyday life. The interest in the situation perhaps emerges as the pieces of the amorphous and intricate puzzle are put together, but it is a difficult task in which the pieces are not defined.

Without exception, in these agencies the practitioners allowed me access to their world. It was obviously important to be non-partisan; neither affiliated to particular staff nor to particular child-care ideologies. I was at pains to share my time with all members of staff and to avoid the temptation to affiliate myself to the higher echelons of the staff hierarchies whose anxiety to create a good impression might have afforded extra comforts and protection. Because of this attempt I provided the staff with an opportunity not only of confiding in someone but also of converting someone to their side. As a result, the staff in all the agencies repeatedly approached me to discuss their work, the problems they encountered, and the solutions they achieved. My own observations were used to confirm or deny the credibility of the accounts so offered by placing them in perspective.

The questions asked
Conversation with the practitioners was invariably prefaced by my asking them about previous experience in child care or related occupations; it seemed important for me to gain some idea of the person I was talking to before I could use their comments in any sensible way. One would have

to consider a comment about girls being much 'worse than boys' or 'much more difficult to handle' from a practitioner who had no previous experience in child care or with children at all, very differently from a similar comment made by an ex-approved school teacher who had a family of sons and daughters, or by a local youth club leader.

Other questions generally revolved around the practitioners' feelings about the girls. Did they, for instance, think it important to consider certain physiological factors which might affect a girl's temperament? Did they see women and girls as more emotional creatures than men and boys? Were problems thought to originate in the family, for instance?

Some of the questions related to the commission of criminal offences, the kinds of offences which the girls committed, their subsequent behaviour in the agency and the practitioners' perception of their problems.

Another group of questions concerned the practitioners' own response to their work. What shocked them, for instance? What was the most difficult kind of behaviour to deal with? What was thought to be the most appropriate response to difficult behaviour?

Thus my concern in the interviewing and questioning was to find out about practitioners' typical understanding of the girls' behaviour and of how the girls came to be there. I was interested in their understanding of how offending might be related to other problems, and in how they thought they ought to respond. Within this framework of concerns I attempted to construct a picture of what 'difficult', and conversely 'normal', behaviour on the part of the girls might look like through the eyes of the staff. For instance, if 'femininity' in various forms was seen as desirable, which girls in the agency were seen as the worst 'offenders' against this criterion and why? My aim here was to consider how far the action on the part of the practitioner relates to a stereotypical picture of the girl's behaviour and how far it corresponds to the notion of the 'gentle sex'.

The questioning did not always include comparison with boys but this was an implicit aim and comments relating to this were encouraged, especially where staff had experience with both boys and girls.

The interviews: a note
In spite of their wide use, interviews are limited in execution and analysis by underlying assumptions. One assumption is that respondents use the same language and similar conceptual framework as the interviewer. For example, commentators suggest that social class, as one system of shared social meanings, underlies styles of affect and mood which differentially come into play, making, for example, unspoken, unexpressed feelings as meaningful as the answer given and a lack of response as valuable as the long, factual discourse. Moreover, they point out that the interviewer is

'a pervasive symbol of the demand to be opinionated'. Indeed, the interviewer has to be aware that probing, the structure of the questioning and the soliciting of responses perhaps crystallizes the respondent's self concept, thereby soliciting previously 'unheld opinion'.[24]

Further difficulties arise from the assumption that it is possible to study complex areas of knowledge without substantive training in those areas. For instance, how much do missed nuances distort the meanings sought? In addition to these potential difficulties informants may consciously and unconsciously distort or conceal information from the interviewer. Writers have described this phenomenon as the 'defensive' and 'evasive' style of responding. In the former type of response, informants may retreat behind the protective cloak of a 'line'; in the latter, informants may give the interviewer the type of information they think he or she is looking for.[25] Further, in the interview the informant reveals only a 'partial self' which should be checked where possible against other sources of information: what action is taken, for instance, or what the informant writes.

Using documents

Official biographies are frequently used as a valid source of data, yet it is important to be aware of the social processes involved in the construction of official data. Madge (1965) has written about the unthinking use of it by looking at the limitations of using personal documents and case work reports.[26] Indeed, Hirschi and Selvin (1967) advise the researcher to ignore completely official documents and accounts in the initial stages of the research so as to avoid forming preconceived ideas prior to meeting the respondent. This strategy has been termed by Bramham (1980) as 'using ignorance to prevent error'. In contrast, however, it has been argued that written data can be used effectively to ease the researcher into the life of those s/he wishes to study. This was a strategy adopted by Millham *et al.* (1975) for example. The strategy I used was to make reference to the case work files only towards the end of the research. In this way, whilst avoiding the process of colouring perceptions, it became a useful technique to generate data by comparing the spoken account of the child's behaviour with the version supplied in written material. Reading files also crystallized the images the staff had of children, which crucially affected their dealings with them.

A final note on data collection

In describing the data collection methods used in the research (abstracting information from records, reports and memoranda, interviews and observation) it is important to stress that they were not used as separate research strategies. While this eclecticism may have epistemological limitations (see Rock, 1979: 217–38), it is also possible to argue that, by using these techniques together, the researcher may attempt to compensate for the weaknesses of any single strategy used alone. Denzin (1970) has noted this in his discussion of methodological triangulation. Hence, throughout my research I attempted to use systematically different types of data in complementary ways in order to investigate the issues which emerged. Thus any questions and issues which emerged from one area of practice and from my observation were 'retested' in a different area, for example, in discussions with the staff.

Having gathered research material, however, the researcher is left with innumerable problems of validity and reliability. The researcher has to be able to remove her own 'rose-tinted spectacles' which may have coloured the kaleidoscope of patterns within the agency which she has been observing.[27] This problem of validity of accounts has created much debate in the literature. The validity of most sociological explanations is perhaps assessed in terms of (a) the internal logic of the explanation and method; and (b) the availability of sociological data from the same or other studies which confirms or supports the explanation. As Phillipson puts it, the real question here is 'what is the relationship between the retrospective reflections of the sociologist and the past realities he is trying to understand?' (1972: 149).

Indeed, validity is perhaps inseparable from what is acceptable as competently and properly arrived at. Such acceptability rests upon ideological assumptions and traditional social practices and conventions. Since the natural history of academic sociologists differs from that of their research subjects (i.e., the actors) we might expect different criteria of acceptability from them and thus different notions of validity. Schutz (1962) sets out the problem by arguing that 'objective' explanations of social scientists as second-order constructs, must remain consistent with the first-order constructs of common sense which the actors use in creating and sustaining social reality. Schutz proposes three postulates to accomplish this (1962: 43–4). First, that one's account should be logically consistent, clear, distinct and non-contradictory; secondly, that it should enable action in the real world to be understood by the original actors. This later point has been termed by Schutz (1962:43–4) as the 'postulate of adequacy', whereby each term or concept in the model of actions must be constructed so that an act actually performed in the world in the way indicated by the construct would be understandable for the actor him/herself and for his/her associates in terms of commonsense schemes of interpretation.

Phillipson (1972) has argued that it is really only this third postulate which is crucial for the establishment of validity, although he recognizes a certain tension between the first and third postulates as Schultz expresses them. For example, if the reasoning of the actors is not logical and clear then generating an 'adequate' account would not, in Schutz's terms, be possible. Hence, the first postulate is often ignored. A second difficulty arises from the social scientist's need to generalize. The solution suggested by Phillipson is to limit context specific meaning while

ensuring continuity and compatibility between the sociologists' interpretations and the researchers' common sense interpretations. (Phillipson, 1972: 151)

As a consequence, validity may be established by showing that, for all practical purposes, the second-order constructs of the social scientist are consistent with the researchers first-order constructions. As Wiseman has described:

In this type of study... the validity problem is *not* whether the empirical indications used to operationalise concepts are indeed valid representations of this phenomenon from an objective or scientific point of view, but whether or not the investigator has represented the social world of the actor *as the actor sees it*. [Emphasis added] (Wiseman, 1970: 280)

In other words, the suggestion is that the sociologist's or ethnographer's account should be translatable back into the researcher's commonsense meanings.

There are obviously several ways of testing validity and representation here. The first method I used was to adopt a technique frequently utilized in psychotherapy or other such situations, where the intention on the part of the therapist may be to 'slow down' discussion so that the full import of what is being said can be realized or to test the accuracy of his or her understanding of what has been said. This is the simple technique of repetition. Thus, a statement might be rephrased with the addendum of 'is this how you see it?', or 'is this what you are saying?'. At the end of my discussions and interviews with practitioners I also attempted to summarize what I had been told in the hope that any apparent misunderstandings on my part would be revealed. Of course, there was the danger here of giving scope for the practitioner to change his or her view about some matter and to retract words they wished they had not spoken, but since in my daily discourse with the staff I tended to rephrase and repeat those questions presented in the interview, there was always some evidence of consistency in the views proffered.

A second method of testing entailed open meetings with the staff in the concluding period of my research when I presented preliminary findings. This provided an opportunity to test not only the content of preliminary conclusions but also their representativeness among all the actors. Discussion with staff was of importance here because I had to ensure that the data I had obtained was not idiosyncratic or unrepresentative. In other circumstances it might be possible to test this out by 'passing as a native' in similar social settings (Wiseman, 1970: 270), but since this was not a comparative study, in the sense of visiting a number of police or assessment agencies, for example, there were no comparative data to aid the reliability of the material collected previously. At least, any comparisons to be made could not be made by virtue of the nature of the agency.

A third method of testing was to let the actors (or subjects) read my account of their practices and views and to invite comments. Those who read the material gave no indication that I had misrepresented their views and, indeed, concurred that their practices had been correctly represented.

The methods I used, of course, are not 'watertight'. Whilst they might seem to guarantee that the researcher has correctly represented the actors' practices as the actors conceive them, and that they therefore avoid selective editing and biased interpretation, it may be that many different accounts would be accepted by the actors as descriptions of how they think, experience and act in the world. Max Weber, for instance, argues that actual action occurs in a state of inarticulate half-consciousness or actual unconsciousness of its subjective meaning. Thus, researchers may sometimes persuade actors to agree that they thought particular things which they had not, in all truth, previously thought of. Also, as the sociologist is obliged to generalize and illustrate, to edit out context-specific meanings, congruence with subjective meanings may sometimes be lost.

One way out of this problem is, of course, to allow the reader her/himself to judge the extent of congruence or compatibility of the researcher's account with the actors' meanings. The researcher might facilitate this not only by uncovering the actors' interpretive schemes, rules and background tacit knowledge, but also by making explicit her own methods of data collection, her own schemes and background relevance or taken-for-granted cognitive assumptions in her recognition, selection and interpretation of data, in her selection of examples as illustrative of her concepts, and in her generation of an account. To this end, my description of the methodology employed is an honest description, if all too revealing of its inadequacies.

Notes

1. See Chesney-Lind (1977), Casburn (1979), and Moulds (1980), for instance.
2. For discussion on the influence of social inquiry reports or court room decision-making, see White (1972). See Hardiker and Webb (1979) for discussion on practitioners' interpretations of crime.
3. The absence of detention centres for girls and young women, for instance, may affect the sentencing of females.
4. See Douglas on this same point (1971: 11).
5. Interactionism was one of the central elements of the 'new sociology', that rather inchoate opposition movement to the dominance of positivism, which emerged in the 1960s (see Taylor, Walton and Young (1975); Rubington and

Weinberg (1968); Turner (1974)).
6. See Blumer (1969: 1–60).
7. See also Shibutani (1955) for his descriptions of situations which require the application of the actors' perspectives. 'Perspective' is very similar to the notion of 'ideology' used by Strauss et al. (1964: 8) for example, when talking of the perspective of professional groups.
8. See Scott and Lyman (1968).
9. See for example Etzioni (1964); Weber (1947); and Parsons (1960).
10. Blumer argues that it is impossible to tell what determines a formal organization scheme contains prior to the time that questions are actually addressed to it (1973: 272).
11. See Parker (1974) and Young (1971) for instance. In addition, interactionists have insisted that the definers of deviance, the media, for instance (see Cohen and Young, 1973), the education system (see Cicourel and Kitsuse, 1968: Hargreaves, 1971), and the police (see Piliavin and Briar, 1964) be closely scrutinised and their role in constructing and sustaining the meaning of juvenile delinquency elucidated.
12. Reynolds and Sullivan (1980) and Karabel and Halsey (1977) have reviewed these developments.
13. A truly interactional account needs to interrelate the worlds of the various actors involved, both in terms of the content of each group's social world and of the product of each group's interactions with others. Wiseman's (1970) study of the treatment of Skid Row alcoholics is a rare example of such an analysis (see also Bramham, 1980 and Ackland, 1982). The study of two mental institutions by Strauss et al. (1964) provides another example, though there is greater weight given to 'professional actors' in this analysis than to others.
14. My original intention was to talk with 'clients' or 'residents' too, but access was denied on grounds that this would be too intrusive for the practitioners to be able to carry out their work in normal fashion.
15. Wilkin's (1964) notion of the spiral of deviancy amplification provides an example of this, whereby actors have free will to choose the activities in which they engage and the definition to which they subscribe, but at the same time, can be seen as forced into a narrow range of interactions which shape and sustain their social world.
16. As in the tradition of Becker's school of deviance, for instance, (see Downes and Rock, 1979).
17. See also Pearson (1975).
18. Despite this initial limitation it soon became apparent that the most useful position to adopt was that of 'active observer'. I make reference to this realisation in a further note on the methodology (see Appendix C).

It was my initial intention to examine agencies within one geographical area but this proved impracticable. However, whilst I realized that I would not achieve a coherent picture of images of female offenders in any one area it was still possible to examine images within separate and distinct organizations no matter where they were. So whilst I could not follow through cases on their frequent passages between agencies and look at the general understandings and inconsistencies in this kind of passage, I could still examine the internal logic of the organizations' and practitioners' response to female offenders.

It may be argued that all sociological research occurs in the context of a set of exigencies which bear on how the research is conducted and the data gathered. Ideally, only theoretical and methodological considerations should guide the researcher in his/her quest for data, but the contingencies of social life rarely afford this ideal.

I focused on three agencies, as I describe in the introduction to this chapter, and all three agencies were appropriate choices because they covered a range of entrances into the juvenile justice and care systems. My focus on the assessment process seemed a very appropriate approach to gaining insight into practitioners'images of their clients since their role and work is such that it entails detailed analysis of girls and their needs. Similarly, I was keen to work with the police because of their significant role as 'gatekeepers' (see Thorpe *et al.*, 1980), or decision-makers with regard to entrance into juvenile justice system. I spent a period of three and a half months in each agency, although contact was maintained with them for several months after.

19. See also Cicourel who notes that such people enable the researcher 'to restrict the frame of possibilities in the research design, in short, to attempt to specify and test relevant hypotheses' (1964: 65).
20. Perhaps also to have most influence on what was recorded about the girls.
21. All the interviews were 'in depth' interviews using a loosely structured schedule. Thus, whilst I discussed the same range of issues with practitioners, the issues were not necessarily presented to them in the same order.
22. Or child care officer: the terms were used synonymously within these practice settings.
23. Occasionally, in the first stages of the research, junior staff (e.g., supervisors, residential social workers) commented to me that it was not for them to express an opinion and that there were 'experts' around who were perhaps the people I should talk to. At the same time, they were very eager to point out to me that the so called 'experts' and seniors relied upon their judgements and descriptions to be able to formulate the 'expert' view. I sensed a certain amount of resentment and frustration relating to this; junior staff felt that they were being exploited by the seniors who were rarely around to deal with the normal hub of activity, or in times of crisis. Thus despite my use of 'key workers' I was sensitive to this issue and attempted to avoid fuelling the situation by seeking out informers privately. More importantly, I attempted to make it clear to all staff that I was interested in everyone's views and that I had no particular allegiance to the management.
24. On the general problems of interviewing see Kuhn (1962) and Smith (1972).
25. Holmstrom, cited in Manning (1967), has described this phenomenon in terms of a 'two game' situation.
26. See Kitsuse and Cicourel (1962), for example. Garfinkel notes that such files are not intended to be used as 'actuarial records' and attempts to use them as such are like trying to make a 'silk purse out of a sow's ear' (1967: 190). See also Belson and Hood (1967) and Walter (1977) on the limitations of using files and case records.
27. Wittgenstein expresses this problem of myopia or 'obscured' vision philosophically when he writes that 'But really you do not see the eye.... And nothing in the visual field allows you to infer that it is seen by an eye' (1971: 171).

3 The fieldwork: images in practice – Agency One

This is the first of three chapters dealing with images of young female 'offenders' in practice. Each chapter follows a similar format by, first, describing the setting for the fieldwork undertaken (paying some attention to the explicit aims and practices of each agency concerned), and secondly, examining the images which practitioners hold of the females within those agencies. Initially I look at the content of professional policy and commitments of the agencies' staff where these may be identified, and then at the themes which emerge from their comments about girls and from their interpretations of girls' behaviour. In each setting my aim is to discern elements of practice ideologies which relate particularly to girls and to establish the staffs' views concerning the appropriateness of these practices and ideas.

In a subsequent chapter I place each staff group's comments and interpretations in context and take note of the exigencies of practice which contribute to the shaping of their images of girls. Thus I attempt to observe the interplay between personal views, professional ideologies and organizational constraints and its effect upon the development of understanding of females.

Agency One

Agency One was formerly a children's home. It opened as an observation and assessment centre in 1974 and was extended with educational facilities in the late 1970s.[1] At the time of the research the agency had 32 places comprising 28 assessment beds, two 'holding' beds (one boys' and one girls') and two night admission places (again, one boys' and one girls'). In practice, however, many more assessment places became 'holding' places and the admission of juveniles was based entirely on need rather than on the number of places allotted to that particular gender, so that the composition of the clientele did not always bear close relation to policy dictates. The policy statements also indicated that the assessment facilities were for girls and boys between the ages of eight and fifteen years, who had recently become the concern of the social services department. The statement continued thus:

> It is our job to live with these children for between four and eight weeks, try to gain their confidence and assess their needs. It is also our job to have the children medically examined, educationally assessed and if necessary psychiatrically assessed and to record and document all our findings. (Social Services Department: 1981)

This was clearly in accordance with the 'official' view of assessment expressed some years earlier:

> The process of assessment requires the use of all available diagnostic resources and interdisciplinary consultation in order to make a thorough study of the child and his family relationships and, through observation techniques and specialists skills make a diagnosis of his problems and assess his total needs, emotional, social, physical, mental and educational. (DHSS: 1970)

Policy and staffing

Policy statements stressed that in the centre children were to be treated as individuals and their physical needs provided for. The job of the staff was described in this way:

> staff are responsible for attending to the physical and emotional needs of the children; assisting in the Teaching Unit; involving children in activities; daily recording of observations; writing assessment reports etc.... Staff need to supplement and not supplant the natural parents. Staff need, above all, to enjoy the company of children and to have the need as much regard for the problems of the parents and family as they do of the child. (SSD document: 1981)

There was some variation in job description according to the status of the worker. Team leaders, for instance, of which there were three, were also

> responsible for helping staff with anxieties related to the job; being aware of stresses and strains on staff so that these could be mitigated; attempting to prevent crises or dealing with them if unavoidable; supporting staff in their individual handling of children; helping staff to acquire good skills and attitudes needed for effective job performance; planning with staff their work with individuals and groups of children; discussing with staff their future intervention and plans for each child; developing new skills in working with children; guiding staff with the writing of assessment reports; planning team meetings so that a limited amount of time can be used to everyone's maximum advantage; creating an atmosphere whereby staff feel they can be constructively critical; developing an acute awareness of the necessity for good communication both within the establishment and with outside agencies. (Ibid.)

This description is important in that it gives some idea of the hierarchical nature of the centre and also gives some clue as to the extent to which staff might learn ideas from their team leaders. Cawson's (1978) work suggested that this is generally the expectation of how training will work. The staff composition (child care, excluding the Warden and teaching staff) at the time of my research was seventeen.[2] Figure 3.1 indicates the formal hierarchical arrangement and also the gender division within the centre.

Staff were divided into three teams. This was basically for administrative convenience since the building did not lend itself to division into self-contained units. Each team, however, had its own dining room and children were allocated to a team on admission. Weekly team meetings were usual and staff were assumed to gain the majority of their support and guidance from the team. Although I interviewed all the staff during the course of my stay in this agency and was a 'roving' observer I had a base in group 2 room, where I regularly joined them for meals and team meetings.

The staff: background and training

Residential care is renowned for the absence of staff training (see Carlebach, (1970) and CCETSW (1974), for example). This agency was unusual in having a number of graduates amongst the staff, who, although untrained in child care, were said to alter the ethos of the place. As the warden described:

> Obviously, having a number of graduates makes it a bit more high-powered than usual, not that they're more sensitive or thoughtful than others its experience that counts you see, but they bring a certain enthusiasm and interest to the work.

Most of the staff had previous experience in voluntary social work (e.g., youth clubs, intermediate treatment, Citizens Advice Bureaux) or in teaching or child care. The two exceptions here were an ex-nurse and an ex-police officer (female). Another atypical phenomenon was that only five members of staff had spent less than one year in the agency. Indeed, the average length of stay at the time of my research was 3 years 1 month – though this reflects a variation between one month and fifteen years. This latter figure reflected the experience of the domestic bursar who had been employed in Agency One in its former role as a children's home. All the management officers (the top three posts) had spent over five years in the agency and the team leaders and their deputies all over two years.

Some of the staff had previous experience of working in residential care with children. The three seniors, for instance (elsewhere referred to as the management), had previously worked in approved schools.[3]

Few of the staff could identify or remember any specific details in their formal training (relevant in six cases only) in relation to girls. Two members of staff admitted that they first gained a special understanding of girls from teaching and from literature on child development. They had been instructed that boys and girls mature and develop at different rates and in different ways, but I describe this at a later point. The point to abstract from this is that the staff could not be identified with any one approach to child care (nor would they themselves consider alignment with a particular approach). Other research has attributed basic differ-

Warden (m)

Deputy warden (m)

Third in charge (m)

Head of school (m)
Teacher 1 (m)
Teacher 2 (f)

Clerical Assistant (m)
Domestic Bursar (f)
Cook and assistants (f)
Cleaners (f)

1
Team Leader (f)
Deputy (f)
Child Care Officer 1 (f)
Child Care Officer 2 (m)
Child Care Officer 3 (vacant)
Child Care Officer 4 (vacant)
Child Care Officer 5 (vacant)

2
Team leader (f)
Deputy (m)
Child Care Officer 1 (f)
Child Care Officer 2 (m)
Child Care Officer 3 (m)
Child Care Officer 4 (m)
Child Care Officer 5 (f)

3
Team Leader (m)
Deputy (f)
Child Care Officer 1 (m)
Child Care Officer 2 (f)
Child Care Officer 3 (vacant)
Child Care Officer 4 (vacant)
Child Care Officer 5 (vacant)

Figure 3.1 Staff organization of Agency One

ences in professional orientations to training (Bines, 1978), but this was not the case in this agency. There were few differences in approaches adopted by the staff. Only the psychology graduate adopted a specific stance (a psychoanalytical one) but this was not applied rigorously and at times, other staff promoted this approach more than she herself did.

The juveniles
During the course of this research there were 9 girls and 16 boys in residence. Their ages ranged between 11 years and 16+ years. The average age was 14 years 10 months (girls) and 14 years 6 months (boys).

The girls
Analysis of the primary reasons for their admission taken from descriptions on admission forms is shown in Table 3.1. This picture, however, may be misleading for all the girls had very complicated life histories, five of them having experienced residential care in previous years and six of them having school attendance problems. Three of the girls had experienced court appearances, and one had admitted to thefts within the agency.[4]

The boys
Similarly, what was initially recorded about the boys may be misleading. Very often their 'problems' spanned several of the categories I have indicated. Five boys (out of sixteen) had previous experience in residential care and four of them were noted to experience 'school problems' (i.e., non-attendance or behavioural problems whilst in school). Twelve boys had appeared in court for offending and three of these were awaiting further court appearances. One boy was due to appear in court for the first time. In addition, three boys had been cautioned for offending.

Suitable clients?
My discussions with staff initially revolved around the reasons why those particular children were in the agency. What were the reasons for their admission? 'Family problems' were seen as the cause rather than more individualistic problems or disturbance. Without exception, comments deriving from interviews referred to placement in that agency as being necessary and appropriate for all the children there. M., for instance, although she had offended, was seen to be the victim of parental quarrels, as her team leader described:

> She came here because she did not go to school, also because she had done some stealing and at home they could not control her... but it was her parents fighting which meant they couldn't control or supervise her properly. ... I don't know really ...there doesn't seem much basis for her being here ...but

Table 3.1 Juveniles in residence at Agency One

BOYS	Status of admission	Written comments	GIRLS	Status of admission	Written comments
1	Section 1 1948	Beyond care and control, non-school attendance	1	Section 1(2) 1969 Act	Beyond care and control, offending
2	ICO	Non-school attendance	2	Section 1 1948 Act	Family crisis
3	Section 1 1948	Parents refusing child after offence	3	Section 1 1969 Act	Foster placement breakdown
4	Section 1(2) 1969	Beyond care and control	4	Section 10 1980 Act	Beyond care and control, school refusal
5	Section 7.7 1969	Offending, home environment unstable	5	Section 1(2) 1969 Act	Non-school attendance
6	(No record)	Family problems, offences, truanting	6	Section 1(2) 1969	Beyond care and control, child abuse
7	Section 2 1980	Parent refusing child after offence	7	Section 1(3) 1969	Foster placement breakdown
8	Section 1 1948	Beyond care and control	8	Section 1(2) 1969	1(2) c,d,e and f
9	Section 1 1980	Self-admission	9	Section 1(2) 1969	Beyond care and control
10	ICO	Breach proceedings enacted following failure to comply with IT condition, offending			
11	Section 1 1948	Placement breakdown			
12	Section 1(2) 1969	Beyond care and control			
13	Section 1 1948	Behaviour patterns, offending			
14	Section 2 1980	Beyond care and control			
15	Section 10 1980 Act	Offending			
16	Section 7.7 1969	Offending			

(See Appendix B for details of Acts)

I think she needs to be, just from knowing her. (Team leader, female)

Or as another put it when talking about girls in general:

When parents say their daughter is out of control... it really means they feel inadequate, the girl won't do as she is told, she won't come home in the evenings and they can't make her.... She may stay out for a couple of nights but the parents haven't tried hard enough usually, they haven't had enough influence. (Team leader, male)

The Warden concurred that most children who were admitted had been subjected to inconsistent care and handling within the home, and that rejection from the home was very often an indication of the parents' own inabilities to cope rather than a reflection of the seriousness of a child's transgressions.[5]

One team leader saw admission to the agency as a reflection of the problems which accompany adolescence:

Adolescence and its problems are expressed differently in relation to boys and girls. Girls don't express themselves as delinquents... in gangs etcetera like boys, they're not admitted into care for those reasons like the boys... they tend to come for complicated emotional problems and for family problems. (Team leader, female)

Another practitioner responded in this way:

Why do I think they're here? – well, the majority of the girls are here because they're incorrigible... hard to handle, the parents can't cope. There's a lack of school attendance, they're very hard to live with – going away without saying where they're going and just very, very argumentative. They all seem to have relationship problems.... The boys? The boys have more criminal careers not just problems, but they're also hard to handle. They don't attend school or they're difficult in school and out of school. Overall, they've committed more offences I think ...more 'criminal minded' I think. (Residential social worker, male)

Some of the staff's comments provided clear support for the assertions of writers that 'problematic behaviour of girls' is interpreted as 'role expressive'. (See, for example, Smart, 1977; Heidensohn, 1970.) This was another response:

I think girls are more more closely tied to their families so it upsets them more when things go wrong... they often talk about home and want to go home... their parents, their siblings. (Residential social worker, male)

I think the chief characteristics of the girls here and of their family backgrounds is that there are always bad... stormy relationships with mothers... not so common with boys, their problems are often nothing to do with the family.... nicking stuff, that kind of thing. Many of the parents are divorced, have new partners. But girls are still taught... even if they have bad mothers, that they must not play around... mother may have done it all. ... it's very confusing for them... their mothers may go out drinking etcetera and yet they're told no, you can't be a slut... you're too young for the pill. ... parents are strict with their daughters, especially mothers. (Residential social worker, female)

Disturbance

The indiscriminate use of the label 'maladjusted' was generally rejected by staff in Agency One, nevertheless the majority of children admitted to the agency were labelled in this way. The defined maladjustment by referring both to the evidence of case histories and to symptoms and behaviours presented within the assessment centre. Staff made frequent reference to emotional deprivation and to poor social training. Deficiencies in social training, for instance, were seen to result in impulsiveness, lack of control, impetuousness and aggression. Emotional deprivation was seen to result in an inability to form or sustain relationships. Moral deprivation was seen to result in the poor development of acceptable social values, leading either to a disregard of those values or to a commitment to 'sub-cultural', 'anti-social' forms of conduct and belief. There appeared to be more than one sort of maladjustment suggested, therefore, or certainly more than one way of categorizing it. Although the general label of 'maladjusted' was used without specific restrictions, practitioners were concerned with three different types, namely behavioural maladjustment, emotional maladjustment and social maladjustment.

Essential differences between girls and boys

Subsequent questioning was concentrated on the differences which staff perceived between boys and girls and the implications of these differences for policy and practice. First, the distinctive problems of girls and boys: several themes emerged here, for example, that girls invariably achieve sexual maturity before boys, also that they demonstrate their distress in very different ways from boys and that they are more emotional and vulnerable. Their comments suggested that they subscribed to an analysis of girls' problems which was dependent upon a model of 'emotional deprivation'. As the Warden described:

> girls are more advanced than boys in the 13 and a half to 15 year age group, also hormones are different and girls are perhaps wanting sexual experience more than boys. A girl could perhaps be compared with a 19 year old boy in terms of maturity. Compare 14 and 15 year old girls with 17, 18 and 19 year old boys in terms of promiscuity and it would be the same. With boys, talk abut sexual experiences is their badge rather than deeds, with the girls there is a real need and a fondness.

and his deputy commented:

The girls want a boy, the boys want a badge, just to say they've got a girlfriend – the girls have an emotional need which comes from physiological changes.

Another member of staff, a female team leader, commented that placements often broke down due to girls' sexual maturity.

A lot of these girls are overtly sexual and seem to get on well with a foster father, for example, but keen competition develops between foster mum and the girl.

Another member of staff commented on the psychological maturity which often accompanies the girls' physiological maturity:

Girls' sexuality does tend to be tinged with emotional feelings, not many girls would say they just want sexual satisfaction... boys do though, they just want the activity...there are definite biological and psychological differences here. (Deputy team leader, male)

sexually they have different problems.... I think girls are more aware of what their problems are... periods etcetera... and they're mature enough to articulate them. With boys ... there are just vague anxieties but they're not able to articulate it... they fear being laughed at. (Residential social worker, female)

Another member of staff described the difference in this way:

boys at this age look on the lighter side of relationships, just the sexual escapade... there's no pressure on them. All the girls, however, have told me that they want to get married. (Residential social worker, female)

The boys are infinitely more fosterable... it's very hard to take a girl into a house when she's just entering puberty – she might play for the husband and the mother might get jealous. (Deputy team leader, female)

Another focused on girls' greater capacity for emotion in the comment:

girls need the emotional attention. They take it personally when things go wrong or they're spoken of in a derogatory way. There's more depth ..., it's there without them realising it... it's natural, it's being female wanting relationships, they have an inborn mothering instinct... home-building, tending, caring, colour in their lives... we fight it sometimes and these are tomboy girls. (Residential social worker, female)

The theme which emerged here, that girls and boys approach relationships rather differently, was soon to appear as a pervasive and persistent one. Girls, apparently, experienced relationships in a much more emotional way than boys and this made them vulnerable. Other staff emphasized that girls' relationships revolve around emotional attachments from their earliest years:

I think girls here want a lot of physical attention. That's their way of expressing emotion. They need emotional attachment. (Residential social worker, female)

> Girls naturally turn to people when they're upset. They have this thing about people and so they do, of course, get far more upset than boys. (Residential social worker, female)

The Warden was adamant that the more demonstrative nature of girls' response to stress – in the form of suicide gestures, scratched wrists and overdoses, for instance, were related to girls' greater capacity for emotion:

> I think the main difference is that girls suffer the extremes of emotional swings, and this is a biological thing, they demonstrate the swings much more than boys, so there's a lot of tension – especially when there are a lot of them... they're often completely negative. They get there quicker than a boy... to the high point.

Girls apparent needs for emotional attachments and views of their sexual maturity as compared with boys resulted in the explicit policy that staff should be wary of 'over-involvement' with the girls, though the degree to which this policy was acknowledged and accepted by members of staff varied considerably, as discussion of everyday practice will reveal. The main effect of these perceived differences between boys and girls was illustrated in comments that male staff, in particular, might be vulnerable to the efforts of girls to form attachments. Indeed, the deputy warden made it his business to explain this vulnerability to young members of the male staff, and he commented:

> I don't like males up in the girls' end of the corridor at night, though I don't like rigid rules either. I think a single man going up to the girls' end of the corridor might feel vulnerable.

Asked whether these feelings of vulnerability might be more extreme than those experienced by single women going to the boys' end of the corridor, the response was:

> it's a sociological question whether women do feel more comfortable going to the boys' end... but professionally we do know less about girls in care. There are fewer girls in care and consequently fewer experiments have been conducted; it's just natural not to reveal too much trust in them.

One member of staff who had been with the agency for some years described an incident which happened some six or seven years ago which helped to put these spoken fears in perspective. He explained that a female member of staff and a boy had become 'involved' to the detriment of their working relationship. Whilst the member of staff attributed the policy of 'wariness' to this particular incident, he still felt a continuing anxiety when exposed to risks when with the girls.

> it's less likely to happen if you're married and have children, but still they're

automatically attracted because you're a man. If a girl puts an arm round me I have to judge whether she's flirting – if she is I reciprocate but I say something like 'I'm old enough to be your dad...'.

I would never have a girl on my lap whether flirting or not – unless she was very little, I would put my arm round her shoulder... maybe hold her hand... that's all, though, you never know with a girl, you're never sure whether you're going to be accused of something.

Clearly, the implication of these comments was that the responsibility for the relationship between the staff member and the boy was attributed to the staff member more by virtue of her sex than her position of authority.

The greater maturity of girls, however, and their sexual precociousness, were seen to be related to the idea that girls are subject to far greater stresses and strains during adolescence. Again, the Warden was quite clear on this:

Certainly, girls have a tougher time physically and also it's still a man's ... boy's world unless the girl will accept the traditional role. If she's happy in that role then O.K. and I think she has a good time, but if not then it's tough.

but girls have periods and that plays a part in it all... it is significant, quite a lot of them here have problems... it affects their mood.

One of the team leaders reiterated this in his comment that,

There is a basic physiological difference which emerges at puberty... the girls suffer with periods and things, it's a very turbulent time for them. The physical hormonal balance makes them more emotional, more prone to depression too.

One female residential worker, who had ten years' experience of working in boys' home and schools perceived the difference in problems to carry great significance.

It's there for boys... the problems... but they cope with them in different ways. There's more of an emotional turbulence for girls. A boy may have to cope with his voice descending, but it is not the same scale... he may be embarrassed for a while, but girls have this thing every month and pre-menstrual tension. Puberty is a very bitchy stage too ... a depressing stage... psychological changes. It's a much harder period... adolescence is much worse for girls than for boys I think.

Views of offending

My questions relating to offending sought first to establish general views of offending and the significance which offending was accorded within the agency, and secondly, to reveal any differences that there might be in the staff's images or understanding of male and female offenders.

Discussions with the staff essentially revealed that the commission of offences in itself was not necessarily seen as an indication of 'disturbed' or 'malajusted' behaviour. Indeed, it was recognized that the majority of juvenile offenders who never came to the agency were very probably 'normal'. As one experienced practitioner described:

> Loads of kids appear in the juvenile court I wouldn't call delinquent, and who wouldn't be disturbed either. (Team leader, male)

But as Stott points out (1950: 363) delinquency is a legal, not a psychological, concept and the commission of offences cannot be regarded as enough evidence to label a child malajusted or disturbed. Also, because practitioners are expected not just to present a history of offences but to distinguish reasons for them and symptoms of general attitudes and behaviours, the commission of offences will rarely be enough to sustain the labelling of a child as malajusted or disturbed. In some cases, therefore, offences committed were hardly considered relevant at all. The only exception might be in the case of particular offences which are atypical, not only in relation to the juvenile population as a whole, but in relation to the population admitted to the agency. D's age and sex, for instance (female, aged 14 years), coupled with the nature of her offence (possession and use of cannabis), made her single offence a clear reflection of 'disturbance'.

Assumptions about the different patterns of offending by boys and girls were made very clear, however, and the following comments were typical of the staff's comments about offending behaviour:

> I think the offending patterns reflect degrees of aggression. The girls' offending tends to be shoplifting, etcetera, sexual promiscuity, that kind of thing. With the boys it's criminal damage, theft, burglary, a broader spectrum. (Deputy team leader, female)

> TDA [taking and driving away] and theft is part of the boys' status thing... like being good at fighting, it's a way of being a man, part of having fun. Boys are expected to get driving licences, to drive. Stealing a car is just a way of demonstrating manliness. (Deputy warden, male)

> A lot of girls steal for no reason... they take stuff they never use or need and they steal a lot... it's irrational. Boys, well... they steal in groups, it's planned out... the act is thought out, they're on stage, acting for each other. It's just 'let's go and nick', girls tend to do it singly or in pairs – a reflection of their normal life-style – they're always in little cliques. (Residential social worker, female)

The general understanding of girls' offending was that it was 'irrational':

> Stealing by girls is like acting out. [Acting out?] Yes, promiscuity is what I mean, it stems from an unstable home life where there's not enough attention within the home – so they seek it outside. Girls resort to shoplifting for the same reasons. I think a girl shoplifter has probably got far more worries and

troubles inside her... it's more of a cry for help from a girl. (Residential social worker, female)

A lot of the girls have been involved in shoplifting... it's always petty shoplifting I think, They're not out to gain very much, it's just silly shoplifting – a packet of biscuits, a pair of tights... it's just an expression of how they feel. ...With boys it's much more due to peer group pressure, it's more complex – they try to impress one another, they break into places. They don't need or want the goods, they just do it for the status. (Residential social worker, female)

This theme, relating to the offending of boys, found further expression in the comment that:

Boys have to prove themselves in action, as they do things which are fun, dangerous, exciting... which provides something to brag about. Few girls have to do this, girls have a quieter temperament perhaps, they have no need to prove themselves in that way early in their life. Girls prove themselves in appearance instead, so they tend to steal, if they have to, to improve their appearance. Generally, the girls have more acceptable outlets to prove themselves. (Residential social worker, female)

Further evidence of this apparent difference, in the staff's experience, was provided in the kinds of articles which girls and boys stole. Respondents continued their comments in this way:

Girls steal make-up, clothes, jewellery. Boys steal batteries, pens, records, clothes sometimes. (Residential social worker, male)

The girls steal cosmetics, clothes, things of use to them; boys may be clothes now, because they're now more clothes-conscious but sports, electronic things, batteries. (Residential social worker, male)

Offences involving elements of aggression were clearly viewed as 'unnatural' when committed by girls, aggression on the part of boys being seemingly more acceptable. As practitioners described:

The offence I most dislike to see in a girl is fighting. I think this shocks me most too... in a girl. [Why?] It's because a female has more open to her... over the years females have taken on more of the male roles, but being aggressive is not natural for a female... it's a kind of trying to impress. Skinhead haircuts, jeans etc. ... they do it because the others do it ... to be mistaken for boys, to be tough, scrap with anyone. (Residential social worker, female)

being loud, verbally aggressive and physically aggressive is dreadful in a girl... it sounds and looks worse from a girl and trashy. Swearing doesn't bother me too much, but it's more acceptable coming from a boy. (Residential social worker, male)

Another residential worker expressed her 'tolerance' level of girls' aggressive behaviour in this way:

they shouldn't swear or fight, I can't abide it. You expect boys to thump one another, it's part of their growing up – it's hideous in girls, the girls really want a more feminine role... the maternal role (Residential social worker, female)

Despite the predominant view that girls' offending was an indication of 'irrational' or 'disturbed' behaviour, however, and that it was frequently a 'cry for help', a number of staff were of the opinion that in general terms females committed an equal number of offences to males.

Women have been protected in the past, they were expected to play with dolls – marriage, children, the little woman staying at home – little opportunity to steal and if she stole it was because she was hard up. Now we've got Women's Lib, and equal education – they're breadwinners and out in the world – they're just as criminally inclined now. (Deputy team leader, female)

I think we are more aware of their delinquency now, girls do a lot of petty things, some of them remain unnoticed, it's just that the things men do are more noticeable, out on the streets for instance. (Deputy team leader, male)

Being difficult and defining 'trouble'

The practitioners' experience of girls 'difficult' behaviour in Agency One proved similar to the catalogue of experiences previously described in residential institutions (Catalino, 1972; Hoghughi, 1978, and Ackland, 1982). In group situations, for instance, the girls were described as being more prone to violent mood swings; the common experience was that once one girl had 'blown' others would quickly follow suit. The girls were apparently more easily frustrated, they became 'fed-up' sooner than boys with the activities offered and were seen to be more 'explosive' and aggressive when frustrated. Further, the girls were described as more defiant, abusive and aggressive than boys towards staff when they did 'blow'. A male residential social worker described the problems in this way:

I think part of the problem is that girls are less good at communication – they don't show anything through boisterousness... chattering away. This goes back to their straightforwardness but every now and again they'll just 'shoot up'. [Shoot up?]

there'll be a huge emotional outburst, they'll blow and be extremely angry and irritating for a while – girls are immediate with their violence, they get so pent up – when she gets going, there's no stopping her— she's quicker, more agile, her arms and legs flay out all over the place. Boys are not so wild, just vicious.

Female members of staff, too, referred to the sudden emotional outbursts:

The girls let off steam less often, but when they do it's quite hysterical – berserk. A, especially just loses her head... becomes insolent, verbally abusive and physically... they lash out. (Residential social worker, female)

Another theme to emerge with some persistence was that of the girls' manipulativeness:

> The main problem with girls is that they are so devious and manipulative, you can never trust them. (Residential social worker, team 3, male)

Whilst a colleague put it this way.

> they play people off against one another. It's all in relation to I.Q. With boys it's related to I Q , intelligent boys are manipulative, girls just are. If you have boys who have been brought up in a very female oriented environment they're often manipulative. (Team leader, female)

In discussing this, even the team leader who had previously suggested that girls were 'more straightforward and honest', and therefore easier to deal with, went on to qualify her first statement by saying that all she had meant was that girls were 'more practised at the emotional level'. Indeed, the team leader felt that this capacity to exhibit emotion and to talk about emotional problems led to frequent emotional blackmail on the part of the girls.

> They know how to get you feeling sorry for them by using emotion and often they will talk about emotional problems as a way of getting to something else ... something they want. Let me give you an example. Mo., for instance, came back to me after I had been saying to her that she needed some space.,, a quiet time to resolve her conflicts about her mum. She came yesterday and said very glumly, 'I do feel all mixed up about my mum and that... I think you're right, I've got to have time to think about it on my own.' ... she went on for a bit getting me to feel sorry for her and then she said, 'Well can I go out of ... [the agency] tonight, I think I need to get away for a while to be on my own'. I knew for a fact that she'd already asked two members of staff if she could go the the village disco. Crafty eh, they're all like that.[sic]. (Team leader, female)

The warden, however, believed boys and girls to be equally manipulative and devious. He stated:

> All children in care are as devious as anything, but all children in care are in great need. It's their way of getting needs fulfilled. The boys' aggression sometimes overshadows the manipulation and if he's a bully that's what he'll be labelled even though he's manipulative. The girls just appear to be more manipulative because that's what stands out.

Another member of staff responded to my question about the deviousness of juveniles in this way:

> Girls are much more so ... you can't trust them so easily. In relationships all females manipulate. You know ... the male struts, the girls does all the

manipulating... a girl has to wait to be asked out but she manipulates things, she makes her wishes known, she has to project her emotions. (Residential social worker, female)

A young male member of staff expressed the view that it was the girls' manipulative behaviour which caused staff members to experience stress:

they try to sweet talk you ... the girls, they play on my paternal instincts. A. would just say 'Let's go for a cycle ride, Mr. K'. I know she'd just want to go to the shops and nick things. They're like this – disguise what they really want or feel, give 'em an inch and they take a mile, they really do. Some of them can turn on the water taps too, when the mood strikes them. It makes our life here hell, it's a real strain for all of us, you must see that... you can never be off your guard and it's very stressful. (Residential social worker, male)

Nice girls

Another approach to gaining a picture of what 'trouble' meant to staff and what 'difficult' girls did to make them distinguishable as 'difficult' was, of course, to establish what 'nice' girls were and did in the eyes of the staff. By gaining a picture of what 'normal', acceptable and nice girls were usually like it would be possible to define more clearly how those labelled as 'bad' or 'difficult' had fractured the boundaries of acceptability. Indeed, this approach was to add to my knowledge of how and why certain girls or, indeed, all the girls in the agency at times, came to be seen as 'difficult' and 'problem' girls. In pursuing this line of questioning, moreover, it was possible to establish a definition or collection of definitions pertaining to 'femininity' and to gauge to what extent girls were expected to conform to these images. 'Nice' girls, according to staff members were

very feminine and caring, sensitive, you know they don't rough you up, push around, swear a lot – that kind of thing. (Residential social worker, female)

I like femininity in females. ... I think we should keep our feminine sex, treasure it. I'm not a women's libber. The woman, the female is the caring one, protector, homemaker, the one who looks after the children, home-going... 'behind every successful man is a successful wife', you know the saying I'm sure. (Residential social worker, female)

The following extracts of dialogue which occurred between the staff members and myself serve to illustrate the distinctions between 'nice' girls and girls who were 'trouble' too.

Nice girls?... well we don't see many around here ... this lot... well they're O.K. but not exactly nice. [Why not?]

They're so rude... swear a lot, they're uncouth. You should see their table manners... the manners of a pig some of them and they'd sooner punch you if you disagreed with them than discuss it. If you pull them up on anything you get an earful of language. (Deputy warden)

and he continued:

it's the way they look too, if they look tartish it's not ideal... you know they're on the look out for the lads.[?] You know, loud colours, short skirts, that kind of thing, half an inch of make-up and cheap flashy jewellery. My own daughters... they're the same age but look much younger because they dress very differently... in sensible clothes and school uniform for the day time too. They don't answer you back all the time. What is more they're pleasant and active... keep themselves busy... don't just hang around like they do here a lot of the time.

Two younger female members of staff described 'nice girls' in this way:

I think girls are just naturally more caring... independent now yes, but caring and wanting to look after others. They're open too... I mean friendly, and they make an effort to look nice. (Residential social worker, female)

I like girls to be responsible... sensitive, caring and attractive too, I suppose. They should use their intelligence too, though many try to hide it. The girls I like best are bright and lively and look that way. (Residential social worker, female)

The distinctions made between different girls within the agency helped to 'sharpen' essential differences between 'nice girls' and difficult or 'not so nice' girls. I asked staff members to describe the girls they were working with in the agency (usually those in their group) and received the following responses. First, the 'difficult' girls:

J. I see J. as a tomboy because she's so aggressive and likes to dominate wherever she goes... she's rude very often and always likes to be the centre of attention. She has no self-restraint. (Residential social worker, female)

The worst girl here is A. She's just uncontrollable, uncouth, loud and violent. She wants everything her own way... it disgusts me the way she tries to manipulate people... especially the boys. She's twelve years old and acts like nineteen years old, far too curious about sexual matters for her age. Go out of the room and she'll be on top of the boys in no time. (Residential social worker, female)

A. tries to be a boy most of the time and even the softer side of her is very selfish. You can't take her at her word. She might appear interested in others, but it's all for herself really and you should hear her filthy language. There's no restraint, she doesn't control herself at all. She's always sidling up to the boys... the older ones, egging them on. (Team leader, female)

In contrast, M. was seen to be 'nice' girl:

M. is very quick tempered and very moody but that reflects her family background... parents' rocky marriage... rather than anything about her in herself. [A tomboy in the same way as J.?] No, she's more feminine. M. would willingly accept the role to be dominated by a man. This is what she wants, she's said... she'll be happy to find someone. She's very insecure... inside she's sensitive... very lovable and caring. [Promiscuous like A.?] Yes, she's definitely seeking love... it's because she didn't get much at home... she needs physical attention – cuddles. (Warden)

Clearly, it was interesting that although labelled as 'promiscuous' this was interpreted as a demonstration of some unsatisfied need because M. qualified as 'feminine' in several other ways. A. on the other hand received little sympathy for her 'promiscuous' behaviour, even though staff members attributed it to her family background and the poor relationship she had with her parents. This 'unsympathetic' attitude could, perhaps, be explained by reference to the seeming lack of other 'feminine' qualities in A.

She's a scheming little so and so ... so devious that you can't get near to her. No, she's crying out for attention in all of this but her behaviour is so repulsive it's difficult to tolerate her. (Deputy warden)

Surprisingly, D., who adopted punk clothing with shorn head and boots, was seen as 'feminine', but for the following reasons:

D. is OK... she looks dreadful, but she's one of our successes, she's always responsible and interested in what you're saying. Yes... despite her appearance she's a sensitive soul really, quite caring about people. She sort of has a hold on the others because they respect her... she's perceptive, you see, and tells them things about themselves which they wouldn't take from staff. (Deputy team leader, female)

S., too, was essentially 'nice' in this way:

S. is a proper schoolgirl and very girlish. Slightly immature I'd say, but very affectionate. She's got a room full of dolls and furry animals. Well, in fact most of these girls have. It's a reflection of their character really... the maternal instinct almost. As you might expect, A. just keeps a football in her room or the latest craze of the boys... to keep in with them, I suppose. (Residential social worker, female)

An, is very motherly, a proper little woman I'd say, she is very good with children. She likes to look nice and spends hours working on that because she's concerned about her weight... you know the way girls and most women get worried about it. You can easily imagine An, as married with kids of her own, shopping and taking care of everyone. She'd love it. She tries so hard here and she's very good, always helps you. (Deputy team leader, male)

One girl, who arrived at the end of my stay in the agency, was immediately described as 'very feminine' because, in view of her pregnant condition, she was 'extremely upset about it, she feels very guilty'. She also cried about it when the results of tests came through and this was a telling part of her character for a number of staff:

> She cried about it when G. told her... I think when most girls cry it's a good indication of femininity, it reveals their sensitivity you see. You've asked me about femininity and I guess that's how I'd describe it, a special softness or sensitivity, not hardness, brashness but concern and worry about others. I think St. feels very guilty because she knows her dad will be upset, she has an unmarried sister you see and there's a child there. (Residential social worker, female)

> You can get near to them when the guards are down and her crying was a way of saying I'm sorry, I think. She's a sweet kid, quiet and compliant – a schoolgirl, really older than A. yet younger in many ways ... doesn't try to be so sophisticated. (Team leader, male)

Joining in this same conversation, another team leader (Team 2) indicated that there were subtle distinctions to be made between those girls who really 'felt something' and those who pretended to feel, those who exhibited 'crocodile tears':

> A. doesn't feel anymore... she has been moved around so much the only way she can cope is not to feel ... she's too coarse. I do wonder sometimes if she has any real fears... whether she knows when she is upset... or distressed, when she laughs it is all false. I have seen her in tears, just once, but I'm not sure it they're real... or what they mean.

Thus, A.'s expression of emotion in the context of other behaviour which she exhibited and which was disliked by staff members, was seen to be false; unlike other cases, it was not taken to be an illustration of the 'natural' behaviour of girls, or of 'femininity'.

Interestingly, the behaviour of this twelve-year-old-girl was seen to be so different from the behaviour of all the others that it acquired a permanence in the minds of staff members where most behaviour was seen as changeable and transient. Indeed, the damage was seen to be life-long.

> She has been sexually exploited for so long, she will be a bad mother... you can't change her... it's too late... she's just twelve years but the mould has been set... it's mother's fault.

The apportioning of blame to mother reflected the moral condemnation of her behaviour; mother was at fault for having children *and* boyfriends, and whilst there was an element of sympathy for A. because she had been exposed to her mother's inappropriate behaviour, the fact that A.'s behaviour was imitative of the mother's behaviour was seen to reflect her own culpability. If, for instance, A. had demonstrated her 'disturbance' in another way, the sympathy extended towards her may have been far greater. As one member of staff described:

> You feel sorry for her because of what she's been through... pushed from

pillar to post, but then she's such a little madam she asks for what she gets. (Deputy team leader, female)

Another, however, was quite clear in his condemnation of A:

Of all the girls she is the one with the least hope... self-centred, selfish... manipulates others to get things for herself. There's very little good in her, if you were kind to her she wouldn't know what it meant. She abuses people, she's totally hard... mercenary. She uses her femininity to be guileful... in her dress, she wants to be feminine, I think, and have a nice little world, dream world... where everything is O.K. but again doesn't know how to get it. She's just like a businessman... wants to screw you to the last. She goes the wrong way about getting affection... she's got nothing to give back... she's all take, that's the problem and she doesn't appreciate what is given. (Residential social worker, male)

Thus A. was perceived to be 'difficult' and 'troublesome', not simply because she did not conform, but because she did not conform even to the stereotypical view of a disturbed child. Moreover, she was unappreciative of efforts to 'help' and 'reform' her. Her behaviour crossed the boundary from a deprived and depraved background to a level of deviation which she was seen to initiate and hence her own culpability was implicated.

A different response for a different kind of 'trouble'

The differential perceptions of boys' and girls' behaviour had clear implications for the practitioners' own responses to their charges. In addition to the general 'wariness' of girls because of feelings that the staff might be vulnerable to accusations from the girls for taking undue advantage of them, the differential understanding of their behaviour and moods meant that different responses to boys and girls were seen as well justified. The greater emotional capacity perceived in girls, for instance, meant that staff could attempt to go beyond the 'playful' relationship they had with boys to develop 'close' relationships. Indeed, there was strong argument from the staff that this was what was required from them. As one female member of staff put it:

You can get closer to the girls because they welcome it. Girls are easier to talk to because they seem to function on a more straightforward and honest and emotional level than the boys. Boys rarely talk about their feelings and this makes relationships difficult. My interest in the work is in exploring feelings, the boys are mostly activity oriented. (Team leader)

There was a clear distinction here, however, in the orientations of male and female members of staff. Whilst the males retained the 'wariness' of girls which I have already described, the females felt they could identify with girls on this emotional level. Moreover, in some cases it meant that they could 'manage' them and effectively deal with emotional outbursts. As the staff related:

> If it's a girl who's about to blow... you know what to do, you know when she means it... just from looking at her... you can judge her mood. (Residential social worker, female)

> When a girl is difficult you know how to talk with her, it's a very individual thing of course, but because we [women] instinctively I suppose ... know the girls better than the boys, you can usually produce some kind of action or words to stop her getting out of hand. (Team leader, female)

> When you work with the girls the relationships are always deeper... you're just with them a lot more than the boys and you get to know their little ways... you can immediately tell if something is 'up' and can work to stop it... respond to their moods, that kind of thing. (Warden)

It was clear that staff viewed many of the provisions available for boys as inappropriate and unsuitable for girls. Most were aware that there were indeed different provisions available for boys and girls, and there was wide expression that this was necessary.

> I can't envisage a time when you would ever want to send a girl to D.C. even if they existed for girls – their problems are so different. (Residential social worker, male)

The fact that two boys from the agency were about to appear in court for their offending, absconding and disruptive behaviour, provided a useful point for discussions here; never before in the agency's history had juveniles appeared in court with a recommendation for a custodial sentence from the agency. The event meant that 'suitability' for custodial sentences in general and more specifically for a detention centre was thus a frequent topic of conversation.

When questioned about 'managing' girls the staff responded in a fairly consistent way. As one team leader described:

> to be honest, I have the feeling that a girl might become very resentful if she was subjected to this kind of treatment [in a D.C.] For a boy it might work, it is different, boys can adapt to it for a time and when they [the boys] go back to society they can forget about it. They can probably just see it as a short lesson whereas with the girls it would have a much bigger impact emotionally. They might get extremely depressed.
> [Why?]
> Well I think it is because a girl needs a more homely atmosphere... a girl takes pride in her surroundings, in their room and she won't have that. She needs a slightly different response... she needs sort of talk therapy. (Team leader, female)

A residential social worker (female) put it this way:

The girls don't respond to the disciplinary line – you have to form a more personal relationship with them. The boys stop if you shout at them. You've got more in common with the girls... You let them know you've gone through it all... because you talk about such personal things it puts you on quite a different wave-length – they trust you more and you have to use that when dealing with them.

Continuing this discussion, a colleague asserted that a spell in D.C. would make a girl 'worse':

You'd make the girls there... drive them to worse things. The short, sharp shock can work with boys... it stops bullying... perhaps... more likely to be of help to boys. Girls would need different treatment, you'd have to be more persuasive with them. (Residential social worker, female)

Another illustrated her views with particular reference to a girl who had previously been resident in the agency:

There was a girl here once, a typical non-conforming female... disobedient, abusive ... you had to make her do everything... she would respond to little, though shouting at her only made things worse, you had to try to manipulate her. She eventually went to a behaviourist set-up... a token economy...earn concessions, that kind of thing, whatever you do it's got to be more therapeutic for girls. You can bully... regiment boys and some of them respond. They respect this... the strength is used... the bigger you are the more right you are. Girls think differently and don't respect this... 'just because you're big doesn't mean to say I'm frightened' is what they think. Females just don't respond to bullying. You have to be persuasive. (Deputy team leader, female)

Another member of staff described his greater difficulty with managing girls compared with boys in this way:

The boys are a lot easier to deal with in that if they 'blow' there's usually a pretty good reason for it, the reasons are obvious. Someone has upset them or whatever. The girls 'blow' for such little things and instead of kicking a table or whatever, they kick you – the girls personalise their anger...it seems more calculated to hurt. (Residential social worker, female)

Even two female members of staff with adolescent sons of their own complained that girls were more difficult to deal with:

My son has given me hell, I'd rather have sons than daughters any day though. (Residential social worker, female)

My own son was more difficult than my daughter but I still think girls are worse – there's just something about them which makes control and power over them very uncertain. (Deputy team leader, female)

All the staff I spoke with were aware that when the agency had been occupied by a greater proportion of girls than boys some months earlier

there had been extreme difficulty in dealing with the girls. There were
several different explanations offered to account for this:

> The problem was that they were very aggressive and very introverted girls
> and they were all together. They all had a high degree of need at the same
> time, that's why we couldn't cope with them. (Warden)

> The girls were left here because there was no place for them to go. The boys
> all moved on to the Community Homes and places. There's never anywhere
> to send a girl, there are many who are difficult to place and they just get
> heaped up here. There were all frustrated in not being allowed to go.
> (Residential social worker, female)

One colleague had a far more pragmatic understanding of the occurrence:

> It was all hell let loose when there were mostly girls here, to my mind we
> didn't cope very well. The staff were all young and inexperienced.... I think
> the girls were difficult, yes, but no more so than most children who come here,
> it was just unusual. The unusual situation just took us by surprise, we
> couldn't think of things for them to do... boys you just send on to the playing
> field ... they'll think of something. (Team leader, male)

Whilst there was evidence of a biological/psychological theme in some
of these comments and an assumption that differences were innate, there
was also appreciation that some of the behaviour was produced by
differences in socialization techniques. A staff member who saw adolescence as a much more difficult period for girls than for boys, for instance,
continued his comments in this way:

> There are lots of commercial pressures for girls... whereas pressures for
> boys, if you can call them pressures... start as soon as he can walk and talk,
> he's encouraged to grow up... be a man all the time. Girls are allowed, almost
> encouraged to be little girls until 8 or 9 and then there's a sudden change for
> them. Their socialization is very different. They're suddenly expected to be
> more adult and to be interested in boys and things. (Residential social worker,
> male)

The warden stressed that the first five years in children's lives were all
important in establishing the differences in behaviour:

> Girls, you see, are taught to relate to adults in a different way. It's all in the
> initial family experiences... the girls in pink, the boys in blue, the boy gets
> a clip round the ear, the girl a finger wagging... and even in the families we
> are talking about where there is some violence, some chastisement, there is
> a difference in the way boys and girls are treated.

Another staff member reflected that:

> there are situational differences more than sexual differences... of course I
> might know the girls better, it depends on your relationship with them. I'm
> female so I spend more time with the girls, I'm bound to be able to elaborate

more on their problems therefore. The relationship orientation in girls?... it's to do with socialization, family controls. Perhaps the boys have just been taught not to show the need, they're still anxious about relationships though. Sometimes they show affection by fighting, play fighting or whatever. (Team leader, female)

Despite this appreciation of the effects of differential socialization patterns and the different expectations placed on boys and girls, however, there was little evidence within the staff's comments that it would be appropriate to challenge any of the assumptions inherent within these expectations. Indeed, my observations of interaction between the staff and the resident children were that traditional role expectations were very apparent.

In my description of the methodology employed for this research I described the importance of 'testing out' different ideas in different contexts. Only in this way is it possible to distil critical themes and ideas from the mass of information presented by practitioners. It is obviously crucial to discern those themes which appear with any element of coherency and consistency. To this end, a further stage of my work in Agency⁶ One was to document what practitioners wrote about their resident charges. As previously described, most of the written comments of staff appeared in behaviour reports and assessment reports; staff in each team submitted short reports on each child for the team leader to compile an assessment report. Reports were discussed with the Warden prior to presentation at review meetings or, in the case of court reports, prior to the court appearance of the juvenile. In addition to reports there was a daily diary for each team in which staff members were expected routinely to record the mood and movements of the children and young people so that staff beginning a shift would have some idea of recent occurrences.

Written material was used, essentially, to corroborate the more general comments about females and female behaviour which were made in interviews. Clearly, a move from general views to views of specific girls and their behaviour patterns went some way to providing the closer and more detailed definitions of behaviour which I required in order to comment on practitioners' understanding of the difference between the behaviour of adolescent males and females and their views on the appropriate methods of dealing with it.⁶

One of the most distinctive features of the reports on girls was that they revolved around 'problematic relationships' in relation to the family, to boys or to other juveniles within the agency. In contrast, written material on the boys tended to focus on their activities, offending behaviour, fights and episodes of running away. Thus, in the main, the written reports reflected practitioners' spoken understandings of the reasons for boys' and girls admissions, that boys were admitted for having committed offences and girls for having problems. I reveal in my own commentary on statements made by staff that these tended at times to be polarized conceptions of boys' and girls' behaviour.

Turning to the reports, the description of An.'s behaviour, for instance, referred both to distinctly 'female' problems or 'relational' problems (as perceived by the staff) and to a more general category of 'children in care problems'. An., who experienced rejection from her mother after her parents' separation, was seen to need a 'mothering' relationship and this was a dominant theme in the written reports.

> An. is a very immature girl who needs strong and careful guidance. She needs reassurance of love and affection and likes being mothered. Residential social worker's behaviour report, female)

> An. is a very domesticated girl, I think she over-compensates for not having a mum around. She misses her mum, that's quite obvious, and she almost treats you like a mum. My view is that she treats the staff as if they are parental figures to make up for the absence of a motherly figure at home. (Residential social worker, female)

Another behaviour report, submitted by a team member to the team leader for use in an assessment report, continued with the view that An.'s difficulties in forming relationships and her preference for female members of staff was only natural because of her mother's rejection.

> An. has shown a distinct preference for female staff rather than male staff from whom she demands attention in an immature and provocative way. This is only to be expected because of her family background. Her behaviour towards females is generally more sensible but even then she has only related well to a few. With these she is able to show affection. (Residential social worker, female)

Clearly, the picture to emerge of An. from written documents confirmed what had already been said about her. Moreover, there was an assumption that An. should be able to show affection, and that she should be able to show affection to more than just a few members of staff.

A critical note was applied to An. in relation to her behaviour within the agency, however, without this necessarily being linked to her background problems. As the final assessment report stated:

> She is sometimes surly and defensive and will use circumstances to her own ends. She lacks confidence and is occasionally aggressive. (Team leader, female)

Indeed, her behaviour was also described as 'attention seeking' without this being linked to former perceptions of An. as a victim of maternal deprivation.

> She is an attention seeker and manipulates staff. (Team leader's assessment report, female)

This label, however, of 'attention seeker' was a label applied to most of the children in the agency and it is possible to discern a conceptual shift on the part of the staff from concentration on distinctive, individual problems to general ones. Thus in An.'s case, the reports included a description of her *distinctive* problems ('female' ones, as defined by the staff's keen perception of 'relational difficulties' amongst the girls) which were both understandable in terms of her social background and her 'femaleness', and *general* problems where her behaviour was seen to be no different from the 'difficult' and 'problematic' behaviour of other children in the agency.

Similarly, D., although described as someone whom the other children respected, seemed to exhibit certain relational problems:

> D. is very much a loner. She is responsive to the staff but that is because in terms of maturity she is very adult. She does not join in the games of other children but watches from the side. (Residential social worker, male)

The team leader recapitulated these problems in her written comments:

> D. is very much on her own for a lot of the time. This is almost certainly due to her sophistication and the fact that she had an abortion, this has made her wise beyond her years. She was used to mixing with older students and it was a shock for her to come and live as a child. (Team leader, female)

Thus D. had her distinctive problems which could be explained, at least in part, by the fact that she had experienced something dramatic which other children could not understand; her 'aloneness' was due to her own experiences. At the same time, however, as the same report makes clear, D. had problems which were seen to be in common with those of other children, particularly those in the agency.

> D. is often selfish, it seems that she cannot share things. (Team leader, female)

Again, D.'s problems were initially linked to a description of former events in her life and the fact that those events may have made it difficult for her to trust other people, but certain aspects of her behaviour which might have followed on quite logically from these events (for example, her alleged 'selfishness'), were not perceived as being related,

In the case of De.:

> A lot of work needs to be done in establishing and stabilizing her social and sexual identity, so as to strengthen her own personality and reduce the risk of exploitation through a need for affection. This is something that all girls experience but De. is rather immature in this respect as she has not yet begun to work things out, this is due to her deprived background. (Team leader, female)

Thus De. appeared to experience distinctive relational problems of her own. At the same time, however, De., too, was subsequently described as 'attention seeking' and as 'manipulative' and these labels were applied in a pejorative way rather than in an 'appreciative' way.

> De. tends to be flirtatious in order to gain attention, she also manipulates staff in order to gain their attention and is very resentful when she is corrected for this behaviour. (Residential social worker, male)

These problems were referred to as general problems of children in care and therefore as indicative of 'trouble'. They were drawn from a general pool of 'child care problems' which, staff members felt, caused difficulties.

The emphasis placed on 'relational' aspects of behaviour in relation to girls was also reiterated in various 'approving' comments. What is important here is that staff thought these aspects of girls' behaviour worthy of note.[7] The report on J., for instance, read:

> She is generally liked and has responded well to some attention from a few boys, both on a playful and sexual level. (Warden)

Whilst the report on M. read:

> She no longer avoids people but relates well to both male and female members of staff. She has a healthy attitude to the boys in [the agency] and likes to spend time with them. (Warden)

St., the girl who was the newcomer, was immediately described in reports as a loner:

> She does not seem to want or need a close relationship with any one girl from [the agency]; this is strange. (Deputy team leader, female)

Again, there was explicit expectation that girls should want to form close relationships with others within the agency, even when they had only recently arrived; it was only 'natural' for girls to do so.

Another indicator of girls' needs for relationships and affection came in the comments that:

> St. always goes to bed when told and likes a goodnight kiss, although she will not ask for this. (Deputy team leader, female)

> I think St. would like to confide in me but she has not yet done so, but the need is there. (Deputy team leader, female)

> It is sad that A. is unable to integrate. She tends to be demanding and overbearing, and she has little trust in children. (Residential social worker, female)

> J. has not formed any strong relationships with staff and although willing to chat in a general sense, she will quickly withdraw and keep her distance if the

conversation becomes too personal and threatens to encroach upon the real feelings of J. (Team leader, female)

Under the category 'relationships with staff' there were further written comments which made clear what was approved of in girls' behaviour, what was sought and what was disapproved of. For instance,

St. has always shown an interest in increasing her domestic skills and will offer to help with domestic chores. (Residential social worker, female)

She will ask female staff for advice on hygiene and personal everyday problems, but has only confided in one female staff member about her sexual activities. (Residential social worker, female)

J. is much tidier now, she used to be very provocative in her dress and very 'tarty', she now dresses appropriately and looks very feminine. (Team leader, male)

We could not get De. to accept any affection at first but she has greatly improved. (Team leader, female)

De. relates on a very superficial level but we are hopeful that as time goes on she will feel able to develop close relationships with the other girls and with the staff. (Deputy warden)

In contrast, although following the guidance of the pro forma requiring the same details on boys as on girls for the degree of parental contact, home relationships and circumstances, a personal picture, relationships with staff, relationships with other children and ambition, written comments on the boys did not concentrate on the same aspects of behaviour. As I have previously indicated, comments on boys revolved around their legal and illegal *activities* and their response to organized activities and their degree of participation rather than on any relational difficulties. Boys were described as immature and as unstable but this was seen to be made manifest in their approach to activities rather than in their approach to other people. Thus the ability to work and co-operate in a team (on the football pitch, for instance) and the ability to persist with various activities (model-making and snooker, for instance) were predominant characteristics of the reports on boys.

P. has matured a lot since he arrived here. He now joins in the activities with the other lads and plays in the games room. (Residential social worker, female)

In my view I would suggest that Th. is now able to cope with other people and with being on his own. He uses his time constructively doing jigsaw puzzles and making models and he now wants to be one of the group. He participates in team events without losing his temper and this is a good sign. (Deputy warden, male)

Summary

Despite giving passing acknowledgment to the fact that it is social situations which lead towards children being admitted into care, staff in this agency referred ultimately to the children's problems being individual ones. All the children came to be seen as suitable clients even though initial comments referred to problems being based within the family. This was especially so in the case of girls, whose problems were interpreted, for the most part, in terms of relational difficulties. But the evidence for this claim lay not so much in the staff's assertions about the causes of the girls' problems and 'difficult behaviour' but in the approach which was adopted to resolve or reduce these problems. In summary, the girls were seen as needing 'affection, closeness and personal relationships' to remedy the 'emotional deprivation' which many of them had suffered. On the whole, a gentle, persuasive and therapeutic approach was seen as necessary to deal adequately with them, whereas boys could be managed as a group. The girls were also seen to have a greater capacity for emotion than the boys and thus to suffer more when there were family or relationship difficulties or when they found difficulties in expressing emotion. Indeed, their problematic behaviour was seen as 'role expressive' and indicative of problems which are peculiar to the female sex. As the staff related, the girls were sometimes very demonstrative and susceptible to 'mood swings' because of their depth of emotion.

Other prominent themes concerned the girls' ability to manipulate and to exploit situations to their own advantage; their greater psychological and sexual maturity compared with boys', and also their vulnerability. But whilst girls were 'vulnerable' in a general way, male members of staff apparently felt vulnerable in the presence of girls especially when on their own, as if it was a natural part of the female personality to be guileful and to crave sexual intimacy with men. This theme hints at the claims and assertions of earlier writers such as Cohen (1955) that where girls are bound to express their delinquency they will do this through sexual delinquency, as if all females are predisposed towards sexual delinquency and the exploitation of men. Interestingly, this theme depends heavily on isolated incidents within the agency and a realistic appraisal of the incidents does not account for the exaggerated sensitivity of some of the male staff on this issue.

The image of femininity promoted amongst the girls in the agency was clearly one revolving around passivity and conformity; 'nice' girls were 'caring, open, friendly, responsive and sensitive' and those who allowed their natural 'maternal instincts and emotionality' to show. By contrast, especially 'difficult' girls were 'loud, rude, aggressive and manipulative'.

These themes and images, it became clear, were not specific to this agency and its staff; they were to appear in all the agencies to a greater or lesser degree. A more rigorous analysis of them is tackled in Chapter 6 but in the next chapter I provide further illustration of images of girls.

Notes

1. Assessment centres were created out of at least four different types of home. The oldest were reception centres, set up in towns during the last century, when long-stay children's homes and foster homes were out in the country. They could take children in an emergency, saved the journey out of town for short-term emergencies and were used as a 'breathing space' for decisions to be made. After the Curtis Report of 1946 and the Children's Act of 1948, reception centres took on a key role of observing the behaviour of children taken into care and preparing them for fostering if they were not to return home. Assessment centres, since their inception in 1970, have also taken on the function of former remand homes and classifying centres (see Hudson, 1975; Tutt, 1977; Bines, 1978 and Bookbinder, 1982).

2. One child care officer was away on leave, another was attending a course, thus I interviewed 15 of the staff in addition to management officers, teaching staff and the domestic bursar. NB: the terms child care officer and residential social worker were used synonymously by staff in this agency.

3. Most of the staff were in their twenties, whilst group leaders and 'managers' were somewhat older. The staff were working a basic forty hour week, either 7–3 pm with a break at lunchtime, or 2–10 pm. This shift system meant that staff experienced frequent changes in their routine, never being sure when their days off would be, for instance. Staff frequently communicated their frustration to me about these working arrangements and the poor conditions of service in general.

4. All the girls within this agency had admitted to having committed various offences, according to the staff. So although 'official documentation' may not have placed emphasis on the offending behaviour of these juveniles it was entirely appropriate to refer to them in some situations as 'juvenile offenders'. In discussion with them it was clear that they saw themselves as 'being in trouble' and they did not make distinctions between those who had appeared in court and those who had not. This blurring of the distinctions between 'offenders' and 'non-offenders' is not a new phenomenon. Indeed, the fact that girls are sometimes likely to be dealt with through 'care' procedures rather than the criminal procedures of court (see LITA, 1983; Campbell, 1981), even though boys and girls may be equally involved in offending, has been well rehearsed.

5. Surprisingly, the apparent contradictions within these statements were not observed by those issuing them. Thus, despite the emphasis on the families' contribution to whatever problems there might be, their daughters were seen as the most suitable recipients for 'help' through their removal from home.

6. Whilst I carried out a traditional content analysis of the material, here I merely report on the common themes in the writing which pointed to broad categories of understanding and images of the juvenile behaviour.

7. As Belson and Hood (1967) point out in their evaluation of case records, it is frequently the case that social workers preparing case records usually adopt the practice of making no mention of some factors if he or she considers it 'normal', but concentrate on factors which either have in the past concerned them or which currently concern them.

4 The fieldwork: images in practice
– Agency Two

This agency has a long history as a public institution. At the time of my research it comprised four more or less independent units. Unit A was a closed unit for six girls.[1] Unit B was a newly founded long-stay unit for girls who had been assessed and who required immediate placement. Units C and D were for girls who were on remand from the court or who were sent to the agency to be assessed.[2] As Agency Two's brochure explained, the 1969 Children and Young Persons Act changed the role of the agency from a remand home to a community home, though it was later described as a regional observation and assessment centre.

The explicit aim of the agency was to provide a place of detention for alleged offenders not released on bail, and a place of safety for girls who were to appear before a court or on whom an interim care order had been made by a court. The centre also provided a place of assessment for girls already subject to a care order so that the most suitable placement could be selected. The intensive care unit within the agency catered for girls who were thought to be in need of a high degree of individual care and/ or treatment or for girls who were seen as too violent to be held in an ordinary community home or school.

The staff: background and training

The staff in Agency Two totalled 46 (excluding ancillary staff – cooks, secretaries, clerks, cleaners). In addition to this there were four women and two men who worked in the school unit (part-time), and two educational psychologists (one full-time, and one part-time), a social worker, a consultant psychiatrist and usually one or two registrars, a nursing sister, a tutor organizer and a visiting medical officer.

Apart from the superintendent and senior assistant (both male) the staff were basically divided into the four groups A – D. Each group had, at its head, an assistant superintendent. During my stay I had the most contact with the assistant superintendent in charge of C and D units, though I also had the opportunity to talk at some length with the assistant superintendent in charge of the closed unit. Each group had a group leader and either two or three senior supervisors who performed various administrative duties and took care of the security arrangements when all other staff (including the superintendent and his deputy) were off duty.

Of the total number of care staff (41), excluding all 'managers', 32 were women and 9 were men. There were two men in three of the groups and three in one. All the group leaders were female. The women who worked in the agency whilst I was there were predominantly under thirty, whilst the men (barring one) were over thirty years of age.[3]

A number of staff were clearly career orientated, using experience in this agency as a stepping stone to other possibilities within the child care system. Other members of staff were content to remain in the agency and could not foresee any reason to transfer elsewhere; they tended to have been in the institution for over four or five years. About six of the staff who had been taken on within the last year did not have any previous experience of working with children and young adults. Most of the younger staff were keen to pursue training possibilities.

The girls
Of the 35 girls who were already there when I arrived or who arrived during my stay, most were 14 or 15 years of age. The average age was 14 years 6 months.

Analysis of the primary reasons for their admission (from descriptions contained within the files) provided the following picture:

Prior placement breakdown – 15
Beyond care and control – 7
Place of safety order – 1
Non-school attendance – 1
Family conflict irreconcilable – 1
Court reports (for borstal suitability/breach of bail, etc.) – 10

This picture is misleading, for only one girl (the non-school attender) fitted into only one category. All the others had very complicated life histories, 23 of them having been in and out of care for many years and 11 of them having had school attendance problems. In most cases the girls had been described as 'beyond control' at some stage in their progression through the child care system, and many came from families where conflict was either temporarily 'irreconcilable' or a permanent feature. Of the girls 22 had been charged with offences; where charges had not been brought there were accusations of girls being 'light fingered'.

The picture which emerges from this analysis is rather complicated, and whilst I have charted the primary reasons for admission there were further details on admission sheets which suggested that the girls' 'problems' were numerous. For example, a girl might be on remand from the court for reports to be prepared in relation to her offending behaviour, but also be listed for non-school attendance and glue sniffing. Fifteen out of the total of 25 girls in C and D units, where I spent most of my time, had previous experience of residential care. Twelve had appeared in court for offences.

Suitable clients?

My discussions with staff gave me the impression that there were few girls there unnecessarily, in their opinion. At the same time, the staff found it difficult to identify ways in which the girls differed from those in the community. A male member of the staff in unit C who had recently turned to child care in a mid-career switch commented:

> These kids are quite normal, I try to treat them as I treat my own kids... the rough, the tumble and everything. They're normal kids in abnormal circumstances, they're the unlucky ones... there are many more like them outside. (Residential social worker, male)

Others described the situation as 'this lot got caught'. A few staff, however, made more general comments that the agency was perhaps an inappropriate response to the girls, that there was very little to distinguish them from those outside.

Close questioning about the girls encouraged reiteration of the view that their admission to the agency was not always due to the girls themselves or to any problematic behaviour on their part. The social worker, for instance, claimed that the matter of admission depended to a large degree on the field social worker, and whether or not that social worker had heard of the agency and whether the relevant borough had previously used the agency with any degree of success. She also stated:

> social workers take kids away from home too soon, the ethos is that social workers are namby-pamby creatures, but they recommend custody, care orders very frequently, though I know some are very anti-custody and will recommend probation orders and things.... A lot of girls come here without having been tried elsewhere... in IT groups and things... there's no questioning of the process. Their social worker happens to have heard of CL... or the magistrates think of it... once a social worker uses [Agency 2] they tend to use it time and time again, sometimes inappropriately, for there's nowhere else to send girls.

A number of staff remarked on the fact that sometimes girls were admitted under the category of 'placement breakdown' when really it was not their fault. Two girls, for instance, had been in children's homes and, although not completely settled there and somewhat troublesome, had been surprised when asked to move elsewhere. It transpired that the homes were due to close, thus the request for a transfer may have been precipitated by this rather than by their problematic behaviour.

Certain homes were directly implicated in the staffs' criticisms. They argued that homes were often responsible for lapses in security which led to children absconding, resulting finally in their admission to Agency Two. This view was expounded by the superintendent in relation to community homes:

We get the kids which others places can't cope with... when they are supposed to be able to. It's very sad when a kid is rejected from a community home... it shouldn't happen at all.

Children's homes were viewed by one deputy group leader as 'breeding grounds for violence' which encouraged transfer to places like Agency Two but the blame could not be attributed solely to the children:

in children's homes, the kids start ruling the roost... there isn't the difference in ages between staff and kids... the staff are often very young and inexperienced. (especially in the C. home)... the kids start taking over... the staff can't control them at all, and the kids just say no. I've seen local authorities do a lot of harm, as well as a lot of good.

This view was similar to views expressed in Agency One where parents were accorded some of the blame for their children's admission to the agency. There was a feeling amongst some of the staff that the girls were there only because their parents were weak and inadequate, and that they had given in too easily; the parents had not attempted to cope with their daughters' 'normal adolescent problems'. It was thought that parents had too easy access to social services.

Others, however, felt that the girls themselves sometimes secured their own admission to the agency; this was not a trend which emerged in Agency One.

It's too easy for girls to admit themselves into care... without realising the consequences... just not   happy at home. Mind you, it's very difficult being a parent these days... kids have recourse to social workers far too easily, you know.

Despite this expression of sympathy for the girls who ended up in the agency (in that staff were aware that the process of arrival for girls was a selective one), most of the girls were (paradoxically) thought to be suitable clients for the agency and deserving of its 'help' and 'control'.

Being 'difficult' and defining 'trouble'

First, it is important to note that the label 'difficult' was not necessarily a comment deriving from observations of the girls' behaviour, but often an indication of girls' reputations and of the staff's apprehension in dealing with them. So a girl need not have done anything wrong before she was described as 'difficult'. Girls who had previously been in care, for instance, were expected to be 'bad' or 'difficult'. They 'spell trouble' was how one member of staff put it.

A girl whom I shall call F. fell into the 'difficult' category on three counts: first, she had had her chance elsewhere; secondly, she was rude and insolent; and thirdly, as illustrated by the comments of the deputy group leader, she was also very aggressive:

> I don't like the girl who puts herself at the top of the pecking order; in this group there is F. and P. P. is verbally aggressive... physically... they both intimidate the others. F. gets into a temper and is vicious... she's very dangerous... very, very strong, she gets extra strength from somewhere.

It seems clear, as a general principle, that those girls who had been to other institutions were perhaps 'hardened' or 'tougher' than those who had not. When I asked why C., a thirteen-year-old, might be too vulnerable in Agency Two as some staff indicated, the superintendent suggested that the others would be tougher,

> a lot of them you see, are well experienced in institutions, or they've committed serious offences. We take the worst, other places can't hold them, care and contain them.

'Trouble' itself

Talking about 'trouble' in Agency One more frequently meant reference to behavioural or emotional maladjustment. Here in Agency Two, it often meant identification of unacceptable or anti-social behaviour. In a sense, the actual behaviour may have been the same, but it was, at times, framed rather differently within the two contexts.

In response to a question about 'troublesome' behaviour I was told by a group leader that it was a matter of

> language, rudeness, and if they run around like children, and try and hide from you, it's not always rudeness... its not being able to share... giggling, silly little games.

The same group leader stated:

> It's bullying, scapegoating... like... the bullying of one girl, they always pick on a weak one.

Other supervisors talked about 'nasty, aggressive behaviour'; one could not stand people being 'foulmouthed, bad table manners – bullying', the 'three things he hated to see in a girl'. Another said that a 'genuine bad egg' stands out, 'they're nasty, manipulating, horrible to everyone'. None the less, some of this behaviour was interpreted, if not excused, as 'attention seeking' behaviour. Interestingly, one of the assistant superintendents told me that she liked naughty girls:

> I quite like it when these girls are naughty... I like them not too placid or anything, but naughty and spirited a bit.

Views of offending

In my attempts to establish an image of someone who might be classified as 'bad' or 'difficult', I frequently asked questions about girls who had offended – thinking that offenders would, perhaps, fall most naturally into this category. I asked about the nature of offences, the typicality of offences and for the staff's thoughts on the motivations underlying offending behaviour.

It became clear, at this stage, however, that initial distinctions drawn between 'bad' or 'difficult' girls and 'nice' girls were not adhered to in any consistent way. Moreover, when it came to 'offending' behaviour, staff resorted to a terminology which meant that they were more likely to be seen as 'disturbed' than 'bad'. 'Bad' behaviour was what occurred within the agency when girls did not conform (though even this might be translated into 'disturbance', as I reveal in subsequent comments); non-conforming through committing criminal offences elsewhere was defined in a different way. The social worker for the agency found this distinction untenable, however. She held the view that shoplifting, for instance, was, in lots of cases,

> pure and simple greed… it's dressed up as a social… problem, and sometimes it's out of need, they say it's boredom, but they know the difference between right and wrong.

She seemed dissatisfied that no distinctions were made in the agency between offenders and non-offenders, understandable and unacceptable offending, irrational and rational offending:

> It's a very cloudy area, and it's made worse by there being no distinction drawn between the girls. It's complicated by the decisions of magistrates, for no distinctions are made there either. We label them here as 'mad' rather than 'bad'… it's unrealistic… we slant it to stress the problems, in a way it's wrong, it means the girls can evade responsibility for their own actions.

This dilemma was epitomized for her by the case of K. who had committed a number of offences, including 'mugging' (where the victim subsequently died) and organized shoplifting. K. was variously described as very 'wicked' and very 'disturbed' by the staff in the agency. The social worker was inclined to think that K. deserved the borstal training for which she was being assessed (initially anyway),[4] but could not deny the huge handicaps which K. had (her mother, for instance, was described in reports as a prostitute and an alcoholic). But she also expressed the view that the agency looked far too deeply into the problems of the girls, and if anyone's life was looked into with the same degree of intensity then numerous problems would emerge. She stressed that many in the community were suffering similar deprivations to those in the agency, but did not resort to criminal activities.

Another member of staff shared a similar dilemma. A long-standing member of Agency Two who, at an earlier point in her career had been a security officer with a large departmental store, responded in this way when I asked her about motivations underlying shoplifting:

> If you'd heard as many pleas as I have ... of 'Oh well I was just taking it outside to look at it ... to look at the colour ... or I'd forgotten it was there' ... and you'd seen them looking around to check that no one was watching them ... they would put it down their coat and then into a holdall and then they'd disappear very quickly up the road ... you'd be very suspicious ... you'd get sick of it.

But initial punitive or retributive thoughts gave way to an understanding of the offences in a different light: 'they get bored', staff commented, and parents were seen to be at fault for not having taught them to develop their own resources to occupy their time, and so on.

At the same time, when I asked these two members of the staff to describe the girls more generally, they immediately referred in a very sympathetic manner to such factors as poverty, single parents, over-strict parents, parents out of touch with their children, and parental emotional and material neglect. Offenders were not identified as a distinct group in their descriptions and the overall tone was one of understanding. The message appeared to be that the girls must be made to feel responsible for their actions, but that, in context, their actions could be understood.

Staff attributed offending to poor school supervision, inappropriate schooling, the prohibitive cost of sports and youth centres, lack of parental interest, family lifestyles of offending, poverty, boredom, group pressure and the need to be accepted, getting caught up in gangs, the need to 'get back' at authority. Some staff members emphasized that 'delinquency' and delinquent acts were just a passing phase which everyone goes through in some way or another. The philosophy of 'offender as victim' was crystallized in the view of the consultant psychiatrist. He commented that:

> organized crime on the part of females is a recent phenomenon. With shoplifting and things I suppose the reasons are the same as with boys – emphasis on material things ... acquisition is terribly important in our society unfortunately, and there's less discipline in schools. I'm concerned with the problematic way of life, however, prostitution, drugs, sniffing and things like this. In the Leicester Square life girls are more vulnerable than boys ... boys are stronger in some way, the girls like to be looked after and they have to compromise to achieve that. The boys remain independent. It's also difficult for girls because they become contaminated in a way ... they can't mix in this kind of circle as easily as boys. It's a bit like the homosexual boy, he's trapped.

Comments about the type of crimes which had been committed pointed to an assumption that with girls it was usually a matter of shoplifting clothes and food or soliciting. Where a more unusual crime had been committed, K.'s 'mugging', for instance, the staff were all aware of it.

Defining 'trouble' and 'difficult' behaviour involved some consideration of 'aggressive' behaviour too. In response to general questions about aggression I received a number of accounts from staff which emphasized that this was something particularly associated with West Indian girls. The conclusion of a group of four supervisors in D unit was that

the West Indian kids are much more violent, it's just in them.

The awareness of aggression was made very apparent to me; most members of staff could recall incidents in which aggression was extreme, though not always from first hand experience.   Sometimes too the aggression tended to be verbal rather than physical. The senior supervisor went on to say:

when they are aggressive there's a lot of verbal aggression ... these girls are frightening when they fight too ... much worse than we used to be when we were lads.

The distinctions drawn here were enlarged upon:

they'll bite, kick, pull your hair ... everything, you have to protect everywhere, with boys it's just boots and fist ... the girls, they bite – ram each other, it's much more savage ... animal fighting.   (Senior supervisor, female)

Unlike some members of staff, she denied that there had been any increase in girls' aggression, however.   Rather, she felt that there might be an increased awareness of girls' violence as they were now more visible in the community and tended to stay at home less often than previously. The aggression in Agency Two, she felt, was in many cases simply fighting between the girls and it was very often to do with their being around all day with little to occupy them.

Aggression was also seen as a sign of disturbance in some cases. It was explained to me by one of the senior supervisors in C unit that this was why F. was going to the Youth Treatment Centre.

It's because of her temper ... foul temper, explosive, she loses all control, it's uncontrollable ... she lets fly, kicks out ... doesn't care what she says ... even to Mrs A. [assistant superintendent] ... she needs help ... psychiatric help. (Senior supervisor, female)

Explanations for the aggression ranged from a theory of simple arguments between the girls to physiological causes.   One supervisor argued:

Kids feel as if they've got to be aggressive to find a place ... otherwise they'll be walked over.

Another,

It's usually just due to quarrels between them, it happens a lot in the work period and in school, it varies with each girl ... the longer a girl has been here the more fed up they are ... and aggressive when they are ready to leave. (Supervisor, female)

Both the superintendent and an assistant superintendent (the former senior matron) referred to physical causes as contributing factors here. The superintendent claimed that:

> If you get a consistent pattern of abuse, aggressive behaviour, violence, etc., it's often their periods, if there's regularity [in this kind of behaviour] the first thing that comes to mind is the physical thing. I'm often the first to notice this link ... in extreme cases it's perhaps physical, perhaps we don't give enough attention to this. You would look at psychology, of course, as you would with boys, but physiology is an additional thing to look at.

The deputy superintendent expressed a similar view that girls' menstrual cycles may have contributed to outbursts of aggressive behaviour:

> I think with girls, emotional disturbance is very likely ... certainly they have more emotional problems in their make-up ... the menstrual cycles they go through are all-important. Sometimes it's pre-menstrual strain.

Apart from bullying behaviour, condemnation of aggression was not in evidence in what the staff said; there was more a tone of acceptance. Sometimes the aggression was viewed as wilful, sometimes as out of frustration, sometimes as an indication of disturbance, but it was always set against clusters of problems relating to family background; these were never far from the forefront of conversation.

Promiscuity

Despite an abundance of written notes suggesting promiscuity in numerous instances, this subject was rarely brought into conversation. In only one case (F.) was the matter raised without my questions. Certainly, staff talked about when they should be in at night, but they were hard put to identify 'transgressors' with any conviction. F. was the only one to 'lose marks' in any sense on this count, and even so there was medical evidence which suggested the contrary, though some staff doubted the accuracy of this evidence. Staff appeared to assume their knowledge more from the fact that she had been 'on the run' for five months, and, perhaps more significantly, she talked about sexual activity and exploits a lot. She was also thought to be very crude. It seems that only where the girls themselves reminded staff of 'sexual activity' with crude jokes and innuendos did the staff remain aware of the possibility of particular girls being promiscuous. It is likely that the fact that it was a single sex and enclosed agency had some effect on the staff's views, too, as the opportunity to be 'promiscuous' would not arise.

These conversations with staff tended to be very general ones; their comments did not appear to relate to anyone in particular. Once encouraged to express views, however, there was a flood of opinion. The deputy superintendent made it clear that 'at risk' was not easy to define:

> We're told girls are at risk ... when I've talked to girls I very often wouldn't share some of the anxiety as the parent or social worker. The West Indian families, I think the parents' attitudes are somewhat different to our own ... they have high expectations and assume the girls to be at risk.

When pressed to tell me what he thought 'at risk' meant and how one would recognize promiscuity he answered:

> It's deviation from fairly normal behaviour...if there's definite proof that she's putting herself at risk, soliciting or whatever, sleeping around...then we need to do something, smoking pot, drugs, wild parties... they put themselves at risk some of them.

At this point 'at risk' and 'in moral danger' were used interchangeably:

> They're in moral danger a lot of them... some of them take overdoses and you have to be aware of the dangers....you have to take the risk seriously...suicide, pregnancy...etc. etc. With some of the youngsters once they've made up their minds to live their lives in a certain way, they will. Some are very wilful, they block off, you can't get through to them...it's a cycle of self-destruction, often they have no control.

This oblique reference to 'victim behaviour' echoes the comments of the consultant psychiatrist and was reiterated in the observations of the former matron (now assistant superintendent) that promiscuity was:

> just sleeping around, from one person to another, she's seeking extra attention and affection which she doesn't receive. Sometimes it's a group thing, it becomes a way of life... pimps make them do it sometimes... it's usually at thirteen or fourteen, this age, due to some pimp, and they're frightened, can't get out. It's more difficult for a girl to get out of it all... they're very vulnerable... some are very frightened of being beaten up.

Despite the general tone of understanding in the more general comments, a number of staff felt it important to mention that sometimes the male members of staff felt quite vulnerable if left alone with a girl – in a bedroom, for instance. This concern paralleled concern felt in Agency One on this issue. Indeed, it was an unwritten law that staff should not get themselves into this kind of situation. I was told of instances in other homes where girls had accused the staff of assault and this seemed to have a resounding effect within Agency Two. Nor was it just the men who were a little wary; indeed, the older male staff denied that they were concerned to any significant degree, being family men and capable of looking after themselves. But the female staff revealed their concerns in asides to me: 'Mr... shouldn't really go in the girls' bedrooms' 'you never know what these girls will get up to, or what they will say'. There seemed to be an assumption that there should always be suspicion where girls were concerned, not just that they would spread malicious gossip, but they might actually attempt to seduce the men.

'It's only natural': the female personality

There were many unfavourable comments about the girls which were seen as an intrinsic part of the female personality. Such comments, which ranged across the two main units, were:

> Girls can be very bitchy with one another, very spiteful, and this is just a natural part of them... that's why you have to think twice about what they are saying, a woman can very often see through another woman, but a man can't... he can't see the same things. (Group leader, female)

> They're very manipulative, very quileful. (Supervisor, female)

> Girls hold grudges, they don't have honest fights like boys... they're underhand, devious. (Supervisor, female)

> With girls they never drop an argument, they're always backbiting with one another... they bitch a lot and that's a sort of female thing. Men bitch too perhaps, but not at the same level... females carry it on a bit longer. (Supervisor, female)

> The West Indians are always crude, it's something in their culture. (Supervisor, female)

These sentiments, clearly, may have had a bearing on the staff's responses to the girls, determining the degree of suspicion with which they were regarded, for instance.

Disturbance

No one was actually labelled as 'disturbed' whilst I was in the agency. Indeed the nearest definition offered referred to the fact that 'really disturbed' girls 'stick out like a sore thumb'. Supervisors were able to recall the admission of 'really disturbed' girls who had exhibited 'absurd and bizarre' behaviour; persistent crying, absent stares and 'depressed behaviour' were some of the indications they used to assess the level of disturbance. None the less, there was a strong feeling that girls were in some ways very emotional creatures, susceptible to radical mood swings and depression.

But there was also some recognition that the 'emotional aspects' of girls' lives were perhaps cultural artefacts, creating a 'false consciousness'. As one of the assistant superintendents stated:

> I think women are more liable to show their emotions than men, this is a cultural thing... it's education which is suggesting that the woman is weak whilst the man is dominant, forceful... it's socialisation. Girls are allowed to

be moody, it's more acceptable for them to be moody. We say 'leave her alone'… 'she's alright', excuse this behaviour. With boys we might say 'snap out of it'.

There were those who related general 'disturbance' to the girls' problems; however, as the senior supervisor in C group commented:

> women emotional… yes, and these girls are moody, but it's due to the enormous amount of stress they're under.

Indeed, it was obvious that the terms 'difficult' and 'disturbed' were used interchangeably. The definitions of girls changed from day to day. Their behaviour might be 'bad' but it was because of emotional disturbance – all understandable in view of family backgrounds. Behaviour loosely referred to one day as disturbed would be labelled as 'disruptive and difficult' the next. Some days behavioural problems were less deserving of sympathy than 'emotional problems'.[5]

Nice girls

There were some exceptions to the general view of the 'suitable client' in Agency Two. One such girls, S., was a non-school attender who had experienced none of the usual passages in and out of care; moreover, she did not display any of the more typical attributes of aggression, 'disturbance' or bad behaviour. She was presumed not to have committed any offences. She was instead generally seen to be a 'good' girl because of her natural attributes. In arguments she was said to reveal an allegiance to the staff, and was 'quiet but not withdrawn', 'responsive', she was 'always willing to help', 'sensible'. Furthermore, S. was thought to have made progress; 'she knows herself to be very lucky', 'she has realized her mistake', and having been able to compare her parents with the parents of others, 'she's realized her parents are okay'. A staff member in one of the groups put it this way:

> S. is a very nice girls, one of the nicest girls we have had here… not like these bloody silly fourteen year olds, but she shouldn't be here.

When I asked how she was different, I was told:

> She's not abusive, she's responsive, keeps out of trouble, doesn't give you lip… doesn't pull you about.

A further example of a 'misfit' amongst the clientele, and of a 'nice girl' was a girl in D group who was clearly thought to be 'more sinned against then sinning', and it was felt that because of her very quiet personality the agency was an inappropriate placement. The group leader stated:

> M. is very nice… she should never have been here, I can't understand why M.'s boyfriend has been sent to prison because of her… all the girls who pass through here… it's all sex under the age, the same thing. It's doing her no

good here... I don't know whether it's true about her father [who had been accused of 'chasing after' M.] – perhaps that's why she can't go home — but she's extremely fond of her mother, they're very close to one another.

Certainly M. was not viewed as delinquent in any way.[6] She was viewed as one of the very few who were 'apart' and even 'above' the main group; she never instigated trouble and was rarely, if ever, on the fringes of it. She was well thought of because she criticized the others about their table manners, for instance, through her silence and separation. However, I was to discover that M. was not popular amongst the staff. She was thought to invite the other girls' ridicule because she was so pathetic, as if saying 'poor old me' all the time. Thus, although she avoided reprehensible behaviour and was in some way approved of, this should not be confused with likeable qualities. Practitioners also reiterated comments made in the previous agency, that 'nice' girls were 'feminine, naturally caring', and so on.

Dealing with difficult girls: a different response for a different kind of 'trouble'

Many differences were highlighted between what was perceived as appropriate for girls and boys. The staff clearly thought that boys and girls had to be handled differently. They also reflected upon their particular areas of difficulty in their handling of the girls, and on the strategies they adopted to overcome these difficulties. The following response of the deputy superintendent was fairly typical, and it reflected comments similar to those offered in Agency One.

I find it easier to deal with boys in the control situation, it's much easier to tell a boy to do something and reason with him... you get a better, positive response. The girls I find are far more argumentative, temperamental and hysterical, and therefore need to be handled in an entirely different way [to boys]. I've never had any major problems, though perhaps this is due to the fact that I am mature and have a family... perhaps they see me as a father figure. I try to talk things through in conflicts.

One member of staff was very clear on his strategy:

if the worst comes to the worst you can always take a boy aside, glower at him and warn him that if he doesn't step in line you'll pull one on him... so there's direct conflict which is resolved in this way... you have to be so careful with girls ... you can only restrain them, if you just take them by the elbow or something they'll say 'you're not allowed to touch me'. (Supervisor, male)

The consultant psychiatrist expressed the view that boys' and girls' needs were quite distinct.

Boys' needs are much simpler, they're younger in a way... they differ greatly, whereas boys might be criminal, girls are wayward. Girls are much more individualistic and have to be treated as individuals. They're interested in clothes and fashion at this age.... You can treat boys as a group almost... they'll adapt to institutional life quite easily... they're used to institutional, community life... they're used to doing things as a team ... from learning games together. CHEs are therefore more appropriate for boys than girls. When girls reach 14 or 15 or 16 they are much more independent than the boys... they are into boyfriends and things, the boys haven't reached that stage yet ... whereas the girls are ready for independent life... girls have emotional maturity. Boys' needs are simpler, they're into sports and competition... even at school they are eager to show that their house is better than another... obviously it's easier to discipline them because of this.[7]

Other views were simply that:

with girls you have to be more cautious, more suspicious... give them plenty of room when they're about to blow. (Senior supervisor, female)

girls are much more likely to rebel against any concentrated form of corrective treatment [than boys]. (Supervisor, male)

You have to spend a lot of time talking with girls... with boys if they're acting up you can take them off to do something physical... a cross country run, for instance... there are more possibilities with boys... you have to talk girls out of aggression, talk them down, you can't be particularly physical with girls. (Assistant Superintendent, male)

In connection with this tendency of girls to sustain levels of tension and possibly aggression and the need to 'talk them down' the use of the detention room was mentioned. I was told that this room essentially existed as a 'cooling off' place and that it was only used as such. Numerous instances of it being used to talk to the girls were cited, for 'therapy' and so on. Staff denied that the detention room was ever used as a place of punishment although there were instances when this was fairly obvious. On one occasion two girls were sent into the room because they had had a water fight in the bathroom; a playful fight had occurred which caused no physical damage to people or property. When staff stopped them they were told that they were to be taught a lesson by being sent to the detention room.[8]

Further discussion with the staff on what they felt to be appropriate responses to girls led to comments that they felt the agency was very much used by magistrates and social workers as a place of punishment. Indeed, the use of the agency in this way was seen as an attempt to equalize the treatment between boys and girls. Staff felt that the agency was being used to provide a response similar to that more typically meted out to boys. Agency Two was being used to provide a 'short, sharp shock' in much the same way as detention centres. The social worker put it this way:

it's partly due to the fact that there are few dispositions for girls. Magistrates don't know what to do with them.... There aren't a lot of sentences for girls ... I suspect very strongly that magistrates use this place as a punishment. I think borstal is seen as the extreme for girls...girls run out of chances, they force their chances with the magistrates. I think everyone is very concerned to look at the alternative dispositions to borstal. The whole system is geared to that. My experience with boys is that they reach the stage much earlier... it's available for them... but magistrates use this place in that same system.

Others went on to point out that although boys and girls might have similar problems, 'you wouldn't want to send a girl to borstal because it might harden her up', as one of the assistant superintendents remarked. This same assistant superintendent thought that in their handling of girls perhaps more attention ought to be paid to their need for affection. Also

girls attach importance to things...they are very sensitive to surroundings... what a room looks like, a boy might expect an army style – a girl needs softer things, soft toys and belongings are very important to them. A girl might be very weepy and homesick and she'd want these things... girls are sensitive to colours too.

Staff emphasized these 'feminine desires' in the importance which they felt should be attached to the girls' self-images. They were clearly concerned that the girls should 'not let themselves go' in terms of appearance, for instance. They felt it was an important aim for the girls both to 'look nice' and 'feel nice'.

Written reports

As in Agency One, much of what the supervisors wrote about the girls was shaped by their obligation to complete a standard behaviour report. Such reports were then collated by the group leader and presented at the assessment conference, or passed on to the superintendent if the girl was there for a court report. In C and D units the reports were reviewed by the assistant superintendent who was particularly concerned to improve the standard of report writing and to introduce new measures of assessment which would perhaps move away from the standard form. Nevertheless, whilst I was there these reports were the main 'instrument' in the staffs' assessment of the girls. Some discussion took place in review meetings (held about half-way through the assessment procedure) and no doubt there was much informal discussion which I was not a party to, but frequently staff would write these reports under pressure of time, asking what each other had written as they 'searched around' for things to say. Consequently, many of the reports were simply 'mirrors' of others, but interestingly they appeared to contain a greater degree of criticism of the girls than conversation with the staff had led me to expect. This was, I suspect, because the reports tended to be more descriptive of behaviour than of anything else; there was only a short space under the heading of 'general comments' for supervisors to articulate their understanding of how the problematic behaviour might be approached with a view to remedying it. Moreover, the assistant superintendent explained to me that it was the supervisors' role simply to report, observe and describe.

Judging from the tone of the reports, it appears that supervisors had very clear ideas about what was desirable in the girls and within the institution, and what was not. The 'nice' girl, for instance, would talk about more than just 'superficial things', she would be communicative (and give staff some reward for their efforts, incidentally), she would share things and would generally be responsive to staff – if they were teasing her, for example, or if they had a 'rough and tumble' or 'playfights' with her. More obviously, the 'nice' girl was not a bully and was not aggressive; she 'knew when to stop' if she was 'ragging' others or 'pulling them about'. The 'nice' girl was also able to occupy herself – by crocheting, knitting, doing crossword puzzles, and so on; she would not just sit around and watch TV. She might volunteer to do things for the staff and would certainly do her housework without supervision. She would definitely take care of her appearance. Also, she would have some insight into her own problems or at least be working hard towards the recognition of them.

This list of 'approved' attributes is by no means exhaustive nor did any of the girls fulfil *all* of them. But the staff's overall image of a girl was derived from a balance of 'positives'and 'negatives'. The 'difficult' girl was generally obstructive and needed much supervision, she would perform very few of the above 'positives' and would probably be aggressive. S., who was described as a 'misfit', was classified as a 'good' girl because she fulfilled many of the above conditions whilst she was in the agency. For example, she looked after her appearance (and was, significantly, thought to be very attractive, looking older than her years); she was quiet, but willing to talk to staff, and she did not participate in any 'bad' behaviour. Moreover, she rejected 'crude and rude' behaviour by not joining in with it; staff did not hear any 'bad or abusive'language from her. As one supervisor described:

> She's a very easy girl to talk to simply because she enjoys talking to the staff rather than the girls... this is because she is a very mature girl for her age... she has very little in common with most fourteen year olds.

Furthermore, she was 'helpful' and did her work without staff supervision; she was willing to talk sensibly about her problems with some degree of success: 'One of her virtues is that she is able to see both sides of the story'; 'She seems to have had time to realize where she has gone wrong and I think she will step back into line if given a chance'; 'She appears to regret not going to school', were some of the comments offered in the reports.

The group leader's summary of her problems was that:

> She has matured too quickly for her parents to be able to deal with it, home is not the answer, it is over-crowded and restricted anyway. (Group leader, female)

Thus, to some extent her appearance and her ability to talk to the staff had acted in her favour.

Another sign of improvement in a girl was if she 'settled in well' and 'adapted' to the system. Thus L. had improved because:

> initially she spent days crying and pleading to be returned to... [the children's home where she had previously lived], now however, she has settled in well, this is improvement. She is co-operative, polite and helpful. (Group leader, female)

One theme which emerged much more in the reports than in the interviews and in conversation was that of the girls being manipulative. The staff's suspicion of them is clear. R., for instance, (West Indian British, 16 years) was described by a supervisor in the following way:

> She is a very sly girl... well aware that we are watching her and consequently shows the kind of behaviour we want to see. She is quite obstinate at times... but no behavioural problems. But I feel very strongly that we are not seeing her as she is outside. She is resentful of staff and has 'selective deafness' she chooses when and what to listen to. (Supervisor, female)

Of the same girl it was said.

> She is polite, co-operative and friendly... (she presents to me as quite a mature, self-assured young lady).... However, I feel we have only seen the side of which she chooses to present to me, she is playing her stay with us very coolly. She is possibly a silent stirrer. (Supervisor, female)

Such comments were not founded on palpable evidence. To some extent, staff must have been relying on what they already 'knew' about girls or felt about them. The staff were employing an image of girls as being 'devious and manipulative'as a basis for their comments.

Summary

Many of the images of girls in this agency, like those revealed in Agency One, resemble images identified by earlier researchers and writers.

Although initially seen as 'no worse' than other girls on the 'outside', the reasons for these girls being there were quickly established. They were all seen to have 'family problems', for instance, and to need the special care and attention which this agency could offer. Whilst there was rather less emphasis than in Agency One on the 'relational problems' of girls, their essential 'emotional deprivation' or 'emotional disturbance' was recognized and became inextricably linked to all other interpretations of their 'bad' or 'difficult' or 'offending' behaviour. Being female itself was seen to contribute to problems and to any behaviour revealing those problems; staff frequently implied that the girls were 'victims of their sex' in that they could not escape from those essential characteristics of female biology; they were, generally speaking, 'emotional and temperamental' as a consequence. Combined with other problems and stresses this sometimes led to explosive and aggressive outbursts of behaviour.

For the most part, the staff's view of the girls was sympathetic, their behaviour was seen as 'understandable', and they needed the special 'individual attention approach' which earlier writers and practitioners had described. The inimical 'female personality', however, meant that girls were always seen as difficult to deal with and a response from them, when angry or upset, frequently hard to gain. Girls who were identified as 'likeable ' and 'likely to achieve growth' in the general 'therapeutic' aims of the agency, were those who responded quickly and clearly to the efforts of the staff. These were the girls who were communicative, gentle and helpful to the staff. In general, these characteristics too were those characteristics of the 'nice' girl and such aspirations for the girls were shared by the staff. The image of the 'nice' girl was essentially that of the 'natural female' as passive, sensitive and caring, and any step towards this was a step towards 'improvement' and the 'resolution of problems'. The staff wanted the girls to care for their appearance, honour their parents (despite acknowledgement that parents' behaviour often contributed to the girls' initial admission to the agency), be non-aggressive and moderate in manners and general behaviour. Looking beyond the confines of the agency, the ultimate goal for the girls was a steady relationship, marriage, home and family.

Notes

1. The 'closed' or 'secure' unit was a self-contained setting for those young people deemed 'unmanageable' or a danger to themselves in an open setting.

2. In unit C there were twelve, and in unit D fourteen places available for girls.

3. Most of the girls were from the London boroughs; those who were not tended to be the girls who had absconded from other homes and who remained in the agency only a night or two prior to their return. Of the girls, 21 were White British, 9 were Black British, 1 was Scottish, 1 was Guyanese, 1 girl was Spanish and 1 girl was a Greek Cypriot.

4. The assessment report on K. which was submitted to the Crown Court recommended that a Care Order would be far more appropriate and, indeed, this is what she subsequently received.

5. My adoption of these working terms, although a reflection of the staffs' 'working images', proved to be less useful than I had anticipated as the definitions and images shifted all the time. Staff repeatedly contradicted themselves in different situations.

6. The case of M. is interesting since she was classed as a 'really nice girl' and yet general depictions of a nice girl were of someone who did not 'sleep around'. The contradiction here is striking since M. was the only girl proven to have had sexual intercourse under the age of sixteen, despite the numerous accusations about

other girls. Perhaps it was acceptable to have one steady relationship without opprobrium, however, whatever the age of the parties involved, and that the meaning of 'promiscuous' for the staff was literally 'sleeping around' with numerous partners.
7. This view proved reminiscent of traditional theories expounded by criminologists and practitioners.
8. In October 1983 an investigative committee appointed by the DHSS reported that this particular agency had used the detention room excessively. See Children's Legal Centre (1983).

5 The fieldwork: images in practice – Agency Three

The location for this part of the fieldwork was a large and busy police station in central England. There were two male and two female constables assisting the male sergeant in the juvenile liaison office (JLO).[1] Overall responsibility for the office was in the hands of a Detective Chief Inspector, but it was the sergeant who organized the day-to-day running of the office and its affairs. In theory, the two WPCs operated the missing persons bureau located in this office, whilst the PCs were specifically juvenile liaison officers; in practice (because of the shift system, apart from anything else), the officers shared all the responsibilities.

All three male members of this team had children of their own, two of them with adolescent children, whilst one of the two women was married. Both PCs were in their early forties and had worked in youth clubs during the course of their careers, one of them still being professionally involved in the local attendance centre. Both WPCs were in their early twenties and neither had any relevant experience with juveniles outside of the juvenile liaison office setting. No specific training had been given to any of these officers regarding their work in the juvenile liaison office.

Why work in the juvenile liaison office?
Despite the frequent and widespread claims from chief constables that 'beat policing' is an important part of police work, studies of police behaviour and police organizations have invariably revealed that there are conflicting definitions of what constitutes 'real police work'. Indeed, it has been pointed out that whilst 'police ideology' stresses the view that the 'bobby on the beat' has the most important role, manpower allocation within police forces reveals that this is not the case; the front line of police organization is staffed by probationers and includes those who perceive themselves to be failures (Jones, 1980). Moreover, it has been suggested that police hierarchies generally create expectations which are not sustained in practice. Despite this primary role of the 'bobby on the beat' in theory, in practice police constables are motivated away from routine patrol work, even when they may find it satisfying, through persistent pressure on them to apply for promotion. Those who do not pursue promotion are frequently seen by others to be failures (Jones, 1980).

The juvenile liaison office, according to the juvenile liaison staff, is often seen as a place for such failures, though for younger constables a period in it can form an essential part of their training. Indeed, in Agency

Three the sergeant was described by his staff as a 'failure' who had passed his Inspector's examination some twelve years previously but who had not been promoted due to the lack of personal ability. Moreover, the sergeant was approaching retirement and his staff revealed to me that this job was a way of 'sending him out to pasture' before his departure from the police force.

Whilst the two WPCs viewed their posting to the juvenile liaison office as part of their training, the PCs suggested that they were probably there because they both had relevant experience with juveniles. It was of interest to discover, however, that neither had wanted to sit promotion examinations despite the length of their service in the police force (16 years and 9 years) and so they may have been perceived as 'failures' themselves.

To clarify the role of the juvenile liaison office within this particular police force, I was particularly concerned to discover the views of senior officers and other constables on the juvenile liaison office and its staff. Whilst senior officers[2] presented the view that the juvenile liaison office was an essential part of police work which could make a valuable contribution through the formal and informal contacts it forged with the community (e.g., social service departments, doctors, schools), other officers argued that it was nothing more than 'window dressing' for the police force. There was a further contrast in the views held about officers selected for juvenile liaison office work. Whilst senior officers suggested that police officers were selected for their special abilities, my more informal contacts with officers (in the CID, for instance)[3] elicited the view that the juvenile liaison office staff were indeed 'failures' or 'misplaced' personnel, thus confirming my earlier comments. As one detective constable put it, 'they're all misfits in the juvenile liaison office, people who are difficult to place, they're not "go-ahead" coppers but "nice", but that means they won't go anywhere, not within this police force anyway'. Walsh (1977) would undoubtedly label them as 'street cops' within his framework of police styles: those who simply wanted secure work to enhance their family and private leisure goals.

The juvenile liaison office staff were aware to some extent that they were viewed as 'soft cops' by the others, but they were quick to defend their work as 'real police work'. Indeed, an underlying theme of their own perceptions of their role was that they were police officers and definitely not social workers. PC M., for instance, described his work in this way

I think the juvenile liaison office is important first to show kids that the police are human. To me, the most important work is going round the schools and meeting the kids… just chatting with them. I want those kids to know that I'm just the same as their own dads, and the same as a lorry driver or a milkman only I'm a policeman. None the less we're here to stop juveniles offending, to point out to them what is not allowed in society.

The police sergeant viewed the work in a similar way:

> I suppose we're helping the social workers really by looking at home background and things, but it's a good chance to pick out the trouble-makers, the ones who'll be back, and we do this ... do it very effectively... and we keep our eye on them ... it's good police work. Social service departments sometimes contact us with their views about 'potential delinquents' and that's good too ... we can then check up on them and stop them.

All the staff in the juvenile liaison office resented the fact that CID officers saw themselves 'above' the uniformed section; they believed this to be an 'unfair' and inaccurate assessment of the uniformed section's role in the detection of crime. They argued that the juvenile liaison office itself had a very good detection rate which contributed positively to the CID detection rate. While my main task was to understand how the juvenile liaison office police officers perceived and dealt with their clients, this apparent rivalry was significant in leading them to defend vociferously their role in police work. More importantly, this defensive attitude led them to 'be hard' with those juveniles deemed to be 'hardened', as one officer put it. The staff unanimously agreed that having found a villian they should seek to 'nail him or her' in no uncertain way. Most of my work in this agency was thus an attempt to discover how judgements about male and female juvenile offenders were made, and more particularly, to establish which of the female offenders, if any, were seen as 'hardened', and the reasons for this.

A different response for a different kind of trouble
Staff in the juvenile liaison office viewed girls' and boys' offending behaviour as different. Girls were seen as predominantly 'shoplifters' whereas the most frequent offence of boys was seen as 'taking and driving away'. This view prevailed despite documentary evidence showing that there were more boys than girls shoplifting and that both girls and boys referred to the office had committed a wide range of offences.

Offences in which girls had been involved included theft, shoplifting, criminal damage, breach of the peace, actual bodily harm, travelling without paying fare, grievous bodily harm, robbery and traffic offences; the range of offences in which boys had been involved was similar, but with the addition of taking and driving away offences, burglary, under-age sexual intercourse, indecent assault and indecent exposure offences, arson, forgery and deception, and going equipped to steal.

Interestingly, with reference to the shoplifting, staff in the juvenile liaison office suggested that boys and girls were stealing very different things. PC M. described how girls generally shoplift little things, sweets, make-up, jewellery, clothing, that kind of thing, whilst boys tended to steal cassette recorders, tapes, records, sports gear... sweets, food.

Similarly, WPC J. believed that girls

take little things but usually for themselves, make-up, and skirts and things, whilst the boys took...magazines, toys, crayons, tapes... really a lot of things which they don't always want... they just chuck them around a lot of the time.

Once again, these beliefs did not accurately reflect the detailed information that was available. Details relating to each offence, e.g., value of goods, type of goods, were recorded in minute detail in the offender register. Analysis of the register revealed that boys and girls stole very similar kinds of goods: foodstuffs, sweets, stationery, cassettes, records and clothing. None of the girls in the 1981 referral list had stolen make-up. There was also an understanding that girls committed offences in large, organized gangs, when most of the offences appeared to have been committed singly or in couples.

the girls are much more scheming, they're organized... there's seldom less than three of them, they use a 'look out', you see. They're a sneaky lot. (PC A.)

I agree, the girls seem to know what they are doing more, they're organized. It's not spur of the moment stuff though most of them try to tell you that. They work in gangs very often. (WPC H.)

Again, however, analysis of details available revealed discrepancies between what the officers believed was occurring and what was happening in practice. Indeed, only 7 per cent of the girls' shoplifting offences were committed in groups of three or more; 93 per cent of the offences were committed either singly or in pairs.

Moreover, my interviews with officers revealed that their understanding of the reasons for offending amongst boys and girls was very different in each case. The boys, they claimed, offended for the 'immediate rewards' and status, and sometimes for no reason at all:

Very often the boys do it as a dare, they egg one another on to do things and I suppose it makes them look good in front of their mates. (Sgt N.)

They do it on the spur of the moment, just when the mood takes them. I suppose ... some small trigger when they're out on the street... a lot of the time they don't know why they've done it. (WPC J.)

Offending on the part of the girls was seen essentially to stem from the pressure placed upon them to look attractive and they too were seen as greedy, but it was felt that girls more than boys stole less impulsively.

Some of the girls even have shopping lists. They go round several shops just as if they were shopping and not stealing. With the boys it seems to be more impulsive. The girls just want to look nice mostly I know, but they're little devils really. (PC M.)

The juvenile liaison officers made a number of general comments, too, which were pertinent to their understanding and treatment of female offenders. Some of these comments referred to an increase in the number of violent offences committed by females, although there were no such increases recorded in the work of the juvenile liaison office. I examined records for the previous five years, looking for possible increases in the rate and type of female offending. Whilst there were increases in the amount of theft recorded, an increase in the number of violent offences committed by females was not revealed. Yet the officers argued:

I think girls are very much more violent now. We see them in here. I'm not surprised by it and I suppose it's mainly due to Women's Lib, and that lot. Much more violent than five to ten years ago, much more assertive. (PC A.)

It's regrettable that girls now think that they've got to be like the boys. Girls were much nicer five or so years ago. I blame the Equal Pay Act myself, it's been a major cause of crime; not only did it lead to more women going out to work and consequently neglecting their children... increasing juvenile crime in this way, but women themselves are less satisified with their lives...equal pay forced prices up... therefore more women had to go out to work. Career women... it's all wrong. If women were content it would solve a lot of problems...certainly regarding juvenile crime anyway. You see, girls don't receive the attention that they used to receive at home. More and more of them get anxious about money, it made them very materialistic. (PC M.)

PCA continued:

Girls today are much more involved in youth movements and the like, in fact quite aggressive youth movements... the British movement for instance, and the skinhead girls are there right in the middle of it all. The girls go round in gangs much more too.

Whilst the sergeant put it this way,

The girls are spiteful really... they don't fight, they scratch... they're worse than boys. You know ... they motivate the boys... get them going from behind the scenes. A lot of the trouble – even in Brixton – was caused by girls. The boys might shout abuse and throw things but the girls were there at the back of them. (Sgt N.)

I think girls are behind a lot of the trouble, you could see them when we had the riots, there they were 'egging' the boys on... pushing them to do things. They're very manipulative, very devious are girls. (Sgt N.)

As regards appropriate responses to girls, all the juvenile liaison officers were adamant that girls should be treated in the same way as boys, if indeed they wanted to behave like boys, as they believed was the case. For example, they said:

> If girls want to behave like boys then they should be treated like boys and they should expect to be treated in this way. (WPC J.)

> They should receive the same penalties. There ought to be attendance centres and detention centres for them and fewer supervision orders perhaps; we need to show them who is boss. All too often the social workers are really soft with them. The girls who get into trouble today aren't the talking kind at all, it's no use trying to persuade them to be good... you've simply got to make them toe the line. (WPC H.)

Another theme, that girls might in some way be worse than boys, was one which was reiterated in all my conversations and interviews with the officers. One of the WPCs argued:

> The girls we get today are ten times worse than boys and they keep coming back. They didn't used to very much, but now it's the same old faces time and time again.

Another officer put it this way,

> Nine times out of ten the girls are worse, they're spiteful, they're canny and 'know-alls' to boot. What's worse is that they know you can't touch them. (PC M.)

Dealing with girls

One of the questions put to practitioners related to their ease or difficulty in dealing with girls as opposed to boys. In general, the juvenile liaison officers reiterated the view that girls exhibited a greater facility for deceit and would tell elaborate stories to cover up their misdeeds. Moreover, it became clear that, despite the fact the there were no policy dictates that women officers should deal with the girls, the PCs often felt that the WPCs could 'see through' the deceit more easily than the men. One of the women, however, when called in to interview girls as a last resort, viewed things in this way:

> I think in fact that girls will often talk to an older man more, they look up to men more. I suppose they see a fatherly figure, perhaps it's not something they've had at home. I think females have a natural respect for males so it helps that way. They certainly don't have any respect for us... in fact they're really lippy but part of that is because we're young as well as female. (WPC H.)

Despite this view of girls, the officers felt that most girls would ultimately be very worried about police processing and possible court appearance and this was believed to have a salutary effect on them:

> I think boys come back eventually. I think a girl's weighed it up by then and thought 'no, it's too much'. So you can get through to them, and most of them are sensible enough to respond. It's just that you have to be tough with them,

I usually say to them that if after all their opportunities to tell the truth that I find they've been lying, they'll have me to reckon with as well and that I'll be watching them like a hawk. And I think it probably does scare them, the sort of thing they have to go through, whereas a boy, I don't think he's scared, or at least it doesn't show that it scares him quite so much. (WPC H.)

And this was confirmed by male colleagues:

the girls don't like sitting with you in the interview room... very aware of what people think of them. I think girls are more aware of that, and what their parents will think of them. Boys are worried to a certain extent but I think it's more a case of you know dad might well pass it off as 'well, he's learned his lesson in getting caught, let's hope he's going to behave himself now'. For a girl it's a bit more. It's a worse experience for her, more of a slur on her because so few of them get taken to court. (PC M.)

Most of these girls will attempt to become shop assistants and a criminal record will stand against them. With boys who go into labouring, tiling and this sort of thing pilfering is accepted to a degree but not in a shop. Whereas a girl, to take garments out of the shop, or money out of the till is a far different thing, isn't it? (PC A.)

The method by which the police officers were able to discern anxiety on the part of juveniles or, alternatively, 'resistance' to police pressure is described below. Continuing on this theme of defining what 'trouble' meant to the staff of this agency I encouraged them to identify who the 'difficult' girls were for them, what was 'difficult' about their behaviour and how this ultimately affected their practices. I approached this topic via their policies and practices on cautioning, which served as a key to their judgements. My questions to the officers were essentially designed to ascertain which kinds of offences and offenders 'qualified' for a caution, and whether or not there were distinctive features about girls which made them more or less eligible for this response to their offending behaviour.

In my discussions with them, the juvenile liaison officers responded to my questions in this area by referring me first to the official rules and policy regarding cautioning. In addition to the type of offence, the admission of guilt, and parental consent to the caution, which constitute the core of this policy, the officers were keen to point out to me a number of other factors which they felt ought to be taken into consideration. These included the age of the offender and the absence of previous offences. They believed that any juvenile who was referred for offending a second time was essentially a 'waster' and thus did not deserve the option of being cautioned. Exceptions here would include juveniles who had not committed an offence for over a year or those who had committed entirely different offences leading to the second referral. Family difficulties or reference to some other source of stress at the time of the second offence was also accepted as an indication that the juvenile might still be worth 'working on' without resorting to the court. More importantly, however, it became clear that, as a general rule, 'deserving' offenders had supportive parents. Thus the decision whether or not to caution depended in part on the character of the offender, of his or her siblings and of the family. Indeed, if the family showed interest in the offender and was 'surprised' and 'concerned' at the time of the child's interview then the offender would be considered a likely candidate for a caution.

> If the family is likely to do their utmost to prevent a reoccurrence of the event and seems to support the child in keeping out of trouble. (PC A.)

Or as another described,

> You can tell a lot in the visits. You know, for instance, that if dad is out at the pub or stares at TV or if mum is out at bingo or at work then there's not much hope for the kid without any kind of action from us. If they turn the TV off though and attempt to discuss things with you and look worried it's worth working at. Sometimes there are other kids around and you can tell what sort of parents they are by the way they control and talk to those kids. I'm always suspicious of TV zombies. (WPC J.)

The character of offenders, it seemed, was established from questions about leisure time, attitude to school, attitude to parents and moreover to the offence itself. If the juvenile had few hobbies or interests and was doing poorly at school then he or she was usually considered a 'waster'. Alternatively, if the juvenile showed remorse, by crying when questioned or by apologizing for the offence, then the chances of being given a caution were increased. This was especially so when parents, too, were communicative, friendly and 'obviously very caring parents' by professing to be ashamed to hear of the offence.

There are two important indications within this routine processing of delinquents that responses to girls may have been rather different from those of boys. The first concerns the general view that adolescent girls are inclined to be rather more communicative than adolescent boys. This generalization is not without criticism (cf. Hemming, 1967; Davies 1979) but youth leaders, social workers and other practitioners have commented on the greater taciturnity of boys compared with girls and on girls' relatively greater linguistic ability. In essence, this means that those girls who were relatively articulate were likely to create a good impression upon the police officers dealing with them. Secondly, since girls are, throughout their childhood and adolescence, encouraged to express emotion, it may be the case that crying over wrongdoing comes easier to girls than to boys. Certainly Maccoby (1966) has described that there is a tendency for girls to be more liable to confess wrongdoing and to express moral attitudes. In my study, boys were likely to be penalized or censored for being unable to express emotion, when their socialization was directed towards inhibiting the expression of any emotion; indeed, in most contexts crying by boys would render them vulnerable to criticism that they were behaving 'like girls'.

This point also has relevance within the actual cautioning of juveniles. Since I witnessed the cautioning of all juveniles I was able to gain information from the officers on their perceptions of the appropriateness and effectiveness of this cautioning. Both officers concerned told me that they could only be sure a caution was appropriate when they could discern that the process of receiving it had made some impact upon the juvenile.

I think the main aim is to achieve effect without making them bitter or anti-police. Some of the cases should never have got this far, but you like to see that it had some effect and you can tell by looking at them. If they stand and glare at you, you know you haven't got through.

The second officer put it this way,

We need to see an effect... I am pleased in a way when someone goes out looking sheepish or tearful, upset... only then has it had impact. I resent it when they go out smiling or looking cocky. It's not worth the effort. I hate it when the little girls cry but you have to get them to that point.

Thus once again, considering the ways in which girls are encouraged to behave – as submissive, respectful of authority, passive and emotional (Sharpe, 1976) – it may be that girls are more able to satisfy the expectations of police officers on the effectiveness of a caution, and their 'pathological potential' benefits them in this way. Whilst this had no immediate consequences, documentation of the juveniles' responses to the caution could have played a part in determining whether or not the juvenile should receive a second caution for a second offence, though second cautions were only recommended under special circumstances.[4] Further, it is possible that evidence of the impact of cautioning upon girls may have created a general impression that this was usually an effective way of dealing with them, thus encouraging officers to use this method more frequently. In addition to there being a greater likelihood of girls receiving a caution in the first instance (I matched offences for offence seriousness), the figures produced by this office suggested that girls were indeed rather more likely than boys to be cautioned for second and subsequent offences.

Problem behaviour
Much of the work which the juvenile liaison office carried out was investigative work concerning cases where a juvenile had not committed a specific offence, but was known to be in some form of 'moral danger': causing problems at home or missing from home, or subject to abuse and

neglect at home.[5] Some of these cases resulted in the police recommending to the court that a Place of Safety Order be imposed upon the juvenile. I chose to follow and document information relating only to those cases concerning 10–16 year olds where the police sought a Place of Safety Order on the grounds that the parents could not exercise appropriate supervision and control or where parents were seeking help and advice from the police in an attempt to find or control their adolescent children.[6] It was striking during my stay that most of the police activity in connection with 'problem behaviour' concerned girls rather than boys. Indeed, this was deemed to be the usual experience of the juvenile liaison officer and police officers. When asked why this might be the case, they argued that 'well, boys do different things, don't they... they commit criminal-type offences'. Moreover, as one officer described, 'for a start, when kids go missing we assume that the girls are being "legged", we assume that boys of 13 and 14 can look after themselves'(PC M.) Thus the three cases of boys who fell into this category of 'problem behaviour' were not seen to demand action from the police except for documenting personal details and subsequent movements if sighted whilst 'on the run'. The details on these cases indicate the different levels of concern and how the police seemingly dismissed the need for them to become involved.

Boy 1, 14 years of age, was first referred to the juvenile liaison office for offending at the age of 10 and had subsequently received attention from the police and courts regarding offences of theft, burglary and traffic offences although he had made only two separate court appearances. The main concern, however, was the fact that he frequently absconded from home for periods of up to three weeks. On one occasion, after being missing for some two weeks, the father took his son to the police, who sought and were granted by the court, a 28-day interim care order. This was preliminary to applying for a full care order on the grounds that the boy was in moral danger and beyond the care and control of his parents. Two days after the interim care order had been imposed, the boy absconded from the observation and assessment centre where he had been placed. Although other juveniles at the centre indicated where he might be, the police did not try to find him. The sergeant argued:

> There is no point in chasing a waster like that, he's probably safe and can no doubt look after himself. If his father comes in again we'll probably do something but not unless people get concerned about it all. If the newspapers get hold of it we'll shift ourselves into gear. Of course we're concerned but we're very busy. (Sgt N.)

Boy 2, aged 14, had three offences of theft (shoplifting) recorded against him and was well known to the juvenile liaison office for running away from home. The police made no active searches for this boy.
Boy 3, aged 13, similarly had three offences (traffic and theft) recorded

against him. He too had been missing from home. The police felt unable to use time to search for this boy in view of his reputation and because they perceived that, despite his age, he was well able to look after himself. The records revealed that the police were seeking an order on the grounds that he was beyond the care and control of his parents. These applications, however, were not 'active', merely 'on record'.

In contrast, there were six *active* police applications for Place of Safety Orders on girls in the course of my work with the juvenile liaison office. These orders were sought on the grounds that they were in moral anger (three cases) or beyond the care and control of parents (two cases) and one order was sought on both grounds. These were the grounds that were specified on paper, but, in practice, the officers argued, either 'condition' could be used to support the application. I shall describe just two cases, which reflect quite closely features of the others, and illustrate clearly that the police thought they should become more involved in these cases even though they resembled the cases of the boys.

Girl 1 had been reported missing by her parents on three occasions in the space of one month. She was brought to the police station by the juvenile liaison officers who were out on a routine school run with the educational welfare officer looking for truants. From the records it is clear that the police decided to take a Place of Safety Order on the grounds that she was in moral danger, the evidence being that she was just 14 years of age and that she had run away on previous occasions. The girl was described as being 'a big girl, tall for her age and well developed'. She was also described as 'sexually provocative'. Further evidence of moral danger, however, was provided in a peremptory manner. WPC J. commented:

> Well, it's just rumour but I'm inclined to believe it... that she's having it off with several characters... she's a nasty piece of work that one, she's horrible.

In pursuing this application, however, it became evident that her parents did not support these claims and they were quite willing for her simply to return home. The social services department were in full agreement with this plan. Significantly, despite written confirmation from the surgeon that the girl was still pre-menstrual, the police officers continued to debate the possibility that she might be pregnant.

> I know her sort... free and easy. I'm suspicious that she might be pregnant. Anyway if the doctor can't provide evidence we'll do her for being beyond the care and control of her parents, no one can dispute that. Running away is proof. (WPC J.)

In view of the injustice here it would be easy to describe such actions as 'sexist'.

The action surrounding the next case arose from rather different reasons, though again, there was a certain amount of concern and perceived necessity to deal with the case in a particular way simply because it concerned a girl. The girl of 15 was well known to the police through her running away, school truancy, and the criminal activities of her older brothers. Unlike Girl 1, this girl was described as being 'slight, waif-like and underdeveloped for her age', she was not perceived to be sexually provocative but indeed rather vulnerable. Her clothing was described by the officers as 'poor... obviously from a jumble sale... old-fashioned'. Girl 2 had been examined by the police surgeon when she had run away from home on a previous occasion; sexual activity had been denied and this was confirmed by the surgeon.

On this occasion the girl was brought to the police station by the educational welfare officer attached to her school because the girl had complained that one of her brothers had assaulted her and that she did not want to go home. The girl's mother had been threatened with court action regarding the girl's very poor school attendance just two days previously. The police visited the home with the intention of hearing the brother's account and also with the aim of establishing the mother's attitude to events. In the home the police officers were faced with 'undeniably bad conditions there... a very unhygienic place'. This assessment of the home was subsequently used to assess the mother's attitude.

> You can always tell what's going on in the home, if it stinks then the family set up usually stinks too. It's a terrible home... what chance does she stand, how can her mother let her live in such terrible conditions. I know she recently had surgery and dad went off years ago, but even so... (PC M.)

The family dynamics, too, had been assessed through previous contact with them. When questioned, the brothers argued that T. (the girl) had deserved her punishment and they were simply doing 'what mum was unable to do'. Furthermore, T. had been 'sleeping around with coloured lads' and had merited a 'good thumping'. Protracted discussions with the family led, not to a charge against the brother, but to an attempt to gain a Place of Safety Order on T. since (a) her health and safety were being impaired (her brothers were aggressive towards her); (b) she was beyond the care and control of her mother (because she did not attend school); and (c) she was in moral danger (it was rumoured that she was hanging around with 'coloured' lads). Their action in this case, however, essentially stemmed from their sympathy for the girl.

> We have to do something for her, otherwise she'll end up like her brothers...heading for the 'nick', and no one will, so we're doing it. (WPC H.)

This illustrates the extent of the police officers' concern and feelings of protectiveness towards some girls, over and above the concern shown for boys in comparable cases, in terms of the juveniles' vulnerability. It shows, too, that the police were not only prepared to respond to girls, but that girls were seen as 'vulnerable' to their own sexual impulses and therefore in 'moral danger'.

It is clear that the police in this juvenile liaison office did have distinctive ideas about girls. First, it was assumed that girls commit particular kinds of crimes, notably shoplifting. In this they were seen as organized and scheming, acting in the full knowledge of what they were doing. Secondly, it was assumed that girls were becoming more violent and this view prevailed despite the lack of tangible evidence from records. Girls were also seen as spiteful and somehow 'much worse' than some of the boys they had to deal with. Thirdly, despite some comment that girls who behave in the same way as boys (committing the same kinds of offences, being more aggressive than expected, or being insolent toward the officers) ought to be treated in the same way as boys, the officers perceived that the police response to girl offenders and the subsequent cautioning or court processing of them had a more salutary effect on them than on boys. Thus despite an apparent 'hardening' of girls' attitudes, the police felt it was easier to make an impression on them. Cautions, especially, were perceived to be effective when applied to girls because they revealed an emotional response to the caution which signalled that the message about offending had been received.

Notes

1. The juvenile liaison offices initially had much wider functions than the processing of juvenile offenders, but since the 1969 Children and Young Persons Act have assumed the same function as the juvenile bureaux set up in response to the Act within the Metropolitan Police area. Despite this parity of function, however, many police forces in the provinces have retained the name of juvenile liaison office. See Mack (1963) and Oliver (1978) for a history of these agencies. Farrington (1983) describes the important role of the bureaux in a text on juvenile justice systems.

2. The rank of Inspector and above.

3. Since there were no restrictions placed on me during my stay with the agency, bar the fact that I had to be accompanied in the operational room, I established a number of contacts with officers outside of the juvenile liaison office. These contacts occurred mostly in the police canteen, an area which senior officers did not use as they had their own private dining room.

4. The officers usually wrote a short note on the cautioning papers indicating the juvenile's response to the caution; these papers were filed for future reference.

5. These problems are referred to as 'status offences' within the literature, though practitioners simply labelled the behaviour as 'problematic' or 'difficult'. See Children and Young Persons Act 1969, ss.1(2)a,b,c,d and e.

6. The purpose of obtaining a Place of Safety Order is to gain legal authority to detain a child or young person for up to 28 days where there is reason to believe that (s)he is in need of care. The taking of this Order may, at a later stage, lead to care proceedings at a juvenile court.

'Place of Safety' means a community home provided by a local authority or a controlled community home, any police station or any hospital, surgery, or any other suitable place, a neighbour, foster parent, or child minder. See Children and Young Persons Act 1969, s.28(1) and (2). Place of Safety Orders may also be granted under other pieces of legislation relating to children and young people.

6 Sexism: 'It's only natural'?

One of the most commonly used definitions of 'sexism' is that it refers to discrimination on the grounds of sex, and sex is seen as relevant in contexts where it is not. Following this, it would be easy to surmise that both the range of theories attributed to practitioners in the three agencies which I have considered and their responses to the young people within those agencies were 'sexist'. Girls' behaviour was clearly examined in a way that boys' was not.

In Agencies One and Two particularly, the girls were encouraged to become gentle; it was expected that they should be more gentle and less rumbustious than boys. And in all the agencies the ideal girl was perceived as 'passive, emotional, caring, sensitive'. Moreover, there was a general expectation that the girls' role in life should be as mothers and home-makers. In the residential agencies (One and Two) the girls were encouraged to discuss their problems, to develop emotional insight and affectionate ties with the staff as a stepping-stone to personal maturity and fulfilment. Boys' maturity, however, would be achieved through visible changes in their behaviour rather than their emotions. In Agency Three, those girls who were deemed to deserve reprobation were those who failed to conform to the stereotypical picture of femininity which the police officers had. Indeed, one 'irrational' piece of behaviour leading to the commission of an offence was more or less excusable, even understandable if linked to family problems or emotional upsets, but persistence in offending, or apparent refusal to express remorse, meant that some girls were castigated as being 'far worse than boys'. More succinctly, it was seen as 'out of place' for girls to offend, and the role of 'offender' as ill-fitting for them.

It was clear from my observations in the agencies that practitioners had very different expectations of girls and boys. They wanted the girls they were dealing with to behave in particular ways which they held to be 'natural' and 'appropriate' for them. But these expectations and beliefs are 'limiting', unfounded and prejudicial to their being justly treated.

My essential argument is that concentration on the concept of sexism may obscure any understanding of the criminal process and dealings with girls; at least, it derives from an incomplete analysis of events. To address this point, I re-analyze some of the observations I have made, by placing them back in their organizational context. My aim is to characterize and comment upon some of the processes which led to the discernment of elements of practice with particular relevance for girls, and to consider more discursively any beliefs we might hold about 'sexism' in these agencies.

Agency One

Despite the fact that staff in this agency had very clear ideas and beliefs about appropriate behaviour for girls, there were frequent comments that in practice the staff did not distinguish between the boys and girls they dealt with. However, my own observations led me to a different conclusion. For the most part the girls were expected to follow the example and guidelines provided by female staff, and the boys the example and guidelines of male staff.

'It's only natural': guidelines for behaviour

One of the clearest guidelines for behaviour within the agency occurred through the role models which male and female staff provided. Role modelling is a well researched and documented area, particular in relation to family life and to schooling.[1] It is less well documented in residential social work, partly because studies have tended to concentrate on boys' institutions where there is typically a predominance of male staff with females occupying only the roles of housekeeper, matron and cook (although this in itself is significant).

The fact that senior positions (the management positions) were occupied by male staff and that both the housekeeper and cook were female also gave the impression that men were in charge of the agency and that all decisions had to be referred to men. Indeed, there was one occasion when two girls, gaining no satisfaction from a female member of staff, were heard to say that they would have to ask a man, when the nature of the decision was not one that necessitated such discrimination.

It was clear, too, that the role orientations of the residential social workers helped to shape and control the behaviour of the young people. As I have described, female staff liked to participate in the 'bedroom culture' of the girls and those girls who did not join in were quickly labelled as 'misfits' or 'loners'. A similar pattern of behaviour emerged throughout the day. The female staff sat quietly watching TV and expected the girls to do the same and not to join in the fights or 'rough games' of the boys. In the morning, lunchtime and afternoon school breaks there was a fifteen-minute period on the timetable designated as exercise time. The female staff interpreted their supervisory role in this period as one of watching over the exercise of the boys who played football or volleyball on the playground, and they stayed together on the sidelines for the most part. Male staff frequently initiated the activity on the playground and regularly participated. Any girl who attempted to participate was immediately labelled as 'rough' or a 'tomboy'. These labels were a subtle form of control over the girls; few wanted to go directly against the wishes of staff and preferred to retain their approval and attention.

There were similar differences in the indoor activities: the female staff organized cooking sessions, sewing sessions and keep-fit exercises for girls. The exercises were conducted upstairs in the bedrooms and were exclusively for girls, though the other activities were open to boys and girls. All girls were encouraged to join in the exercises to keep slim and healthy, and relentless pressure was applied to those girls who were slightly overweight to join in. On the other hand the male staff organized the indoor games, darts, snooker, table tennis, cycle rides, football matches, outdoor running, model-making and art work. One of the male teachers ran an after-school swimming club. None of the activities organized by male staff was exclusively for boys, but again, any girl who attempted to participate was labelled as 'unladylike' if she joined in physical games and as a 'misfit' if she chose activities other than those organized by female staff.

Girls were also labelled as 'disturbed' or 'misfits' if they did not respond to the affection and interest which the female staff showed them. The male staff were guarded in this respect for reasons I have described elsewhere, but the female staff made clear in the way they approached them their expectations that girls both liked and needed affection. It was not unusual for a member of staff to stroke a girl's hair whilst talking to her or to put her arms around the girl's shoulders. I described at an earlier point that boys in care were seen to need affection too, even though they could not ask for it or show it to the same extent as girls. What emerged in practice was that the staff were equally reserved in showing affection to the boys. The rationale given to me was that the staff's reserve was essentially an attempt to be sensitive to boys' embarrassment about any form of affection. Thus although 'need' in this respect was perceived, little effort was made by the staff to fulfil this need and to change the situation for boys. This was a surprising contradiction, given the staffs' alleged commitment to a general 'child care philosophy' which acknowledged the boys' need for affection.

Female members of staff also invited girls (either singly or in groups) to their homes, so that the girls could, as the staff put it, 'participate in normal family life'. They were concerned that the girls should not be deprived of 'normal' domestic scenes. When the staff brought any of their own children to the agency there was an explicit assumption that it would be the girls who would want to meet them and play with them. Moreover, it was seen as a good ploy to get the girls interested in relationships with children, and it was described as 'only natural' that they should want to.

Interestingly, despite their own professional and often 'academic' backgrounds, the female and male staff viewed the girls in the agency as being, for the most part, destined for marriage and family life. 'Work' for the girls would be a short interlude between school and marriage and subsequently a method of earning money for children's school extras and excursions. Career advice was very much on the lines of looking for 'interesting' factory work, nursery nurse training or shop work: even one girl who was considered 'bright' was encouraged to pursue a traditional female role in teaching. Staff defended this approach on the grounds that to raise expectations for girls would make things more difficult for them when they eventually left the agency and had to rejoin their families. Thus staff did not wish to contest the expectations that parents and others might have of the girls, when to do so might increase the girls' difficulties

In addition to the emphasis placed on girls' physical appearance through encouraging them to join in the exercise sessions, there was also considerable emphasis on the way they looked; non-conformity in appearance was frowned upon. There were frequent arguments with the girls about their dress and appearance and they were often sent to change before school if it was thought they were wearing something inappropriate. 'Inappropriate' dress typically meant jeans, boots or short skirts, and the girls who adopted this form of dress were described as 'tomboyish' or 'provocative'. The girls were expected to look smart and 'attractive' on excursions from the agency, but here they had to be careful not to exceed the unspoken guidelines of the staff, for they were not to look 'tatty' or 'like a tart' or provocative in any way. During my stay two girls disobeyed their female team leader by wearing what the staff member described as 'flashy gear, tight skirts and skimpy jumpers and loads of make-up' to a village disco. They were fetched from the village hall after the disco lest they be pursued. The staff member concerned thought that the girls' style of dress made them vulnerable.

Absconding behaviour brought similar concerns about girls' vulnerability. There were four incidents during my stay in the agency, involving three boys in a group (two aged 14 and one 15), two boys singly (one aged 11 and the other 13), and one incident involving a 15-year-old girl who failed to return to the agency after weekend leave. This incident caused much greater concern and consternation within the agency than even the absconding of the 11-year-old boy. My attempts to clarify whether or not this greater concern was related to perception of the girl's and the boy's relative abilities to look after themselves was answered with claims that there was always the danger that the girl would get herself pregnant if she stayed with her boyfriend or another male met casually whilst on the run. The boys, on the other hand, were viewed as being able to look after themselves; the 11-year-old was not seen as being in any special danger.

The politics of 'trouble'
In any institution which involves the full-time care of individuals there is always the temptation to compare the behaviour of individuals with that of others in the institution rather than with those 'outside'. Thus what is

acceptable behaviour or 'acceptable trouble', 'unnatural behaviour' or 'disturbed behaviour' becomes very much a reflection of the tolerance levels of the organization and its staff. Sometimes 'trouble' in the form of a fight or argument can provide 'excitement' in an otherwise dull routine. At other times, if the fight follows a series of fights or occurs at tea-time when staff are harassed, chasing up individuals who have failed to arrive at the tea-table, the fight could be described as an unacceptable nuisance. This example may appear as a simplistic account of events and yet it serves to illustrate that what determines the quality of life within an agency reflects innumerable organizational constraints, staff prejudices and preferences, and individual 'tolerance' levels as well as strands of any one child care policy, philosophy or professional ideology.

In this sense, the designation of a particular child as 'troublesome' meant that the child had become a nuisance or that the child could not be understood within the individual child care perspectives of staff. 'Problem' girls, for instance, were those with whom staff had failed. When the girls were unresponsive to normal appeals to behave more appropriately and to other techniques of persuasion it meant that something was seriously wrong with the girl.

Further, this understanding of how behaviour is defined within an agency means that a successful child is one who makes the most of the opportunities provided by the organization. In the case of girls, they have to demonstrate that they have developed an ability to make meaningful relationships. An ability to relate to the staff in the 'bedroom culture' in the group room and the school implies an ability to relate to others outside.   Those girls who settled in and conformed, 'satisfied' or 're-warded' the staff in some way by responding to their overtures, developing close and affectionate relationships were perceived to have 'matured' and to have seemingly 'developed an ability to make meaningful personal relationships'. Successful learning required that the girls accept the models of behaviour with which they were provided. Failure to achieve this, failure to accept the appeals and expectations of the staff served, in the case of A. particularly, to confirm the immaturity and disturbance in the child.

This agency did not have an explicit policy differentiating between girls and boys. There were some practice differentiations but these were seen to be the result of experience rather than as emanating from any specific philosophical considerations. None the less, the sexual divisions amongst staff, their understanding and interpretation of their own roles in child care, led to a number of practices which may have influenced or shaped the behaviour of the girls and boys in the agency. It is, of course, difficult to say how much the differentiation which occurred was negotiated between girls and boys and staff, but my interest was in the contribution of the staff to any sexual differentiation that might have occurred. As I argue elsewhere, this seemed a valuable exercise in itself since staff are frequently in more powerful positions than 'inmates' and 'residents' in institutions.

It is difficult to judge exactly how much of the perceived difference in girls' and boys' behaviour came from the staff's own socialization and acceptance of cultural expectations, how much was imposed on the juveniles and to what extent the staff's behaviour was redefined and shaped in the light of 'professional acculturation' and increasing knowledge of what was expected from them by senior staff. What is undeniable, however, is that the sexual divisions did contribute to the creation of a different climate of acceptance for boys and girls in the agency and contributed, too, to a different form of assessment. It was discernible that whilst boys' *actions* were being judged, with the girls it was more a case of their '*character*' being assessed. Their 'femininity', which was an essential part of their character, was under scrutiny in a way which the boys' 'masculinity' was not. But I take the analysis a step further from this point and examine some of the general influences which affected the internal life of the agency.

Structure, organisation and practice: constraints on judgement
First, there are a number of general points to make about the nature of this agency and its subsequent effect on the practitioners' understanding of their work. The most obvious of these points was the explicit assumption that to be sent to the agency the juveniles must have had problems. Even before staff had met a girl or boy they assumed that she or he had 'problems' and therefore needed 'help' and 'understanding'. Whilst this would seem a logical feature of practice for an agency whose function it was to 'assess' problems, this approach has to be juxtaposed with comments from the staff about the agency as a 'dumping ground' for children who could not be placed elsewhere, and with comments about it being a 'holding function' of the agency to accommodate children who had been assessed elsewhere. Although staff revealed that they were aware of this contradiction in the policy, in their practice they made no distinctions between children. This phenomenon is not new (see Walter, 1978; Gill 1974 and Tutt, 1974), and can be seen as a clear philosophical orientation, in that it describes how the agency sees its role in the total system of child care. Indeed, professional ideologies, however loosely defined as in the field of child care, may prescribe a preset response to all troubles without regard to the particulars of a given case. None the less, the absence of distinctions between children was strikingly obvious because staff were eager to point out to me the sometimes ambiguous and even otiose role of assessment in dealing with children.

Another contradiction occurred in the fact that practitioners frequently resorted to psychoanalytical explanations for the children's behaviour, although privately, and individually, many argued that the children in the agency were essentially no different from those outside and their 'problems' were 'family problems' rather than individual ones. Indeed, the influence of psychological theories on practitioners was fairly marked. Practitioners were very concerned in their public discussions, at least, with aspects of the conditioning process and, in particular, an individual's failure to be conditioned. References to the poverty of impulse controls or lack of conscience amongst children who were seen as 'real delinquents' as opposed to 'temporarily difficult' illustrate this point.

The difference here between public and private theories was thus essentially a difference between policy or 'child care philosophy' as seen by the warden and other senior staff, and individual 'operational philosophies'. The agency had a clear yet unpublicized philosophy and policy commitment which revolved around psychological explanations when staff members could not express their own discrete and varying ideas.

The orientation towards psychological explanations was made apparent in a number of ways. First, practitioners were encouraged to make observations on the psychological state of mind of the individual through observations of behavioural indications, even though they were not professional psychologists or psychiatrists. Indeed, as my initial examination of the agency revealed, only one member of staff had professional training in counselling. Secondly, there was a subtle reference to psychological dimensions of delinquency in the commonly accepted practice of including the reports of the visiting psychologist or psychiatrist in every assessment, irrespective of need. There was, therefore, a basic assumption that there was always a psychological element to the delinquency or general behaviour of the individual. As previously indicated, this psychological emphasis often worked to the exclusion of other factors, such as environment, family dynamics, 'subcultural' factors and other social dimensions. It would be simplistic to deny that some of those children who were assessed needed some form of psychiatric help (just as in the population as a whole), but to maintain that by virtue of their residence in the agency they should be psychologically and psychiatrically assessed is to accentuate the importance of such psychological factors. Whilst assessment reports included certain social determinants, such as the home, the school and the neighbourhood, these were usually in the form of descriptive background to the real 'psychological' problems; the conclusion of such reports always focused on the *individual's* behaviour, in isolation to other factors.

What emerged was that staff would only refer to debates about sociological factors (peer group pressure on adolescents, for instance) in private discussions. When senior staff were present in discussions there was adherence to the general 'philosophy' of the agency. The subservience of staff in this respect was epitomized in an incident which occurred in a staff meeting at which the offending behaviour of one boy was being addressed. Having outlined a catalogue of offences which the boy had recently committed within the agency and the detrimental effect on other children of his frequent attempts to run away, the warden announced that the boy needed to be taught a lesson and that this lesson could best be given in a detention centre. The 'lesson' to be taught, it was made clear, was that 'agency would not tolerate such behaviour'. Moreover, 'the boy's departure to a detention centre would have a "cautioning" effect upon the other children'. After this announcement, the team leader who dealt with the boy and her team were told to construct an assessment report around the fact that this boy *needed* to be taught a lesson. Clearly, there was a subtle shift between describing the 'needs' of the agency to achieve respite from the antics of this boy to 'accommodating' these needs in terms of the boy's own needs. What occurred was the gradual individualization of a problem.

There is a further point to add, in that dependence upon psychological theories and concepts might be seen to add to the professional status of the practitioners. Residential social work is arguably a body of practice without a discrete philosophy, the principles of which are usually borrowed from other disciplines, particularly from psychology. Practitioners in this field are frequently seen as' second-class' social workers; those who *fail* to become 'proper', that is, generic field social workers. The fact that residential work is relatively poorly paid work adds to its image as a low-status occupation, as does the general absence of training opportunities. Nevertheless, because there is no distinct terminology, the use of 'professional terminology', that is, of psychologists and psychiatrists, could be seen as a way of enhancing the status of the job. Indeed, many of the staff baulked at the idea of being just 'child minders', although they confessed to me that that was how they saw themselves being used by the agency, and the adoption of psychoanalytical orientation was perhaps one way of rationalizing what would otherwise be a fairly monotonous and meaningless task involving the mundane and routine 'caretaking' of children. To make the task interesting staff felt that they had to move beyond physical tasks of feeding and clothing children. It was noticeable too that the practitioners' descriptions of children were infused with psychiatric jargon especially after the visits of the consultant psychiatrist. For example they prefaced comments about children with the conventional introduction of psychiatrists, 'this child presented as ...'.

The essential point of these general observations has been to emphasize that the seeking out of problems derives from the nature of the institution itself and from the staff's perceptions of their roles and status. Such observations led to my recognition of certain elements of this 'practical' or 'operational' philosophy which had particular relevance for girls and I discuss these elements under the heading of 'pathological potential'.

Pathological potential

I have previously described how there were contradictions in relation to the criteria for admission to the agency. Whilst staff privately felt that the resident children were not dissimilar to those 'outside', in the course of their work they strove to elaborate upon problems which essentially did make those children different. One of the striking features to emerge here was that the problems of girls were viewed as more serious than those of boys. There was an assumption that girls must have reached the 'end of the line' in exhibiting behavioural or personality disorders, simply because of a belief that girls were rarely taken into care (or indeed any other kind of institutional setting). The admission of boys because of their offending appeared to be acceptable to staff, especially when the boys were due for their third or fourth court appearance. The general belief about girls was that their home and family problems must have been very severe for field social workers to have advocated admission to care. The route from the court for the boys who have offended was seen as a natural part of the court processing of juvenile offenders, without that route, and the request for social reports which it entailed, being necessarily indicative of the existence of psychological problems. This belief about girls was subsequently to give rise to the exploitation of those deeper and more serious problems, in the sense that the agency's staff were immediately attuned to the task of elaborating upon the problems. They were not questioned, but seized upon and exploited by those members of staff who saw their role as one of counsellor, 'carer', 'mother-figure' or 'older sister'.

Thus, in a sense, the girls were seen to have greater 'pathological potential'. Given that the staff accepted the pathological nature of girls' actions, the assessment procedure and report was used to validate the preliminary diagnosis that the girl was a 'problem'. Evaluation of the girls as 'problems' was thus sustained despite the fact that their problems may have had as much to do with their home lives as with any individual 'pathologies'.

'Trouble'

As comments on the nature of girls' problems and on the nature of 'trouble' indicate, staff were not unanimous on what constituted 'problems' or 'difficult behaviour'. Clearly, the question of whether definitions related to the qualities of girls themselves or to the ability of the staff to correctly identify, understand and respond to their behaviour has to be raised. My observations were that behaviour was labelled as 'difficult' and subsequently distinctions made between 'real delinquency' and 'temporary difficulties or problems' when the staff had difficulty in interpreting a child's motivation and behaviour. This difficulty was, as I have described in the case of A., transposed to the child herself. Rather than the staff acknowledging that they found it hard to interact with the girl, they said that the girl was extremely 'difficult' and therefore she was 'a real delinquent'. To some extent this means that information on family pathology can serve (as it did in the case of A.) as a latent rationale for explaining unsuccessful remedial actions.[2]

More generally, it seemed that 'improvement' on the part of girls was related to their acknowledgement of problems. Thus they not only had to have problems, but they had to be willing to talk about them, otherwise they were seen as 'obstructive' or even more 'disturbed' than the staff initially thought. Some 'acting out' disturbances were acceptable; for example, swearing or shouting and slamming doors, but this changed according to the likes and dislikes and varying tolerance levels of members of staff. The expectation was carried into the staff's dealings with girls at all times, but particularly at bedtime when staff spent time in the girls' rooms. Female staff were keen to exploit every opportunity to counsel and discuss, however, and would eagerly participate in the girls' own 'bedroom culture'. Staff described this 'bedroom culture' to me in terms of the greater needs of girls than boys to have privacy, to 'create a home', to enjoy their 'surroundings' and to be 'domesticated' and 'feminine'. Consequently, they not only allowed girls the privilege of using their rooms when they wished to, but encouraged the girls to stay talking in their rooms.

Personal adjustment is invariably a long process and so it was surprising that the willingness or ability to discuss 'problems' should so readily be taken as indicative of 'improvement'. Moreover, staff saw the 'improvement' as indicative of their successful treatment, their own ability to encourage the girls to develop. Thus a main observation here was that evaluation and 'improvement' depended very much upon the ability of the child to develop and mature through close personal relationships with the staff. Tears, too, were seen by the staff as a sign of improvement. Girls were expected to express emotion, to 'let go of' their feelings. The dilemma here for the girls, however, was that whilst expressing emotion they had to be careful not to express too much. If there was a hint that the expression of emotion was 'uncontrollable' it immediately led to a re-definition of the problem and of the girl as very difficult, or disturbed, or as a 'real problem'. In practice, 'uncontrollable emotion' was that emotion which staff could not control either by their presence or words.

Further, it became clear to me that staff members sometimes resented girls expressing things to other staff when they perceived that they themselves had facilitated the emotional outpourings. Indeed, as one member of staff described, it was only right that the emotional outpourings which were the culmination of several hours' work in counselling and keeping the girl company should be reserved for the staff member involved. One team leader's comment suggests bitterness that she had not received the 'emotional outpourings':

> I thought I had got through to her and in fact I thought we were quite close, but she kept the night staff awake last night by being upset. Sometimes they do that because the night staff are softies ... give them tea and biscuits in the middle of the night. (Team leader, female)

To talk about problems or to express emotion to a wide audience was thus to indicate that the problems were in some way 'uncontrollable' and that the 'pathological' behaviour remained.

It was interesting, too, that the juveniles within the agency became the reference group and if 'success' was achieved with a particular girl then it was expected that the others *could* achieve the same success. 'Normal' behaviour and 'improved' behaviour was thus defined within the agency and children compared with each other rather than with those 'outside'.

Further constraints
The process of data collection and of report writing frequently warrants a study on its own. In this case the pro forma which the staff used can be seen as a constraining factor influencing the report writers on what they could and could not write about to a considerable degree. Another constraining factor was that of time. Staff were often reluctant to write reports because of the time involved. Moreover, they felt that their own views would be ignored when juxtaposed with information from the warden, from visiting psychiatrists, the field social worker and the agency teachers. The importance of this assumed 'hierarchy' was also revealed in the staff's acceptance of 'case papers' as 'plain fact' when a child arrived in the agency. They did not feel that they had the authority to question or to refute the observations and recorded details presented by 'outside' report writers (usually the social worker involved in the case). Indeed, in contrast to the 'investigative stance' or 'critical stance' adopted by Zimmerman's (1974) public agency workers, the residential social workers in this agency (although similarly involved in 'assessment' work) assumed that all records accompanying the children were correct, even though they contained subjective statements or accounts, and they simply drew upon them to confirm their own views. None of the documents was rendered problematic by the agency staff, though in asides to me and to

other staff they acknowledged that their views sometimes differed from those presented in records. Their solution to any discrepancy was to assume that their own view was inappropriate or less valid than others and therefore irrelevant and not to be documented.

The only staff who enjoyed writing reports were the team leaders and their deputies who, having a number of behaviour reports (pro forma style) from residential social workers, were given licence to draw their own conclusions and write at length. But even they were inevitably influenced by the common expectations of a 'reasonably long' court report. Moreover, they were aware that they would be scrutinized by the warden who could amend them, if he so wished, to include his own views. As one team leader described:

> When I write a report I have to incorporate as many points of view as possible from my team otherwise they get offended. At the same time I know that even if we as a team are in agreement about something, if the warden or whoever is chairing the assessment disagrees or has a particularly good relationship with the child, then the report has to make room for that. I mean, I don't want to appear completely at odds with my boss. We may have differences of opinion, that is allowed, but he is the professional, he's been in it ... this kind of work, for a lot longer than me, and I have had to respect his views and wishes. (Team leader, male)

The team leader continued in a whispered aside to me that it was in his interests to do this in terms of his career.

It is also important to note that those staff who submitted reports were usually 'key' workers for a child and therefore invariably of the same sex. Any differences in the management of male and female children was as much a reflection of the staff's own interest and orientation to the work as anything else. Since female members of staff frequently saw themselves as 'counsellors' this undoubtedly had an effect on what they both said and wrote about their charges. The emphasis on 'relational' aspects of behaviour is understandable if placed in this context, and is not directly or simply a reflection of 'sex-biased' attitudes. The male staff were primarily those who organized activities: this tended to be their orientation in the work, how they could best make sense of it, how they could best cope with it and how they could gain satisfaction from it. It was not surprising, therefore, to find that comments about the children centred upon their ability and willingness to participate in activities set up by the staff. Again, the comments do not reflect, in any direct way, a sex bias. This is not to deny that a bias was in existence but to indicate that the processes by which male and female behaviour came to be seen as 'natural' and 'acceptable' were convoluted and subtle processes. Further illustration of this view is provided in a consideration of Agency Two.

Agency Two
In this agency it was more difficult to discern practice features which related specifically to girls (as opposed to boys) since the agency dealt only with girls. Where the two are seen together it is perhaps easier to point out discriminatory practices which might be interpreted as 'sexist'. But it was possible, however, to gain a picture of acceptable or ideal 'femininity' through comparisions made of the girls by the staff. Again, where specific images were imposed it could be interpreted as a 'sexist' practice. Thus my initial comments in this section concern the kinds of distinction which were made between girls and how these reflected particular images of girls and what they ought to be like.

One of my observations about the staff's view of girls was that the older girls or those involved in group crimes tended to be regarded as 'more criminally inclined' and less malleable. One girl, T., because she was sixteen (nearly seventeen), and thus slightly older than most of the girls, was regarded as more hardened. It was assumed that she must already have had numerous chances to opt for a different lifestyle and resolve her problems prior to her arrival in the agency. Thus despite the fact that T. had been admitted because of one offence concerning the possession of a minor drug (her first offence), and despite the fact that her social worker (the field social worker) viewed her admission as primarily related to her parents' impending divorce, she was seen as devious and an experienced offender. As one supervisor put it, 'T is a very naughty girl beneath that smile ... she's a tough nut, and she'll be difficult to reach.' In this case age led to increased suspicion of the girl's activities.

Another distinction made between the girls concerned those who were attractive and those who were not. Those who were attractive tended to receive more attention from the staff in terms of time and comment. On the whole, this was because those girls who were classified as 'attractive in appearance' by the staff were those who had the more attractive personalities and were thus more responsive to staff approaches: they were more rewarding for the staff. Even those girls who were being 'rude' or 'cheeky' (muttering and swearing about the staff within their hearing) could, if they had an engaging smile and wit, 'get away with it', as one girl put it in an aside to me. Indeed, their behaviour tended to be excused; it was at times thought to be amusing. In a sense, their behaviour was interpreted as evidence of 'spirit', and 'spirit' in girls was a desirable attribute so long as it occurred in moderation.

'It's only natural': guidelines for behaviour
There were also explicit guidelines for behaviour presented to the girls. The emphasis on their physical appearance was very apparent. There were frequent comments on girls who were thought to be overweight or

were untidy in any way. Staff commented on the condition of their hair, for instance, and passed judgement as to whether or not it needed cutting. Initial response to a new girl was frequently shaped by her appearance. Supervisors would pronounce that 'she looks a nice girl', or conversely 'she looks a hard case', without any introduction to the girl, and simply on the basis of their observations. The more 'masculine' a girl looked (cropped hair, jeans, an aggressive stance, for instance) the more likely it was that she would receive a less than complimentary comment. An emphasis on hygiene was evident too. On several occasions it was pointed out to me that these things were really important to the girls, to improve their self-image. I once witnessed a long conversation between staff who were arguing that perhaps they ought to pay more attention to the appearance of the girls and that the rule prohibiting the wearing of lipstick for court ought to be changed 'so that they feel better about themselves'. Some of the staff felt that girls 'let themselves go' in the agency, that they did not look after themselves properly in terms of their appearance and that this ought to be remedied. Furthermore, I witnessed staff looking through glossy magazines with the girls and discussing clothes and make-up. Supervisors appeared to participate in the 'bedroom culture' with the girls, although who initiated it was difficult to discern.

From the instructions of staff to the girls, which I heard in the group rooms, it seemed imperative that in addition to 'looking nice' young ladies did not 'run up the stairs', 'yell', 'grab food', wear 'provocative' clothing, 'answer back' or swear. From the activity which was imposed on the girls it was clear that 'young ladies' also needed to know how to do housework and do their own washing, for instance. The girls were required to spend an hour cleaning around the house every morning, and to wash their own clothes (in buckets) frequently. When I asked if there was not a laundry or some such facility I was invariably told that, of course, it would be much easier for everyone (staff included) to make use of a washing machine, but how important it was for the girls to learn to do this for themselves: it was an invaluable contribution to their future role as housewives. This was not claimed simply as an appropriate role for the girls but more an expression of the inevitable. Staff also held the view that the housework gave the girls something to do, too; it kept them occupied. Of course, any significance attached to 'their future roles as housewives' has to be tempered with the fact that the activity was a useful time filler. At the same time, however, it was interesting that this was one of the activities upon which the girls were judged: 'attitude to housework' provided one of the categories on the assessment/behaviour report,

Structure, organization and practice: constraints on judgement
There were several influences upon the staff's behaviour worth noting.

First, much of the day-to-day activity in this agency seemed to be a remnant of its former days as an approved school and remand home. Many of the rules and rituals (for instance, girls washing their clothes nightly in buckets)[3] were, according to the former superintendent and his deputy (who had both worked in the agency for eighteen years), inherited by the agency when it became a classifying centre (and subsequently an assessment centre.[4] It was not that the rules were thought to be particularly appropriate, more that they were viewed 'harmless' and that change was always likely to upset members of staff. Current members of the agency attributed many of the rules to the former superintendent and his wife (the deputy), but probably, in view of his own comments on the matter, this was simply because he had been there much longer than any other member of staff and so it was difficult for them to consider the history of the agency beyond his occupancy.

The overall philosophy of the agency which emerged from their activities and views was one of 'care and control'. This implicitly embodied the assumption that it was not possible to 'care' for the girls without 'controlling' them, hence the emphasis on security and routine. This philosophy was supported by the view that practices adopted in the agency had 'stood the test of time' and the agency was successful in keeping the girls there, where other institutions were not. In one sense 'experience' became the philosophy, and staff shared the assumption that their approach was the right one.

One essential element of the 'control' part of the philosophy appeared to be that suspicion of the girls was justifiable and necessary. They were all in some way difficult and disturbed, otherwise they would not be there. Recognition of individual differences in this instance was submerged beneath the overall assumption that they all required the same treatment, all needed to be subjective to 'care and control'. Their suspicion of the girls was in evidence in what staff said about the girls and also in what they wrote. In day-to-day life suspicion emerged in the form of rules which were designed to restrict movement and the opportunity to do anything 'wrong'. For instance the girls were not allowed to keep very much personal property in their possession because 'it will be stolen'; cutlery must be counted after every meal, because 'they'll steal it to use as weapons and escape tools'; clothing in use must be restricted to two sets each, because 'they lose it and steal it'; every personal possession (including clothes) must be registered, because 'they'll accuse us of having lost it and claim more'; letters home must be read by a senior member of staff because 'otherwise they'll make wild accusations about us and the treatment they receive here'. Further, girls must be searched after visiting time and trips out to court 'because they attempt to conceal things like cigarettes, matches and knives'. Most of the rules, it seemed to me, were applied fairly rigidly. I did not witness any searching but was told about it by both staff and girls. Suspicion of the girls was also evident in the staff's perceptions of activity: 'they're up to something', 'trouble is on the way', or 'they're plotting something' and 'you have to watch the quiet ones' were comments frequently heard in the group rooms. On one occasion the educational psychologist visited a group room to explain to the supervisor that she had spent such a pleasant hour or so with a girl that she had come to find out what the girl was really like. 'I spent such a charming hour with her, she was so sweet and pleasant I wondered why she was here.' The immediate response of the staff that she was 'devious', 'sly', 'two faced' fulfilled the educational psychologist's expectations to some degree, and confirmed the reasons for S. being in the agency.

The essential part of the 'care' philosophy meant looking after the girls' basic needs for warmth and food and so on, but it also meant, as one supervisor put it, 'sussing out their problems'. Indeed, the whole ethos of the agency reflected that of Agency One and was one of 'understanding problems' and this was evidenced by the elaborate assessment procedure, giving girls interviews with educational psychologists, psychiatrists, the nursing sister and school tutor, for instance. It was not considered part of the supervisor's role actually to interview or formally quiz the girls about their past, more simply to encourage them to talk about their problems. This had obvious effects: first, there was an assumption that all the girls had problems (why else would they be there); secondly, if a girl would not talk about her problems this was in itself an indication of a problem or a sign of truculence. It was not unreasonable for the supervisors to want to take part in the professional task of assessment, despite the fact that they were told that their task was one of 'basic caring and observation' (they called themselves 'dogsbodies'). Indeed, like staff in the previous agency they wanted rewards for their efforts. Girls who did talk were seen to be 'improving' because they could recognize their problems.

The concern to identify problems was, however, overbearing in some instances. In one case a supervisor would not even listen to a girl's own account of 'problems' and description of her relationship with parents. In this case, the supervisor's aspirations to become a counsellor made him proceed with a line of argument which both irritated the girl and may have been inappropriate. His concern to be viewed as a counsellor made him 'blind' to any other response which he might have given and, like a railway engine out of control, forced him along a particular line of 'family pathology', a line which he considered appropriate for 'counselling'.

Further, following the same arguments which I presented for Agency One, the professional ethos of this agency was a constraining influence on the judgement of the girls, in the sense that it encouraged the translation of 'common understanding' into 'professional language'. Thus, whilst supervisors might make the remark that a certain girl was 'a spiteful cow' and that 'she needs a thump from another girl to put her in her place', on paper this sentiment would appear very differently; for example. 'Seems to have a false conception of herself ... this needs working through'.

As in Agency One, the borrowing of formal language from the 'professionals' within the agency (the psychologist and visiting psychiatrists) was evident in both the oral statements of staff and in their written comments. Here too supervisors said or wrote 'a girl presents to me as someone ...' which was the standard introduction of the psychiatrists. Whereas the 'professionals' might *talk* in this way the supervisors generally did not. One group leader expressed admiration for a former supervisor who was known for her forthright manner and 'everyday language'. It was described that the former supervisor would frequently comment in assessment and review meetings that, for instance, 'this girl needs a good belt round the ear' or 'this girl is telling a pack of lies'. The group leader continued that current supervisors, without this woman's broad Yorkshire accent, her sense of humour and forthright manner, could not 'get away with it'. Whereas everyone, including the psychiatrists, had understood what she was saying and to some extent shared her sentiments, now, staff claimed, 'they expect us to talk in a different way ... as professionals'. This adoption of 'professional language' was significant considering that the supervisors had expressed some resentment of the 'experts', who 'never came near the kids' and 'only knew half the story'. Indeed, I gained the clear impression that they felt 'professional procedures and commentaries' to be superfluous to the task. Such procedures tended to create an 'artificial' understanding of the girls, whereas they had the 'real knowledge'. This tendency to 'psychologize' problems, to express punitive attitudes in 'dressed up' jargon (for example, as 'needs' or 'best interests') was an important feature to note since it exaggerated the girls' problems. At the same time, however, as in Agency One, there was obviously a certain kudos associated with the 'professional task'. To be seen to be doing something provides status and prestige. Moreover, the professional task of assessment provided the necessary rationalization for their own jobs: 'assessment', no matter how inappropriate they felt it to be, was the basis for their employment.[5] Thus the staff were not prepared to look beyond their own roles within the system to any great degree, for this might bring into question their employment. The system was seen as basically acceptable, needing only minor modifications to iron out any problematic features.

Another feature of life for the staff within the agency was how their work was (for the most part) monotonous and routine, going through the same rituals and activities with the girls day after day. Indeed, mealtimes, schooltime, the clothes washing and cleaning time and bedtime established a set pattern for each day, with very little change in routine. Thus a request from a psychiatrist to see a girl in another part of the building was a welcome change in routine for the staff as well as the girl in question, and often elaborate and exaggerated plans were made to transfer the girl through the building. That changes in routine were a welcome disruption was also evident in the responses to a new admission in the agency. Although staff expressed some 'dismay' when a new girl arrived (meaning potentially more work for them), this dismay was edged with excitement.

Whilst tall and strong (usually male) supervisors complained about being called to the reception area in case of 'trouble' when a girl arrived there seemed to be almost a pleasure in this task; it provided something out of the routine. Elaborate steps were taken to ensure that 'trouble' would remain within the building and staff stood by the exits. Similarly, whilst staff might comment to one another that 'I'm sure — is going to attack me today' it seemed that such 'action' was not totally undesired; again, the 'action' would be welcome in an otherwise fairly mundane routine. The challenge which 'troublesome' behaviour might present did, of course, serve to justify the elaborate security arrangements and concerns in this respects.

There were also constraints on the staff's view and behaviour from the need to find specific placements for the girls so that they could be transferred from the assessment centre. Despite the fact that their role was, in theory, to find the most suitable placement so that treatment needs might be fulfilled, there was evidence of an avoidance of specific kinds of labelling, which (as they had learned through experience) might mean that a girl would remain unplaced. The staff modified their views and beliefs about girls in order to achieve placements for them because some institutions would not accept the girls for admission if they knew the 'truth' about them. There were other cases where labelling of a girl's needs was distorted and exaggerated to achieve a placement 'in a nice place', and, for example, a girl might be deemed 'maladjusted' if it was thought that this might increase her chances of gaining a boarding school placement, though the schools themselves are no longer labelled in this way (Warnock, 1978). The social worker admitted 'assessment' meetings where such decisions were made were very often discussions about specific institutions known to the staff and the possibility of these accepting the girls who were about to be transferred. The so-called 'objective' findings and observations of the staff throughout the 'assessment' period seemingly made little impact on the eventual choice of placement. The girls' 'needs' were abandoned so that the task of transferring the girls out of the agency could be accomplished.

Agency Three

Structure, organization and practice: constraints on judgement
Whilst it is clear the police held distinctive images of girls and that some of their images and practices might be seen as 'sexist' there were other aspects of life in the juvenile liaison office which have to be seen alongside any notions of 'sexism'. One was the need for officers to be seen to be 'busy'; another, the need for them to be seen to be doing 'real police work', or as the officers were heard to describe it, 'bringing in bodies'.

'Being busy' and doing 'real police work'
In addition to the routine processing of offenders, cautioning work and investigations with a view to taking care proceedings, the juvenile liaison office was inundated with requests from parents for officers to go and speak to their 'difficult' children. The majority of these requests, in the experience of this juvenile liaison office, came from parents who were concerned about the difficult behaviour of their daughters. The response of the police was generally one of collusion with the parents in seeing the behaviour as 'problematic' or 'difficult'. It was not clear, however, that this collusion reflected a simple sexist bias in their behaviour towards girls. Indeed, some of the factors already mentioned were of significance in defining the action to be taken. The juvenile liaison officers felt that they were *expected* to respond more to complaints about girls partly because 'girls are usually good so a complaint means trouble', as one of the officers put it, but also because they perceived that if they did not respond they would be berated by the press, in particular.

This collusion had a further dimension to it. The interpersonal dynamics of the juvenile liaison office were such that all the officers sought opportunities to get out of the office. Within the office they felt subject to the critical eye of the sergeant; moreover, the WPCs felt that they were used by the others as clerical assistants as they tended to be given a great deal of paperwork to do. 'The men assume we can type better than them and we haven't even been trained' is the way one of them described this treatment, and so they had apparently even more incentive to seek work outside the confines of the police station. Thus any opportunity to go out was readily seized, and if calls came in from parents they presented ample opportunity to do this.

One incident provided the WPCs with a legitimate excuse to be 'outside' in the following way. During a routine visit to a community-based police officer the officer made a chance remark about some schoolgirls who had been 'skipping' school (i.e., truanting). An educational welfare officer and a parent had brought this to his notice and had asked him to discover their whereabouts. He did indeed observe the five girls going into the home of one of them (after her parents had left for work). He further observed a boy visiting the home, though he believed the boy to be the older brother of one of the girls. With these observations in mind, the two WPCs were able to argue with the juvenile liaison office sergeant that they should spend a week 'on obs.' (that is, observing the house). Their reasoning with the sergeant was this:

> It's obvious they're up to something, five girls and one boy ... can't be bad. There is very strong evidence to suggest that they are offering prostitution services. The local policeman has observed regular visits by one boy and so there are probably many others going in and out too. (WPC H.)

In reality, there was very little evidence and an alternative response to the whole situation would have been to call at the house with the educational welfare officer to ensure the girls' return to school.

The chosen response, however, offered to WPCs the opportunity to work 'outside' and moreover, to work independently, which was seen as infinitely more rewarding than being on someone else's case or merely gathering details from the home regarding a juvenile.

Further, this 'created opportunity' contained an element of 'real police work' within it. It was investigative, 'detective work', not just routine paperwork which the officers grew accustomed to in the juvenile liaison office, and could be used to enhance the status of the WPCs in the eyes of colleagues working in more traditional areas of police activity. In this case, the 'difficult' behaviour of the girls was exaggerated out of the officers' desire to create interesting work for themselves more than out of specific concern for the girls and their behaviour.

A main point to note in this description of events is that the case was recorded as a moral danger/prostitution case by the juvenile liaison office, creating the impression that there was substantial evidence for this alleged activity. Moreover, the police response could, on one level, be interpreted as willingness to 'police' girls' behaviour in a way which they would not 'police' boys' behaviour (the activity being dismissed as unwarranted and not legitimate in relation to boys), from motives which reflects a differential expectation of boys' and girls' behaviour and sexist bias.

Referring now to the case of girl 1 who persistently ran away from home, it may be argued that the police took unnecessary action in dealing with her by seeking (and indeed obtaining) a Place of Safety Order on the grounds that she was in 'moral danger', and consequently that this action was 'sexist'. It is clear, however, that there were other influences dictating the course of action which the police should take. First, their action partly arose from the belief that because they were dealing with a girl 'action' of some sort would be expected more than if they were dealing with a boy. As the sergeant put it: 'Well at least we have covered ourselves ... we feel that this action is necessary so that no one can say that we didn't try to control things ... that we didn't try to stop the running away' (Sgt N.). Subsequent comments of police officers made the reasons for their continued application more explicit:

> She's only 14 and if we don't do something we'll get a lot of stick if things go wrong. If she goes off again it's us the press will have a go at as well as the nibs.[6] (Sgt N.)

> She's a spoilt brat, you should see the home she's been given, everything ... even got her own TV. She is so insolent ... very lippy and she called me all the names under the sun. I expect she's shacking up in tin town somewhere.[7] (WPC J.)

Moreover, the girl had been 'difficult' within the police station itself: 'She kicked me and I'll do her ... she won't get away with it. She was very rude to the police surgeon when she was being examined' (WPC H.). In this case, it was the police officers' awkward interaction with the girl which led to their insistence on pursuing the order, it was their way of ensuring some kind of punishment for the girl's aggressive behaviour towards them. As one of the officers described, 'Even if we can only get her away for a week it will be a lesson to her if she needs it ... pull her up sharp, a short, sharp shock for her' (WPC H.).

A further example of the way in which initial interpretations of an event as 'sexist' might need to be moderated in the light of other possible influences, concerns the case of girl 2 for whom the police sought a Place of Safety Order. Despite the fact that the major problem relating to this girl was her repeated absence from school and an unsatisfactory home background (with the police approving neither the material conditions of her home nor the care or control of her family), the police had included grounds of her being in 'moral danger' in their application for care proceedings. This could easily be seen as 'sexist', by reflecting an assumption that the girl was 'sexually promiscuous' or 'at risk'. The question of whether or not a boy was in 'moral danger' would generally not arise.

Significantly, the inclusion of this condition in the application came not from their concern to impose a moral judgement on the girls' behaviour, nor out of their concern for her wellbeing in this respect but reflected their concern to ensure that a Place of Safety Order would be granted.[8] As they pointed out:

> We have to be really careful these days in the courts. They pick you up on such little things. If we've got evidence at all we slam it in to make our case strong. (PC A.)

> We know she doesn't sleep around really because we have no reason to distrust her. She's a nice kid and she told us the truth the last time, can't see why she would lie, but it makes our case look better. I've just included moral

danger to impress the magistrates. The assault and impairment will have most impact I suspect and I have added the 'e' and 'c' as support and also to save the EWO [Educational Welfare Officer] from having to take mum to court for T.'s non-attendance at school. (WPC J.)

Thus the application was influenced not only by the police officers' views and judgements of the situation but by the administrative and judicial need to present substantial evidence. In this case, although there was no evidence of 'moral danger', the inclusion of this condition was used to support the whole application. Further, the 'beyond care and control' condition was included for purposes of administrative convenience.

Clearly, police intervention in this way was a distortion of the real situation and whilst the outcome (that is, a Place of Safety Order on the aforementioned grounds) could be interpreted as 'sexist bias' on the part of the police in actively imposing constraints on girls' behaviour whilst not on boys', an alternative explanation would depend more on the 'operational philosophy' of the police and on administrative structures. Underlying these influences was the need for the police to 'cover' themselves regarding accusations from the press that they had failed to act when girls are generally perceived as 'vulnerable'. Their own views were thus 'shaped' or supplemented by those of external agents and agencies and their subsequent actions further mediated by organizational contingencies.

From this second level analysis of events in the three agencies under consideration, it is clear that any perspectives or ideologies which the staff held, sexist or otherwise, were subject to many influences.

In essence, both the processes of interaction between actor and subject (practitioner and child in this context) and the professional skills and standing of an individual practitioner within a particular institution may be important in determining the expression of a particular perspective or ideology. Moreover, certain items of information, for instance, could be withheld lest they hold implications for the professional standing of the practitioner involved. The attitude to authority of a particular girl or boy, for example, might be examined in a circumspect manner lest it reflect on the control and discipline exercised by a particular practitioner. The need to exhibit personally acquired knowledge may cause reports to be written with this knowledge accentuated, to the exclusion of other fields of knowledge in which the practitioner is not as skilled. The expectations of others in the agency may influence the content of information put forward by the practitioner, and may also be submitted by the practitioner because s/he thinks others regard it as relevant, rather than because of its importance.

Such expectations may be linked to general ideas of professional standing and skills or they may be linked to direct or implicit guidelines that exist in one particular agency. The demarcation of professional skills may affect these expectations of what information is considered relevant, to the extent that only teachers comment on learning ability, and only residential social workers comment on behaviour at mealtimes. Behaviour that is not specifically included in a checklist may be ignored as irrelevant, or the behaviour of a boy or girl may be re-interpreted to fall into checklist classifications. Also important is the way in which the perceptions of those who are thought to 'really know' children (usually psychiatrists) may influence the professional language and satisfactory diagnoses and assessments by those dealing with them on an everyday basis. Visiting psychiatrists, for instance, are by virtue of position and training believed to have special understanding, though they only occasionally meet the children concerned (see Buckholdt and Gubrium, 1979).

The individual personality and ideas of each practitioner, too, may affect assessment to some degree. Strong views on certain types of behaviour may lead to its accentuation in reports to the exclusion of other noted behaviour or attitudes. A sympathetic and approachable practitioner may learn more about the problems of some juveniles and thus write a different assessment from that written by a practitioner who is less able to make relationships. Some practitioners will be subject to more 'acting out behaviour' from those children they are dealing with because they do not wish or are not able to convey as much authority as other practitioners. As a consequence, their views and reports on individual children may well differ from those of stricter and more authoritarian staff. Simple clashes of temperament and personality between certain children and certain stff may similarly lead to diverse reports and assessments. Professional acculturation in these contexts ensures that the views of staff about a particular child are not too dissimilar. Nevertheless, personal factors may intervene in the development of such views.

Further, staffing problems, the presence of a number of 'difficult' boys or girls, and lack of suitable placements could affect the nature of decisions taken within any one agency dealing with them.

Another factor which may influence the way in which images of children are formed concerns the use of stereotypical images. Thus stereotypes of disturbed children may be appealing because of their simplicity; stereotypes of 'bad' girls and 'nice' girls may be a useful mechanism to ensure social control, not through the images themselves but through the polarization of such images. Following this, it is arguable that images of female offenders as somehow 'worse' than young male offenders reflect a fear of them and a fear that when a girl is being difficult things are very much out of control.[9] This, we are told, is because girls' difficult behaviour tends to be 'less visible' than boys. Girls often assume a passive stance and silent hostility whereas boys are more often hostile in an open, physical way. It is the 'unknown' quality of the silence which poses a major problem for practitioners.[10] The 'good' or 'nice' girl is thus one who communicates, reducing the staff's fear. In this sense, the stereotype of the 'nice' girl is one which alleviates practitioners' anxiety about a relationship rather than one which reflects a purely 'sexist' view.

It is clear that the notion of 'sexist bias' becomes complicated once it is placed in an administrative and organizational context. 'Sexist ideology' is not a discrete phenomenon, but a mixture of personal views, professional policies and practices which are continually 'shaped' by the exigencies of practice and organizational constraints. Indeed, it is impossible to distinguish between professional ideology, organizational expedience and sentiment.

Notes

1. See Sharpe (1976), Deem (1978) and Chetwynd and Hartnett (1978). The female staff tended to reinforce the view of men as dominant by seeking their help in minor practical tasks – changing a fuse, for instance, and in one case by asking a man to change the batteries in a radio. This image of the men was strengthened, too, by the fact that in general (since in the main they were the ones who initiated games and activities) the men were the keepers of resources. Men dealt with the stereo and games equipment, the children's personal property and with the doling out of the weekly pocket money (a task which was left to a man even if he was the only man on duty or the 'weakest' and least liked male member of staff). See Stanworth (1983) on the subtle ways in which male dominance is reinforced in everyday interactions between people.

2. This is allied to what Giller and Morris (1981) have described as the search for 'moral character', where an ideology of individual need prevails until the moral character of parents makes it difficult for the social worker dealing with the case to co-opt them as clients.

3. Other rules related, for instance, to restrictions on the use of radio and TV and to saying Grace at mealtimes.

4. The superintendent of the agency during the period of my research had been in post only weeks. It seemed appropriate, therefore, to interview the former superintendent and deputy.

5. See Festinger (1957) on the theory of cognitive dissonance which explains how incompatible views can be tied together. See also Menzies (1960) on how practitioners rationalize their (often mundane and boring) work activities.

6. 'Nibs' – the superior officers.

7. 'Tin town' – this was a local council estate made up of prefabricated buildings. The area was thought to be disreputable.

8. The 'moral danger' category is section 1(2) of the 1969 Children and Young Persons Act (See Appendix B).

9. See Perkins (1978) on public stereotypes.

10. See Davies (1979) who writes about the fear of girls in the classroom.

7 Conclusion. Beyond intellectual sexism: a comment

It was argued in Chapter 6 that the picture of a criminal justice system and allied agencies imbued with 'sexism' becomes less acceptable once an attempt is made to recognize 'sexism' in the everyday activities of practitioners as an unalloyed expression of belief about females. I suggested that the concept of 'sexism' as a body of beliefs which systematically distorts knowledge about females is affected by a host of organizational and administrative constraints. Thus the practitioners to whom I referred in my fieldwork were as much influenced in their everyday activities by the constraints which derive from organizational settings as by 'sexist' ideology. My intention in Chapter 6, however, was not to dismiss the concept of sexism *in toto*, but to point out that it is difficult to discern distinctive 'sexist' intentions in practice settings. I shall return to this point later in the present chapter.

First, though, I continue my examination of the notion of sexism by considering some of its theoretical underpinnings. Having raised some questions about the acceptability of the concept in practice, I now wish to raise some questions about its theoretical foundation and to point out some of the difficulties which feminist writers must address if they hope to pursue and promote effectively their arguments about sexism. Just as I raised questions in relation to practice settings, here I ask, if knowledge is distorted (and consequently sexist), who distorts it? And for what purpose? And how?

It is upon the 'conspiratorial' aspects of feminist contributions to the women and crime debate which I focus my attention. Writers tend to draw upon 'conspiratorial' aspects of the notions of sexism or 'oppression' without fully explicating these concepts.[1] This is unsatisfactory. In my attempt to expose some of the problems within this area I first examine, by way of introduction, some of the general themes underlying the writings of early feminist writers; secondly, I examine the idea that there might be a logical or unambiguous relationship between the law and the 'oppression' of women. This second part of my argument does, of course, bring us rather closer than the first to questions relating to the treatment of females in the criminal justice system, but in this area of discussion it is important to refer to the general themes as well as the specific and more criminological ones since feminist writers tend to depend implicitly upon these. Throughout this book I have been concerned with the suggestion that ideas about females in the criminal justice system and allied agencies have been 'created' or exaggerated out of proportion to actual differences between males and females. In view of this it is essential to consider those general areas of debate which also emphasize distortion and exaggeration.

In most of this chapter I am concerned with a body of feminist writing which seems to reflect a 'conspiracy'. Authors of this literature tend to believe that any exploitation of women, or of women's position in society is deliberate. Later in this chapter I make brief reference to another body of writing which I classify as 'structuralist'. In this context I am using the term 'structure' to refer to those aspects of society which exist beyond individual control, motivation and intention and to those theories of sexism which are both functional and non-conspiratorial. There are, of course, many differences between writers. My own classification serves merely to mark out those writers who emphasize the 'conspiratorial' aspects of sexism and those who have attempted to refine the arguments about the oppression of females by shifting analyses to a level which utilizes a more discursive understanding of the notion of ideology than the one adopted in this thesis.[2]

'Conspiratorial' arguments

Patriarchy

Some of the emphasis on the notion of sexism of 'conspiracy' has come from general consideration of the concept of 'patriarchy'. Patriarchy has been used in a variety of ways, some of which clearly do not involve the notion of conspiracy. For example, it has been described as an ideology which arose out of men's power to exchange women between kinship groups (Figes, 1978), as a symbolic male principle, and as the power of the father over females (its literal meaning, the concept operating primarily within the psychological realm of analysis; Mitchell, 1974). It has been used to express men's control over women's sexuality and fertility (Edwards, 1981), and to describe the institutional structure of male domination.[3] Indeed, it is a term which has been widely used as a foundation for a specifically feminist investigation of sexual relations. It is often used quite casually, bandied around conference halls and used interchangeably with 'sexism'. It is used sometimes simply as a reminder that there is one sex which dominates, another which is subjected.

The attraction of this term, however, lies beyond its contribution to feminist currency and polemics. It appears in several different theories, all of which can be said to have had some impact on defining the space which women occupy in society. Anthropology, for instance, records the social and political dominance of men over women in a large number of societies and even suggests that some form of patriarchy may be inevitable. Psychoanalysis suggests that it is the history of the patriarchal family which is the essential key to the imposition of sexual identity and the reproduction of that sexual identity. Marxist theory, also, refers to the crucial relation between patriarchy and private property.

Engels (1972) focuses on the concept to describe the first shift in power from women to men (from matriarchal to patriarchal societies), together with the emergence of private property and, hence, classes. Drawing from theories in this way we can indeed arrive at a position where we assume that patriarchal relationships, being in existence for whatever reason, determine the interests of the sexes. But the assumption made is often more than this, it is an assumption which incorporates the idea that the promotion and maintenance of patriarchal relationships has been conscious and intentional, as if men or kinship networks or particular modes of production have immediately seized upon and used any basic sex differences for their own ends. Moreover, implicit in this assumption is the idea that 'patriarchal relationships' are always oppressive.

There are some problems with the concept. It is undeniable, on the basis of anthropological evidence, that in most societies a higher status is awarded to men than to women. This occurs even when there is the appearance of high female status in matriarchal societies. Mead, for instance, recognizes this contradiction and argues that men's activities always attract a higher status than women's.

> Whatever the arrangements in regard to descent or ownership of property, and even if these formal outward arrangements are reflected in the temperamental relations between the sexes, the prestige values always attach to the activities of men.   (Mead, 1935: 302)[4]

A further example which is often used by feminist writers in support of the concept of patriarchy and of oppression is provided by Rosaldo (1974) who reports that among the Tchambuli, women were the traders, controlling family economics, whilst the men were artists and ritual specialists. She notes that although women had little respect for masculine secrets, they still found it necessary to adhere to, and engage in, ritual order that marked them as inferior – in morality and knowledge – to men. Again, in certain African societies such as the Yoruba, women may control a good part of food supplies, accumulate cash, and trade in distant and important markets (Lloyd, 1965); yet when approaching their husbands, wives must feign ignorance and obedience, 'kneeling to serve men as they sit' (Rosaldo and Lamphere, 1974; 22–3). Feminist writers tend to use such examples to suggest that 'patriarchy' implies a relationship which is fixed and intransmutable, or a kaleidoscope of forms, so to speak, within which women and men have encountered one another. But the problem in this perspective is that the term 'patriarchy' does not encompass any suggestions about ways in which women might act to transform their situation as a sex. It may be that the Weberian distinction between power, authority and influence are relevant here in that women may have more power and influence on an informal level (cf. Young and Harris, 1976). Thus feminist writers' use of the term 'patriarchy' suggests a fatalistic submission which allows no space for the complexities of women's defiance.

Moreover, implicit in the term is the assumption that the defining features of oppression have been obvious to all women at all times. This is misleading. There is need for caution in applying our own assumptions to the past. Women may have seen the defining features of oppression very differently at different times. Large numbers of children, for instance, could be regarded as a sign of value and status by some women, whereas others would define this as oppressive, insisting on the right to restrict the number of children they conceive and bear. There is frequently a tendency to colonize women in the past by imposing modern values.

Further, turning now to historical material, it is clear that there are obvious differences between different groups of women and they may have experienced 'oppression' dissimilarly.[5] For instance, the possibilities for women among the higher peasantry in the Middle Ages were clearly quite different from those of poor peasants without land. Changes, too, may not have affected all women in the same way. The growth of domestic industry, for example, is usually associated with an increase of the father's control over the family. But the domestic division of labour here also meant that women's skills were vital to the family economy at certain times in the production process. Thus it may have been easier for women in domestic industry than for peasant women to question sexual hierarchy. Indeed, Alice Clark (1982) and Ivy Pinchbeck (1969), examining the labour conditions of women in the seventeenth, eighteenth and nineteenth centuries, both note in their work that it was single women who were most subject to distress. Whilst not receiving a wage themselves, working wives did at least enjoy stable employment and were recipients of the 'family wage', whereas single women could rarely find stable employment or adequate wages for subsistence.

On the other hand, with respect to factory work, it has been said that it was single women who benefited, by having the opportunity to gain social and economic independence. The change here proved worse for married women who lost their crucial role in the household economy and who were expected to depend on their husbands. As Pinchbeck notes:

> Married women had never possessed a legal right to their own earnings, or their share of the family wage, nevertheless, in the new situation their financial subjection was greater than in the days when they contributed their share to the family income. (1969: 312)

Pinchbeck makes further distinctions between employed groups of women, noting that whilst most working women in the 1800's were working in domestic service, as needlewomen, agricultural workers and in domestic industries, the factory women were better off because they worked shorter hours but received better wages. This clearly marks the difficulty in treating women as an homogeneous group, regardless of the specific regime they were subjected to.

This point is further illustrated by the emphasis on 'sisterhood' amongst women as the subjects of 'patriarchal oppression'. This emphasis is misleading. Some feminist thinking was born out of the involvement of poor working class women in large-scale popular movements at work and in the community in the nineteenth century, where women demanded their rights as a sex while resisting class oppression. But the first movement of feminists was also born out of the domestic isolation of middle-class women, the extreme control of middle-class men over their wives and daughters, and the impoverishment of unmarried women.[6] Indeed, there were very different emphases within nineteenth-century feminism from those today which look at specific antagonisms within sex/gender relationships.

Moreover, there are other variables such as race, class and culture, which cut across the group identity of women as the oppressed. Although patriarchy is evident in nearly all societies which have been studied, there are occasions where men and women appear to have equal interests. Indeed, given women's role in capitalist society as domestic labourers whose role it is to create the preconditions for the production of surplus values, it is important to examine the relationship between domestic labour and the mode of production rather than just women's position. In doing so we can comprehend the emphasis on 'class consciousness' rather than on a 'feminist consciousness'. Thus, when women do identify with other women, it tends to be on a class basis rather than on any basis relating to sex (Bujra, 1978). Consequently, whether through design or practice, such groups act in defence of their class interests at a subjective level. Similarly, McDonough and Harrison (1978) argue that within the capitalist mode of production patriarchy is mediated through class relations, so that while the relations of production may be analytically central to the explanation of the subordination of all women there are differences which arise for women inhabiting different class positions.[7]

This means that although 'patriarchal subjection' exists, it is not necessarily and automatically the case that patriarchy is the main constraining relationship within which women are subjected. Rather, the precise character of the operation of patriarchal relations may be shaped within the historical concreteness of modes of production, even though at certain conjunctures patriarchal relations may operate in a relatively pristine form.

Reproduction

The concept of reproduction, too, has frequently been employed in attempts to understand women's oppression. Indeed some of the emphasis on 'conspiracy' in accounts about the unjust treatment of women in society and in the distorted accounts of their 'needs', is derived from arguments about women's role in the processes of reproduction. There are, of course, different sorts of reproduction;[8] here I am referring to biological reproduction and 'social reproduction', meaning the reproduction of labour power and social systems.

The concept of reproduction has been used to examine the nature of oppression within particular modes of production (that is, it has been closely tied to materialist conceptions of patriarchy, especially those relating to the capitalist mode of production), and in attempts to develop theories about the situation of women in society, in such a way that the particular biological tasks of women are frequently conflated with the overall process of social reproduction. There are, however, a number of problems attached to its use. The first I want to mention relates to the juxtaposition of biological reproduction and social reproduction. Early Marxist (and reductionist) accounts, for instance, took this notion from a passage in one of Marx' letters in which he remarked that

> every child knows that a social formation which did not produce the conditions of production the same time as it produced would not last a year. (Marx, 1868)[9]

This comment, when linked with Engels' formulation from *The Origin of the Family*, that the main influence in history has been the aim to reproduce life, has led to a consideration of the extent to which the forces and relations of production depend upon women occupying a specific role in society. Engels argued that

> the determining factor in history is, in the last resort, the production and reproduction of immediate life itself. This is of a twofold character: on the one side, the production of the means of subsistence of food, clothing and shelter and the tools requisite therefore, on the other, the production of human beings themselves, the propagation of the species. (Engels 1972: 71)

Subsequent writers such as Adamson *et al.* (1976) have assumed from this that biological reproduction is merely one, unproblematic aspect of reproduction as a whole. Biological reproduction is analyzed by feminists as a fundamental part of social reproduction and analyzed within the same conceptual framework. Women are assumed to be 'the means of reproduction' (Taylor, 1975) and 'control over them' becomes of paramount importance because of their assumed significance for social reproduction.

Another criticism of the early feminist conception of reproduction relates to the assumption that reproductive practices will be similar in different modes of production. For example, in the analysis of the capitalist system, various types of labour have been labelled as 'reproductive' in that they appear to maintain and serve the labour force. The best example is so-called 'domestic labour'; in this type of labour biological reproduction is often conflated with such 'reproductive' tasks as washing, cooking and cleaning. This gives some degree of autonomy to the 'process of reproduction' and, consequently, the reproduction of the labour force is easily seen as a specifically female activity, separate from the process of production. The traditional emphasis within Marxist thought on the exploitative wage-contract being central to capitalist social relations has been demonstrated by Seccombe (1974). He has argued that women's unpaid work in the home serves to reproduce both the forces and the relations of production. At an economic level, the housewife's labour reproduces on a daily and generational basis the labour power of the worker, at an ideological level it reproduces the relations of dominance and subordination required by capitalist production. In other economic systems, however, domestic labour may have different meanings attached to it, and a different value accorded to it. Clearly, therefore, concepts developed in an analysis of capitalism cannot easily be transferred to analyses of non-capitalist systems.

Lastly, and importantly, an over-simplistic reading of reproduction tends to lead to the assumption that (a) social systems exist to maintain themselves through time; and (b) that all levels of the system must be maintained through time in the same way. The teleological and functionalist implications of these assumptions are obvious.[10]

The family is often mentioned in relation to women's oppression, particularly by those seeking to understand women's oppression through the concept of reproduction. The suggestion is that the form of the family is determined by the social system or the mode of production. Engels expresses this in his notion of women's subordination through the 'father right', private property and the class-based society. Indeed, as Kuhn (1978) points out, the family is very often invoked as a 'final, catch-all' explanation of the various characteristics of women's position in different societies and at different times. Certainly, within both functionalist and early Marxist sociology there is a tendency to concentrate on the 'fit' between the family and the various needs of society.[11] Kuhn describes how within this perspective the family is seen as the site of 'social reproduction':

> the family is thought of as the non-contradictory site of socially necessary activities such as 'pattern maintenance' (ideological reproduction) and 'tension management' (psychological renewal of labour power) (Kuhn, 1978: 45)

Mary McIntosh made much the same point when discussing the demand of the Women's Liberation Movement for the abolition of the legal definition of women as dependent on men. She argued that underlying any notion of the family as simply a part of civil society which the state recognizes and respects, is a fundamental truth that the state needs the family (1974: 5).[12] Dalla Costa and James put the case more forcefully:

the family under capitalism is a center of conditioning, of consumption, and of reserve labour, but a center essentially of social reproduction. (Dalla Costa and James, 1972: 10)[13]

Once again, there are problems with some of these ideas, McIntosh herself acknowledges some of the difficulties in the functionalist approach inherent in her work and in the idea that all social formations and relationships can be reduced to an economic level. McIntosh's recognition of the 'over-determination' of policy comes in her incisive query as to whether or not the value of labour power includes the cost of reproducing the worker alone or the entire family of the worker (1977). Of course, in traditional Marxist theory the reproduction of labour power does include the invisible costs relating to the family. But there is a tension between this implicit assumption and Jane Humphries' (1977) point that the 'family wage' for the married man, and his wife and children staying at home, far from being a part of the cash nexus, was an achievement of the working class during the nineteenth century. Her claim is that the 'family wage' was the result of hard-fought battles and not the instrument of some capitalist conspiracy to retain control over reproduction.

My purpose here is to dismiss these types of reductionist arguments which revolve around the concept of reproduction. It is clear, for instance, that the family household has a history of its own and roots which lie beyond capitalist society, so that state effort cannot achieve a perfect fit between the household and the various needs of capitalism.[14]

Sexism in the criminal justice system

To return to sexism in the criminal justice system, the writers who allege 'sexism' in its operation do so, in the main, by referring to the influence of the capitalist mode of production. In this analysis 'sexist ideology' indicates the manipulation of reality to serve men's interests and to serve capitalism. This viewpoint is epitomized in the claim of Klein and Kress:

the special oppression of women by the system (the criminal justice system) is not isolated or arbitrary, but rather is rooted in systematic sexist practices and ideologies which can only be fully understood by analysing the position of women in 'capitalist' society (Klein and Kress, 1976: 45)

Kress later provides a variation on this theme by referring to the idea that 'sexist ideology' and practice is rooted in bourgeois morality (1979: 48), but it is only a version of the theme and not a departure from it. One of the essential arguments within this feminist perspective is that all definitions relating to women and crime reflect and reinforce the economic position of women as reproducers and domestic workers.

Some feminist contributors view their approach as a remedial one whereby political analysis becomes of prime importance. Thus for example, rather than paternalism being the innocent expression of 'reverence' and protectiveness for the female sex, it is to be seen as an indication of men's interests and as a vital function of capitalism. It is regarded as insidious that women are treated as minions and as dependants. And it is argued, for instance, that female delinquency is 'sexualized' because of the relationship of women, as property, to the mode of production. Smart (1976), for example, has argued that prostitution arises out of the working-class woman's secondary role to the labour market. The woman is subsumed within the identities of her husband and family where married. The male labourer is the primary producer of subsistence needs and the woman has to serve the reproductive needs of capitalism, in this context, servicing the male within the home. Being relegated to the secondary role in the labour market means that when she enters it, her wages are seen as additional to her husband's; sexuality thus becomes a bargaining power in the absence of any other viable means to achieve economic independence. It is also argued that the protection of female sexuality (through paternalism) arises because marriage acts as a vital service industry in the reproduction of labour power, not only releasing the man to capitalism for the (re)production of surplus value but also by ideologically and emotionally chaining him to what may be described as a contractual relationship drawn up to serve interests outside the domain of marriage. Paternalism thus represents or reflects an anxiety to uphold the *status quo*. This argument is too one dimensional. If in the capitalist mode of production there is so much concern about the female sex role (which some feminist writers argue is demonstrated through anxiety about 'status offences', for example) it is surprising that there is not a great deal more 'policing' of women via the criminal justice system. Interestingly, McIntosh (1978) argues that the state intervenes less often and less directly in the lives of women than in the lives of men. Moreover, if the regulation of female sexuality is seen as a reality for capital it is curious that there is not a great deal more effort to induce women, by rewards, to have children.

Attempts to describe the oppression of women range from the idea that the ideology of oppression is irrevocably rooted in biology (where procreation and its different consequences for men and women is taken as the main cause),[15] to the notion of a 'self-contained' and 'self-perpetuating' ideology as the 'energy source' of patriarchal oppression; there is also the idea that sexist ideology is a reflection of material conditions of male power and dominance.[16]

In this section of the book my criticism has been directed towards the idea that the 'oppression of women' is invariably direct and intentional. These ideas are evident, though not always explicit, in the writings of feminists who examine the treatment of women in the criminal justice system and they underly many of the claims that both theories about female offenders and the treatment of them are in some way due to a male conspiracy and/or the capitalist mode of production.[17] I have tackled the suggestion of a uniform, deliberate and direct oppression of women at this theoretical level to underline the importance of my empirical findings which demonstrate that the treatment of females in the criminal justice system may be due to a variety of factors and not simply to some conspiratorial notion of 'sexism', 'free-floating' or otherwise. There are, of course, more refined approaches to the notion of sexism which are both functional and non-conspiratorial. These are discussed in the next section.

'Structural' arguments
I now turn to 'structural' applications of the concepts of sexism and oppression which suggest that the oppression of women may not be conscious or deliberate, but rather a reflection of structure. I do not propose to pursue these arguments within the context of this book since they are not of prime concern to my critique of writers who emphasize 'conspiratorial' aspects of sexism, but I do wish to acknowledge their existence since my conclusions have some implication for their work. As previously stated, I am using the term 'structure' to refer to those aspects of society which exist beyond individual control, motivation and intention, especially those deriving from the distribution of power, wealth and differential location in the labour market. These are the structural 'constraints', 'contingencies' or 'imperatives' which direct us to behave in the way we do. Such restraints are responsible for the processes of socialization which we all go through.[18]

In these later approaches it is argued that oppression has to be explained beyond its entrenchment in relations of production, that the notion of oppression does not derive solely from economic modes of production nor from reductionist analyses which rely solely on biology. Mitchell summarizes the position thus:

> The longevity of the oppression of women must be based on something more than conspiracy, something more complicated than biological handicap and more durable than economic exploitation. (Mitchell, 1974: 362)

She herself has made strenuous attempts to break away from economic reductionism and to locate sexuality and gender identity in the historical specificity of ideological processes by appropriating the field of psycho analysis. She has generated some interest in the possibility of using the work of Freud (and subsequent writers in the psychoanalytic tradition, such as Jacques Lacan) to develop a materialist theory of gender and sexuality.[19]   Clearly, this approach has certain advantages over the traditional Marxist accounts of gender and sexuality (and the production/reproduction arguments) and also over the early feminist 'conspiratorial' accounts (and the dependence upon biological differences between males and females). Barrett who is one of the protagonists in directing feminist analyses away from crude biological and economic reductionism, offers some encouragement for this move:

> On the one hand it avoids the unsatisfactory reductionism of attempts to explain the very diverse sexual behaviour in terms of a rather forced notion of the 'needs' of capitalism: on the other hand it overcomes the monolithic, at times verging on the conspiratorial, conception of male oppression offered by some feminist analyses and, perhaps most importantly, provides an explanation of the processes by which women come to 'collude' in their sexual oppression. (Barrett, 1980: 60)

We should be cautious in our enthusiasm for Mitchell's suggestion, however, since it denies the cultural influences upon sexuality and subjectivity and neglects the relations that exist historically between economic and ideological structures.

It is important to note that Mitchell's new ideas occurred at the same time as changes in Marxist theoretical approaches to the concept of ideology. Althusser (1972) has been the most important influence in this new approach. He rejects the notion of ideology as a deliberate distortion of reality by the ruling class for its own interest and the view that ideology is simply a mechanical reflection of a determining economic base. As an alternative, he locates ideology as a practice enjoying relative autonomy from the economic level and stresses that ideology is 'lived experience' representing 'the imaginary relationship of individuals to their real conditions of existence'. Thus the rejection of crude economism has facilitated the accommodation of the question of gender division within ideology and it has become possible, within a new kind of Marxist perspective, to see the oppression of women as a relatively autonomous element of the social formation. Recent Marxist feminist work, therefore, has focused on the ideological construction of gendered subjects and on attempts to rethink psychoanalytic theory from a Marxist feminist perspective.[20]

Whilst crude economic reductionism is dismissed, however, the theoretical advances made here do not completely solve the problem of the relationship between Marxist and feminist theory (Hartmann, 1981). Indeed, whilst a discussion at the level of ideology may appear to rescue sexual politics from a position of marginality within Marxist writings, it does so at the cost of excluding any possibility of specifying determinate relations in the real world. The discussions become too abstract, as if it is impossible to identify any specific influences on the shaping of women's lives. Indeed, the challenge to mechanistic relationships assumed by earlier Marxists has had the effect of 'throwing the baby out with the bath water', when the removal of *all* determinate relations may not be appropriate. In a sense, analyses of this type lead us back to notions of 'free-floating' sexist ideologies. I shall return to this point in my conclusion.

This is a lengthy introduction to the points I illustrate later in the chapter. In some instances I have simplified very complex arguments, and I may have glossed over subtle and intricate differences between the different positions adopted by feminist writers, but my main intention in this section of the chapter was not to pursue the feminist debates in depth, merely to emphasize the dangers of the wide assumptions and functionalist approaches inherent in some of their work. Often, they view the exploitation of one group by another as the unfolding of an inevitable plan – all directed against women. My concern in exploring such issues here is merely to emphasize the fact that 'sexism' is a difficult concept to deal with. The complications which occurred when I searched for sexism in practice are mirrored at this theoretical level of debate.

The relationship between the 'oppression' of women and the law
In this section of the chapter I provide an illustration of some of the problems by referring to the implicit {and sometimes explicit} claims of feminist writers that there is a logical or unambiguous relationship between the 'oppression' of women and the law. This claim is often used to account for the range of images of women and girls within the criminal justice system and allied agencies which I described in Chapter 1. Thus images of female offenders as 'weak, passive and disturbed' for instance, are seen as a direct illustration of 'oppression'.[21] Discriminatory practices operating between women and girls within the criminal justice system are seen as a symbolic reflection of the 'oppression' of all females.)

To assist my analysis of the relationship between the law and the oppression of women I shall use the helpful framework provided by Elizabeth Kingdom (1981). In this framework she suggests that there are three basic models which might be used to describe the 'distortion' of images of females. First, sexist bias as intervention in the law. Secondly, sexist bias in law. Thirdly, sexist bias as an effect of law.[22]

The first model suggests that there are non-legal elements which somehow intervene in the legal sphere of activity in ways which are, in some sense, improper or disliked because they work to the disadvantage of women. The model suggests that there are 'outside' influences which get in the way of the proper functioning of the law and that these influences contain elements of sexist bias.[23]

The problems with this model are, first, that law is seen as independent of other practices; for example, economic or political practices, and there is frequently a concomitant assumption that the law can be impartial, neutral and fair. Secondly, there is some difficulty in identifying the occasions on which the alleged economic or political (or indeed any other interests) make their appearance. The neutrality and impartiality of the law, however, is not something easily accepted by modern criminologists. Indeed, within this claim, that 'sexism' somehow infiltrates or intervenes in the law, is the assumption that the law is not biased against or towards other groups of people and this is an untenable analysis. The claim assumes, for instance, that men and boys have been, and are, treated fairly; it misses inequalities between women and men. Indeed, accounts of practice which discuss 'sexism' need to incorporate a much wider spectrum of evidence. Law is not only 'biased' against women, but also against the poor and racial minorities, for example (see Hall *et al.*, (1978)), and these 'biases' are not merely additive but sometimes work together. Women are treated differently from each other by race and class at the same time as being dealt with differently from men.[24] Datesman and Scarpitti (1980a) analyzed over a thousand cases of juveniles appearing before the American family court. Their work revealed that for felonies and misdemeanours, black females received harsher sentences than whites;[25] this difference was apparently greater than that between black and white males. Conversely, for status offences white females were treated more harshly than black females (Datesmann and Scarpitti, 1980).

In considering these issues Kress (1979) felt it pertinent to characterize feminist criminology as 'classless'. She criticizes the fact that class distinctions are frequently neglected in analyses of sexist ideology and argues that:

> feminism ... treats the state as a classless monolith that somehow operates neutrally outside of class relations. Thus the contradiction becomes one of women and the state instead of a contradiction between the classes. (Kress, 1979: 45)

The second main assumption within this model refers to 'interests' which intervene in the law and has been indirectly dealt with in a previous section of this chapter where I examined the links between capitalism and women's oppression. There I offered some criticism of the assumption that the oppression of women is invariably in the interests of men and/or capitalism. But there is a further point that we need to note in any reference to 'interests' which intervene in the law (or any other institution, for that matter). If it is assumed that there are specific 'interests' which work within the law it is difficult to explain anomalies where practice or the operation of the law does not fulfil those interests. Kingdom's example of the Married Women's Property Act 1882 is a useful illustration of this point as she considers some of the explanations that might be put forward to account for a piece of legislation which was undeniably in women's favour. She states:

Consider the explanatory options: male partiality momentarily displaced by female partiality, male partiality miscalculating its economic interest, male dominance in the legal profession briefly overcome with guilt at its history of male partiality, male partiality shrewdly calculating a mere gesture at female equality; the belated appearance of gender free impartiality and so on. (Kingdom, 198: 102)

It is useful to turn briefly to a different example of anomalies in the 'operation of the law', and one which has provided the focus for some illuminating historical analyses. In theory the eighteenth-century criminal law was a rigid and harsh penal code laying down the death penalty for a broad range of property crimes. In practice it was a flexible and highly selective system. Douglas Hay, in an essay entitled 'Property, Authority and the Criminal Law' (1975) has argued that it was this very 'selectiveness' in the operation of the law which reinforced and protected the authority and interests of a small ruling elite. He suggests that the law was both an instrument of authority and an ideological weapon. Through the discretion available to them at various points in the judicial process, the ruling elite were able to use the levers of fear and mercy in a way that encouraged deference and maintained their authority. The analysis of Peter King (1984), however, questions the importance of these motivations and, in looking at the operation of 'selective justice', shows that the law was also used by the poor and operated in certain situations to protect them and to constrain the power of the elite. There was not one central motive force representing specific interests which governed the way in which the courts and justice were administered.

Similarly, it is difficult to assume that there is only one set of interests underlying the law in its application to women. A suggestion that anomalies in the law are simply there to appease women and perhaps to encourage respect for their male benefactors is difficult to sustain. If the law is seen as distorted by male interests in some way, in ways which disadvantage women, we have to be able to formulate very precisely what these interests are, how many men recognize them and how they translate into legal practices. It may be plausible, for example, to argue that women are not sent to prison because men benefit from the unpaid labour which women perform in housework and childcare. But how do we then account for the fact that imprisonment rates for women were very much higher in the nineteenth century than they are today (Greenwood, 1981)? This leads us to the view that men must have more 'benefit' from the work in the home now, or that they value it more.   Such a viewpoint is clearly questionable, since imprisonment rates are affected by a host of factors, not least public attitudes towards offenders and the development of alternative sentences.

Moving on to Kingdom's second model, the claim is that the law *per se* is sexist, and that the elimination of sexist bias from law involves a complex process of law reform (1981:   103).   This is something which Mawby (1977) explores in his comment on sexism and the law and both Temin (1973) and Armstrong (1977), for example, in the United States, adopt this approach in relation to the discriminatory sentencing of women. Carolyn Temin summarizes her argument on this issue in an essay entitled 'The Case for ERA [Equal Rights Amendment] in a Nutshell' (1973).   Gail Armstrong reiterates the importance of the Equal Rights Amendment and suggests that its passage would render the law in its present state as unjust and unconstitutional (1977: 120).

The main problem with this model, of course, is that the promotion or existence of formal equality does not guarantee lack of discrimination in practice.[27]   Moreover, it fails to recognize the complexities of social relations outside the legal sphere.   This may be illustrated by those cases which are perhaps dealt with under Pearson's (1976) 'social casualty' model, whereby magistrates attempt to be 'sensitive' to women's difficulties and adopt a 'soft' approach. As Pearson relates, 'legal rights have little meaning when avoidance of punishment involves proving social disadvantage, or lack of other rights' (1976: 270).

There is a further problem in identifying, or wishing to identify the level or standard of equality to be sought.   Cousins (1980) makes this point when he argues that (feminist) accounts of the discriminatory treatment of women in the criminal justice system set up male criminality as the norm. He criticizes the fact that in feminist analyses of patriarchy and the law, for instance, male criminality is assumed to be adequately represented in court (1980: 114).

Thus the implication of this second model which assumes sex bias in the law itself is perhaps to treat women like men or vice versa, girls like boys or vice versa.   Surprisingly, some protagonists in the fight for the Equal Rights Amendment in the United States, have indicated that a 'levelling down' would be acceptable in relation to conditions in prison, meaning that women should lose the favourable treatment and conditions which they apparently receive (Price, 1977).[28]

In her third model, which suggests that sexist bias might be an effect of the law, Kingdom is concerned with the wider influence of the law. She views the law as potentially neutral, but inextricably bound up in the economy, politics and ideology (1981: 106).   There are two alternatives posed in this model; on the one hand, that the law may be considered to be always and necessarily effective in the wider sphere of activity, and on the other, that the law may sometimes be, though not necessarily, effectively 'sex biased'. The first alternative is similar to the first model which I outlined regarding sexist bias as intervention in law, and is equally reductionist. The second alternative, however, emphasises the need for focused analyses of prevailing relations between legal and social practices.[29]

It is clear that these models have only heuristic import. The message contained in these models, however, that the law is not simply an instrument of women's oppression[30] reiterates the main theme in this book that any distortion in our knowledge about female offenders and any discriminatory treatment of women and girls is not necessarily due to a set of clearly defined, discrete 'interests' or 'biases'.

Clearly any ideas of an unambiguous relationship between women and the law is inappropriate. Feminist critiques which tend to rely on this idea frequently fail to account for the historical and material determinations of the phenomena they seek to explain. Moreover, such critiques, which promote the concept of sexism in the law, fail to take into account inconsistencies and illogicalities in the 'march for male supremacy' which is often seen to be the motivational force underlying its operation.

In the concluding section of this chapter I draw together some of my criticisms of the views of female offenders and their treatment in the criminal justice system and allied agencies, with some comments on new approaches to understanding sexism.

Conclusion

Students of women and crime inherit from early commentators a legacy of images of female offenders which has generally remained unexplicated. There has been little by way of explicit theoretical or conceptual breakthrough for the interpretation of data. Yet it is important to ask questions of the 'accumulated wisdom' about female offenders, since this influences both our current understanding and practice in relation to female offenders. We need to evaluate that 'wisdom' and not simply accept it. For example, early commentators see distinct differences between female and male offenders. We may argue that the perception of differences may reflect research methodologies which have exaggerated differences between the sexes rather than actual differences. Where 'essential truths' about females have been proffered, we should relate those truths to the social, political and cultural contexts in which they were formed. Where claims were made about distinctive behavioural characteristics of female offenders we should refer to a focused surveillance and 'policing' of females' activities, leading to an overemphasis on females' sexual and emotional proclivities in analyses of their offending behaviour.

In sum, 'accumulated wisdom' is frequently ambiguous, often flawed, and in many cases, simply untenable.

Additional flaws in the feminists' castigation of criminal theories and criminal justice system practices as 'sexist' may be summarized as follows. First, the neglect of women in criminological theories cannot be viewed as a systematic neglect, since the whole history of criminology reveals an erratic development. Women are not the only 'blind spot' in criminology. Secondly, the frequent concentration on sexism in criminological theory inherently assumes that 'emptied of sexism' those theories remain valid. This view seems to be, as Greenwood writes, that 'if we could rid Lombroso of his conceptions of the sedentary female, if one could eliminate Pollack's conception of women as consistently evil, cunning and deceitful, then the theories would at least be worthy of examination' (1981: 77). Thirdly, critics assume 'sexism' in only those theories explicitly relating to females. This is an untenable assumption. Theories applied to men are also riddled with stereotypical images of what constitutes manhood, the inherent nature of men, with their needs and desires are and so on. Fourthly, and more specifically in relation to the criminal justice system and allied agencies, enough is known about practices to suggest that not all females are equally subject to scrutiny; race (Datesmann and Scarpitti, 1980a), home circumstances (Datesmann and Scarpitti, (1980b), type of offence (Hindelang, 1979; Nagel, Cardascia and Ross, 1980) and perhaps personal characteristics of appearance and demeanour (De Fleur, 1975) are all relevant here in that such factors clearly mediate any discriminatory treatment of women and girls.

My own analysis suggests that there were numerous organizational influences relating to the exigencies of practice which contributed to the development of specific images of the females practitioners were dealing with. Whereas some writers have inferred that criminal justice agencies impose and promote fixed and pervasive sexist assumptions about females as an expression of unalloyed sexism, I found them sustaining assumptions for different reasons. Moreover, where there have been claims that ideas about 'difficult' or 'appropriate' behaviour would be fuelled by 'sexist beliefs' alone, I found that ideas were affected by the meaning of 'trouble' for the agency, by the micro-politics of institutions, so to speak. Thus 'sexist' beliefs, where they existed, were mediated by administrative and organizational factors.[31]

With these further difficulties regarding idea of sexism exposed, there was reason to re-examine the claims about sexism on a theoretical level. Here, too, considerable problems arose in attempts to follow through arguments that it is possible to identify, without equivocation, the 'culprits' responsible for the treatment of women and for the theoretical conceptions of them. In the radical feminists' analyses men are labelled as key instigators of sexism, though an equally strident account in feminist writings is that promoters of the capitalist mode of production contrive to exploit women to their advantage. Close examination of the claims at this theoretical level disclose several inconsistencies and illogicalities within arguments. Neither men nor the capitalist mode of production can be singled out as chief conspirators in a plot against women. However ideas about women have been shaped, it is clear that there is no one unified motivational force underlying the shaping.[32]

But my attempts to grapple with the claims of feminists leads to evaluation of a different kind too. Not only can flaws in arguments be exposed, but we can criticize the abstract nature of the arguments. We can, perhaps, argue that all theories are, by nature, abstract, but this would be to gloss over an important distinction which can be made. This distinction is between 'grand' theories or 'integrated conceptual structures' which attempt to accommodate all theories, and theories which have more specific application. This latter group of theories are what Merton has referred to as 'theories of the middle range' (1957: 9). The main aim of these theories is to focus on a specific problem to be studied on the basis of a limited range of data. The intention of the feminists in their theorizing is to do just this and to focus on specific problems. Rather than their theories being 'stepping stones' into the middle distance, however, in effect they may be likened to 'grand theories' since they pitch analysis in the far distance.

This criticism applies even when social, political and economic contexts, patriarchal relationships or simply men, are identified as 'the oppressor', as the source of sexism. Many theories of sexism in both general commentaries on the position of women in society and in descriptions of the criminal justice system contain only generalizations; they have lost the particularity of the reality which feminists presuppose the theories to represent. They are divorced from the exigencies and intricacies of everyday life. Moreover, theories of this genre presuppose a particular kind of relationship between the individual and society: the individual is frequently cast in the role of the passive recipient, and experience is not fully taken into account. We are left with 'tidy' theories floating free from the reality of an 'untidy' world.

A useful analogy here refers to the difference between a televised performance of a play and a live theatre performance. In the one we observe the actions and words of actors who necessarily stylize their performance to achieve maximum impact through a screen; our eyes focus on their words and movements. In the other, we are there. This too is a representation of reality, but we are closer to it, we observe the actors and the setting, we hear the squeaks on the floorboards, the offstage whispers, we see the cracked paint on the scenery and the imperfect costumes. As they are presented to us, we view theories about 'sexism' through a screen; the more we are able to look at those theories 'on stage', or in practice, the more we see the imperfections. But those imperfections, it may be argued, are too important a part of reality to be glossed over.

The more refined 'structural' arguments to which I made brief reference earlier in this chapter are also of an abstract nature. But at least these theories bravely and importantly shift the analysis to 'how' questions in relation to the perpetuation of women's oppression and sexism. With such questions in mind we might expect them to be accessible to analysis which is grounded in practice. Without doubt, such theories improve upon the conspiratorial notions of some feminist writers, but they still demand of us the 'intellectual acrobatics' involved when considering the causes of oppression. The problem is that we are bereft of examples to test out the notions. Such theories somehow divine the social totality, and their models have an oracular quality; it is as if writers in this group assume that they can grasp reality without the mediating and distorting effects of consciousness. Explorations of landscapes in the realms of cultural ideology (Barrett, 1980) almost become field guides to false consciousness, there is no consideration of conflicting evidence, there are no obdurate obstacles which defy the exploration in thought. Thus there is a curious paradox, in that the movement away from conspiratorial strands of thought leads us not to a more accessible analysis of reality, but to a world in which ideology is the controlling puppeteer.[33]

To suggest that feminist writers have not begun to explore the problem with the discursive and distant theories referred to above would be unfair. Indeed, one example is that provided by Stanley and Wise (1983). They are aware that it is insufficient to talk blithely of 'capitalism' or 'men' as the cause of women's oppression, but more importantly criticize the macro-level approach to analysis of reality. They exhort us to consider the personal experiences of women as the basis for understanding how and where oppression (or sexism) occurs and are vehemently critical of research and analyses which appear to be 'all-encompassing' and to have all the answers. Such research, they write, is 'dishonest' in the sense that it pretends; it is based upon an ideology which legitimates the pretence of being representative (1983:169). But the movement to return to 'personal experience', whilst overcoming the false impressions which current analyses at the level of structure and ideology create, like many micro-sociologies before, becomes vulnerable to criticism that it is too 'inward-looking', that it lacks 'vision', and that it is simply impossible to generalize from the experiences of single or small groups of people, or from how oppression occurs in one small area of life. Indeed, some critics might easily 'write off' the experiences of oppression as the product of emotions or false perceptions. However, I would not go this far in assuming that such phenomena disqualify us or prevent us from 'knowing what we know'. To make such an assumption would lead us into the trap of believing that all representations of everyday life can be seen as 'false consciousness'. Thus, whilst the macro-level claims of feminists writers (whether relating to 'conspiracy' or 'structure') lack depth and remain at the level of rhetoric because we cannot see how sexism 'works', focus on micro-level activities lacks breadth. It is unacceptable to categorize the actions or intentions, thoughts or whatever, without referring to a broad social context, outside of which they have no real meaning.

It is almost a truism to say that in sociological literature relationships between different levels of analysis, between theory and practice, 'structure' – or, as Giddens (1979) terms it, 'agency' – and 'action' have largely been ignored. Those schools of thought which have been preoccupied with action have paid little attention to, or have found no way of dealing with, conceptions of structural exploration or social causation. Similarly, as I have indicated in previous arguments, large-scale theoretical explorations have tended to neglect the actions of individual actors, influences upon those actors and even the actors' own interpretations for those actions.[34] It is this very relationship between 'action' and 'structure', between micro and macro levels of analysis, which criminological researchers intent on explicating the notions of sexism or oppression need to address.

There is a remedial option available for researchers to attempt to reduce the gap between different levels of analysis. Writers outside the sphere of feminist theory have been more successful in approaching the issue of the dichotomy between levels of analysis and it is possible that future feminist researchers could learn from their methodologies. Willis (1977) in the mainstream of sociology succeeds in demonstrating the interface of cultural ideology. He is able to show, through a clear depiction and explication of the lives of working-class lads, how ideologies are mediated and transformed in practice. He shows both the structural and ideological influences and responses, interpretations and experiences of the lads involved, and thus illustrates the central role of cultural forms of ideology in shaping and reproducing practice and experience.

Of the feminist writers who have made advances in this area, Barrett (1980) recognizes that 'how' questions are as important as 'why' questions in seeking to explain the shaping of knowledge about females, but she fails to illustrate this. She leaves us stranded on an ideological island, albeit one which has a sign pointing across the water to the mainland.[35] Where Willis (1977) particularly succeeds is in taking us across the water and showing us that it is possible to draw links between the two land masses. He shows us that it is possible to draw correspondences between levels of action without insisting that everything is lived out at the level of practical consciousness and without imputing to the individual actors any particular critique or analytic motive. Importantly though, more recent feminist writing demonstrates these kinds of correspondences. Smart (1984) achieves this in her analysis of law, marriage and the reproduction of patriachal relations,[36] and both Mary Eaton (1986) and writers in the Pat Carlen and Anne Worrall (1987) collection demonstrate this in their work on 'gender and justice'.[37]

There have been important developments in feminist thinking about female offenders in recent years. Among the most notable achievements are the development of a critique of 'accumulated wisdom' about female offenders, and the attempt to answer broad questions as to why knowledge about them is shaped in the way it is. On a general level, without specific reference to female offenders, there has also been acknowledgement that there is a need to concentrate on questions relating to ways in which knowledge about females is sustained and mediated. The important shifts which have taken place to encourage us to think about structural constraints and the broad contexts of ideas, however, have not yet achieved impact within criminology. In the attempts to theorize about sexism and the shaping of knowledge, chief 'culprits' are still identified with the erroneous implication that their motives underly all action . There is no room for other motives or other influences in this analysis. In the other attempt which I have briefly referred to (the structural arguments) we are all encouraged to think about oppression or sexism at the level of a discursive cultural ideology, at the level of 'structure', but we are given no demonstration of what oppression means subjectively or of how it is continually shaped in practice. My own findings and my analysis of sexism in practice add impetus to the need for criminological writers to move on from sweeping generalizations about the treatment of female offenders and to adopt a more appreciative stance in their analysis, but a stance which can be built upon and placed in a broader theoretical context. Writers in this sphere would do well to learn from feminists looking at other areas of social practice and from sociologists and educationalists who have made important advances in promoting analyses in which macro- and micro-worlds are drawn together. Unless this can be achieved, there is a danger of perpetuating myopic claims and approaches which do research in criminology a disservice.

Notes

1. See, for instance, Sachs and Wilson (1978), Ellis (1980), Casburn (1979 and LITA (1983).
2. This distinction is proposed solely for heuristic purposes. I am aware that there are many ways in which the writers might be classified. Within the field of 'structuralism' itself there are clear differences between writers, but this is a complicated area and not one which needs to be explored for the purposes of my

argument. Giddens (1979) provides an illuminating guide for some of the complex issues in this area. Ann Oakley presents a useful categorisation of feminist positions in *Subject Woman* (1981: 336–7).

3. Rubin (1975), Atkinson (1979), Barrett (1980) and Coward (1983) all explore the origins of the concept of patriarchy.

4. One now has to acknowledge that some of Mead's anthropological observations and findings may be dubious. Freeman (1983) argues that some of her fieldwork suffered from 'response bias' because the women she interviewed were a selected few and they may have given her misleading replies to questions.

5. Though the usual assumption is that *within* each class, women are the 'less advantaged' or more 'disadvantaged' group.

6. As well as Evangelical Christianity and the Movement for Moral Reform. See Banks (1981) on the origins of the British feminist movement.

7. See McDonough and Harrison (1978: 26) where they describe the relations of human production as 'the privileged site for all patriarchal relations'.

8. For a more complete discussion, see Kuhn and Wolpe (1978); Barrett (1980), and Sargent (1981).

9. Like Mary McIntosh, I discovered that the statement does not appear in the letter which is usually given as a reference for it, at least not in the English translation (letter to Kugelman, 11 July 1868, Selected Correspondence). McIntosh (1982) resolved the problem by referring to the statement as 'Althusser's dictum' since it was he who first introduced the statement to British readers.

10. Some of the problems with the concept of reproduction have been tackled by Edholm, Harris and Young (1977) in their attempt to distinguish between different uses of the term. Whereas I use the term 'social reproduction' to refer to the reproduction of social systems *and* the reproduction of labour power, they introduce further distinctions regarding the use of the term. In their analysis 'social reproduction' is taken to mean 'reproduction of the conditions of social production in their totality', that is, the reproduction of 'structures'. They refer to the 'reproduction of labour power' as just that. Although their analytical distinctions between social reproduction, reproduction of the labour force and human or biological reproduction are useful in making matters clear, it is questionable that such distinctions avoid the problems of functionalism. Also the relationship between the three forms of reproduction and production is not clarified.

11. See, for instance, Farmer (1979), cf Morgan (1975).

12. This argument is also reflected in McIntosh's later analysis of the relationship between the state and the capitalist mode of production, and the part which the state plays in the production and reproduction of the conditions of production. In arguing the case for the oppression of women via the state she focuses attention on the maintenance of the family household (1978: 255).

13. See Bland *et al.*(1978), for a discussion of attempts to develop theories about women's position under capitalist social relations.

14. See Kuhn (1978), and McDonough and Harrison)1978). Paul Corrigan addresses the assumption that everything is serving the needs of capital quite wittily. He argues that if we accept that welfare is controlled by capital (and this may really act against the welfare of working people), then there should be common interest in *not* fighting against 'welfare cuts'. Indeed, any such cuts might represent a cut in the power of the ruling class over the working class (1978: 88).

15. Where male dominance is seen as homogeneous, universal and transhistorical.

See Shulamith Firestone (1979) on this point. She sees nature as part of the great conspiracy against women.

16. One might also consider the influence of religious doctrine here. Biblical precept is seldom taken seriously by those who fail to see its significance other than in terms of of its fulfilling a social function. To question the authenticity of an epistemological position, though, does not mean that ideas propagated within the position have been limited in their effect. Ideas about women in the Bible have been clear and commanding. This is not to assume a widespread and wholesale adoption of these ideas; rather, to note that some of the ideas, about the inferiority of women, their passive nature, their 'deceit' and the images of them as both 'virgin and whore' have been sustained within popular ideologies. See, for example, the commentaries of Agonito (1977) and Figes (1978) on the influence of biblical precept.

17. See Klein and Kress (1976), Rafter and Natalizia (1981), Sachs and Wilson (1978) and Figes (1977).

18. Again, see Giddens (1979) for a clear exposition of the meaning of structure and the different interpretations placed upon it.

19. This perspective is sometimes referred to as 'psychological materialism'. See Burniston et al., (1978) and Chodorow (1978), for example.

20. See Adams (1979), MacIntyre (1976), McRobbie (1978), and Winship (1978).

21. See, for example Klein and Kress (1976), Datesman and Scarpitti (eds.) (1980).

22. The models, she acknowledges, are simply heuristic devices useful to divide the literature. Indeed, elements of all three models may be found in one work.

23. That is a position adopted by Sachs and Wilson (1978) and Kuhn (1978). For instance, Kuhn argues that patriarchy is a structure which intervenes in social relations and in institutions (including legal institutions) in ways which are determined by the prevailing mode of production.

24. See Greenwood (1981) and Jeanne Gregory (1987) on sex, race and the law.

25. This finding is given some support by the work of Casburn (1979) on the practices of a juvenile court in England.

26. Carol Smart provides further illustrations of anomalies in the law as a main instrument of women's oppression in her essays on the relationship between law and sexuality (1981 and 1983).

27. We need look no further than the British Equal Pay Act of 1970 for evidence of this (see CIS Report 1975 and Gregory 1987).

28. Johnson (1977) has discussed a similar question in relation to the treatment of boys and girls. She raises the issue of whether law reform should mean that boys are specifically included in any references to status offences, for example, or whether girls should be judged only on their criminal behaviour. The issue is more complicated than it seems to be since there are differing views as to whether boys or girls are treated more leniently.

29. Carol Smart (1977) argues that it is futile to think of promoting attempts to redress the balance in favour of women, in the context of their traditional legal status as comparable to 'children and animals' in any way which does not involve both focus on law *and* social practices. Her position is that anti-discrimination legislation must be combined with attempts to make existing discrimination obvious and visible in order to question women's traditional roles.

30. Cousins too, rejects any analysis based on a 'singular, interior and essential relation between the law and women as such' (1980: 119) and confirms the suggestion that it is often difficult to identify specific 'interests' underlying the

criminal law since the actors in the legal scenario change so frequently. Both men and women are sometimes defendants, sometimes plaintiffs; and sometimes actors merely represent corporate bodies in legal activities, for instance. Clearly, the operation of the law cannot be made reducible to men or women and their attitudes.

31. There is a useful parallel to this situation in various educationalists' analyses of schools and teaching whereby management takes over from pedagogic principles and survival on a daily basis becomes the prime concern for teachers. See, for example, Sharp and Green (1975)

32. The model of linear causation implicit in some feminist writing has been severely criticized by Joan Roberts (1976). She singles out those feminists who search for the singular moment when males are alleged to have asserted their supremacy as deserving of criticism. The assumption that all men or capitalism are sole causes of women's oppression or sexism is clearly based on an erroneous view of social reality. Further, suggestion that it may be possible to discover one single cause for the inequality of women in all times and all places led Coward (1983) in an important contribution to the debate on patriarchy to claim that all feminist theory has now reached an impasse. The diverse feminist arguments have resulted in a polarization of theories into an essentialist versus culturalist debate.

33. Rock (1979) has made similar criticisms with regard to the development of the new or radical criminology which he argues is organized around a massive tautology. He argues that analysis in radical criminology is 'unregulated by any canon but that furnished by the new consciousness, ideology gives objective reality and objective-reality gives ideology' (1979: 79).

34. This dichotomy is well exemplified within criminological debate by the problems with both symbolic interactionism and the theories of the new criminologists (Rock, 1979). Much the same is the case between social psychology and 'micro-sociology', dealing with small scale interpersonal relations and the more embracing 'macro-sociological' task which American sociological functionalism addresses (Merton, 1957).

35. It would be unfair to be too critical of Barrett (1980) since her chosen task was to explore problems in the Marxist-feminist analysis of the oppression of women. My comments reflect a frustration since she strongly hints that it is ideology and the culture of gender, the construction and importance of gender differences, which we need to explore at different levels of analysis to create a coherent picture of oppression, but she provides no further comment on how this approach might be addressed by researchers.

36. Writers in the field of education, too, have explored and illustrated how ideologies are mediated and transformed in practice. Sharp and Green (1975) have, with some effect, shown how wide, discursive ideologies penetrate the education system. Indeed, the substantive study in which they are interested concerns the relationship between the construction of pupil identities and the practice of the teacher within the context of social structure in the classroom, school and wider society.

37. See also the critical contribution of Frances Heidensohn (1985) in *Women and Crime* where she shifts the debate from women and crime to women and social control.

Appendix A: Pilot work

Prior to carrying out fieldwork within the organizations and agencies described in the book, I investigated the attitudes and perceptions of both field social workers and probation officers regarding their female clients.

The aim of this pilot work was, firstly, to establish whether or not it would be possible and fruitful to complete an analysis of reports and case work files only, along the lines of Hardiker's (1975) research and in accordance with the traditional designs of content analysis (see Mayntz *et al.* (1969), for example). Secondly, it was to enable me to establish an appropriate interview schedule and to help me to decide whether or not a fixed interview schedule or an open-ended schedule would be appropriate to the task. Thirdly, the aim in the preliminary work was to see how easy (or otherwise) it would be to identify any themes which guided and preoccupied these groups of practitioners in their dealings with women and girls.

To accomplish these aims I interviewed those social workers (male and female) in a London Borough who were currently supervising female offenders (either on a statutory or voluntary basis). Thus I interviewed thirteen social workers on two occasions about their young female clients. To supplement this material I studied the case files of each juvenile involved.

This approach quickly proved inadequate to the task. I could not gain any sense of why the practitioners thought as they did, how their views related to other pressures within the working context, or how the local resources available for female clients might influence their perceptions of clients' needs; case files were massive, chaotic and incomplete. As a second stage to the preliminary work I decided to interview and examine files of a group of practitioners who worked in the same setting. I realized that I would only be able to gain an understanding of practitioners' perceptions of their female clients if I could relate those perceptions to the practice setting. I anticipated that my discussions and interviews with ten probation officers who all worked in the same office, alongside the usual case file explorations, would provide me with sufficient information on how the organization or agency itself might contribute to the development of distinctive images and understandings of female clients. In the event this proved inadequate too, and I subsequently realized that my method and approach would have to be along the lines of the interactionists as I describe in the methodology.

In addition to this 'methodological enlightenment' the pilot work proved important in two main ways. First, it sensitized me to various themes which occurred and reoccurred in the practitioners' images of their female clients (such as deviousness, immaturity, sexual precocity and promiscuity, irrationality, mental and emotional instability, greater emotional capacity than males, loneliness and manipulativeness). Secondly, since in the second agency practitioners were dealing with female clients of all ages (over fourteen) and I had not revealed any preference as to which females I was interested in, it became clear that these themes were not only consistent in interviews, informal discussions and in case files, but the themes cut across age boundaries too. It was not the case, for instance, that younger clients were considered sexually precocious and promiscuous and middle-aged shoplifters psychologically unstable because of the menopause (as might be expected, see Gibbens (1971) and Gibbens and Prince (1962)). Each client was viewed and defined in a mixture of terms. The implication of this is that practitioners do not conceive of female offending as a distinctive phase in females' lives; offending behaviour is not dismissed as 'something she'll grow out of ' or described in terms of 'it's her age' as might be the case with boys.[1] This finding confirmed the assertions of Hudson (1981) that theories referring to female delinquency lack an age perspective.

Note
1. See West (1967), West and Farrington (1977), and Wadsworth (1979), who argue from a theoretical perspective that male delinquency may frequently be viewed as part of adolescence. See also the similar arguments of sub-cultural theorists (for example, Downes (1966), and Wolfgang, Savitz and Johnston (1970)).

Appendix B: A note on sections of the Acts referred to in the text regarding children and young persons

Children and Young Persons Act, 1969
Care proceedings by local authority, police or NSPCC
Care Orders

s. 1(2)(a)	Health and development
s. 1(2)(b)	Already applies to another person in the household
s. 1(2)(bb)	Person in household convicted of offence
s. 1(2)(c)	Exposed to moral danger
s. 1(2)(d)	Beyond control of parents
s. 1(2)(e)	Not receiving full-time education
s. 1(2)(f)	Guilty of an offence, excluding homicide

Other Care Orders

s. 7(7)	Committed serious offence – in need of care and control.

Child Care Act, 1980

s. 2	Voluntary Care (formerly Children Act 1948, s.1). Parents retain rights.
s. 3	Parental Rights Resolution (formerly Children Act 1948, s.2) – already in voluntary care. Local authority assumes full parental rights.
s. 10	Provisions as to children subject to care orders, etc. Section 10 sets out the powers and duties of local authorities to receive children into care, restrict liberty, and other matters.

Place of Safety Order
The purpose of obtaining a Place of Safety Order is to gain legal authority to detain a child or young person for a period of up to 28 days where there is reason to believe that s/he is in need of care. The taking of a Place of Safety Order may, at a later stage, lead to care proceedings at a juvenile court.

'Place of Safety' means a community home provided by a local authority or a controlled community home, any police station or any hospital, surgery or other suitable place, the occupier of which is willing

orarily to receive a child or young person, (i.e., a neighbour, foster
t, or child minder).

l Authority
egal authority for the removal of a child to a Place of Safety resides
following statute law.

Jren and Young Persons Act, 1969

ocial workers and NSPCC
te under this section which
authority for *up to* 28
removal to a Place of
y.

Section 28(1) states:
'If, upon an application to a justice by any person for
authority to detain a child or young person and take
him to a place of safety, the justice is satisfied that the
applicant has reasonable cause to believe that –

(a) any of the conditions set out in Section 1(2)(a) to
(e) of this Act is satisfied in respect of the child or
young person; or
(b) an appropriate court would find the condition set
out in Section 1(2)(b) of this Act satisfied in respect of
him; or
(c) the child or young person is about to leave the
United Kingdom in contravention of Section 25 of the
Act of 1933 (which regulates the sending abroad of
juvenile entertainers),

the justice may grant the application; and the child or
young person in respect of whom an authorisation is
issued under this sub-section may be detained in a
place of safety by virtue of the authorisation for
twenty-eight days beginning with the date of authorisation, or for such shorter period beginning with that
date, as may be specified in the authorisation.'

Section 28(2) states:
'Any constable may detain a child or young person as
respects whom the constable has reasonable cause to
believe that any of the conditions set out in Section
1(2)(a) to (d) of this Act is satisfied or that an appropriate court would find the condition set out in Section
1(2)(b) of this Act satisfied, or that an offence is being
committed under Section 10(1) of the Act of 1933
(which penalises a vagrant who takes a juvenile from
place to place).'

police operate under this
on on the advice of an in-
tor or police officer in
ge of the police station. It
s authority for up to 8 days
oval to a place of safety.

Section 1(2) states:
'If the court before which a child or young per:
brought under this section is of the opinion that a
the following conditions is satisfied with resp(
him/her, that is to say:

(a) his/her proper development is being avoi(
    prevented or neglected or his/her health is
    avoidably impaired or neglected or s/he is bein
    treated; or

(b) it is probable that the condition set out in
    preceding paragraph will be satisfied in hi
    case, having regard to the fact that the cou
    another court has found that the condition is o
    satisfied in the case of another child or y
    person who is or was a member of the househc
    which he/she belongs; or

(c) s/her is exposed to moral danger; or

(d) s/her is beyond the control of his parent or g(
    ian; or

(e) s/he is of compulsory school age within the n
    ing of the Education Act 1944, and is not recei
    efficient full-time education suitable to his
    ability and aptitude; or

(f) s/he is guilty of an offence, excluding homic

and also that s/he is in need of care or control v
s/he is unlikely to receive unless the court mak(
order under this section in respect of him/her, t
subject to the following provisions of this se(
and Sections 2 and 3 of this Act, the court may
thinks it make such an order.'

A Place of Safety Order may also be granted under the Adoption Act 1958, ss. 37
43 the Children Act 1958, s. 7, the Children and Young Persons Act 1933, s. 40
Schedule of that Act.

Interim Care Order
If a local authority is not ready to proceed with the hearing of care proceedings by
time a place of safety order expires, the child is returned to his or her parents unless
agree voluntarily to leave him or her in care. It is possible, however, for the l
authority's lawyers to ask the juvenile court for an interim care order which tran:
parental rights to the local authority, but which lasts only 28 days on the first applica

Further applications may be made, and indeed, there is no limit to the number of interim orders that may be granted.

Appendix C: A further note on the methodology: being there

At the beginning of the field research I explained to the practitioners in their respective agencies that my interest was in learning how they conducted their work and in their thoughts about the girls who arrived in their particular agency. I used some of the historical images of female offenders as, for instance, 'being worse than male offenders' to focus their interest, and to stress that it was the ideas about the girls in which I was interested rather than their work as agents of juvenile justice and child care regimes. It seemed expedient to emphasize that I was not there as a judge of their behaviour. In turn, they knew that I had a certain amount of experience in dealing with young offenders and children in care, and this, I was subsequently told by the agencies, made them more receptive to the idea of my carrying out research there. Personal experience in child care, of course, meant that I had to give extra consideration to the problems surrounding the objectivity of the research. I had to examine my own beliefs and assumptions about children in care, for instance, and consider whether or not these were 'colouring' the questions which I intended to put to the practitioners. To have given personal information about myself as a researcher (although necessary to gain access in the first place), may have encouraged some of the practitioners to assume that I shared their 'understanding' of 'delinquent girls' thus excluding the possibility of them sharing their beliefs with me. I was anxious to circumvent 'tacit knowledge and understandings', however, and I 'played ignorant' to a point of irritation in some instances, with the insistence that they spell out their beliefs.

The practitioners stressed that it would be important for me to be honest with their clients in explaining my presence, but I assumed the role of a student or researcher who was simply interested in girls and in the operation of the agency when I talked with them, rather than give the more complicated and subtle reasons for my presence. I was assured that the 'clients' in the assessment centres would not exhibit much curiosity as they were quite used to having students around. In retrospect this should, perhaps, have alerted me to the fact that although staff and charges alike were accustomed to the presence of students, they were not accustomed to having researchers around – but social work students whose orientation was of a different nature to my own. Where social work students would be keen to assert their presence and skills (for the purposes of assessment, if nothing else) I was concerned to remain in the background of activity.

This initially created some discomfort – for both parties in the enterprise, I suspect – and I quickly learned that 'acceptance' would only come if I took a more active role in matters. It seemed more effective to turn this 'role assignment' to my advantage than to try to remove it from my research activities.

The police are well known for their conservatism regarding the acceptance of civilians within their agencies (Jones, 1980). But even in Agency Three, by adopting a non-judgemental attitude and showing a willingness both to assist where possible (for example, by carrying the police radio on occasions) and to take the same risks as the police officers themselves (for example, by entering the home of a suspect thought to be aggressive and by accompanying the police officers in premises which subsequently required inspection by environmental health officers) I achieved a level of acceptance.[1]

I used a range of data collection methods to accomplish the field-work tasks I had set myself, namely observation, taped interviews, individual and group discussions and the examination of case records. I kept notes of conversations with staff and of observations of staff-child interactions in each of the agencies (usually surreptitiously). Conversations were recorded verbatim as far as possible: in practice, this meant jotting down key phrases soon after they had been spoken and then later recalling the context of those phrases. Although this method of recording is liable to distortion due to failings of memory, I found no particular difficulty in recalling the details of conversations, having learned this skill whilst undergoing professional training.

Throughout the field-work I used a diary which I completed at the end of each day to provide a comprehensive account of all that I had witnessed during the day. To some extent, the process of writing the diary was cathartic and at times I felt it important to record my own expectations and frustrations in relation to the field-work since these undoubtedly influenced my perception of events. At the conclusion of the field-work the diary was shown to a research colleague and my perception, interpretation and understanding of events discussed at length.

All formal interviews were tape recorded. The lengthy transcripts from the interviews were examined in detail and a content analysis carried out. In this analysis I identified and charted the themes which appeared. Those themes which appeared most frequently and which were consistent with themes identified through other data collection methods were chosen for analysis and interpretation. This is not to suggest, however, that the least mentioned comments about girls were insignificant.

After the completion of pilot work (described in Appendix A) in which I focused on social workers' and then probation officers' perceptions of girls, I embarked on a study of Agency Two. This was a single-sex agency which I chose to visit because I had anticipated that study of an agency of this type would highlight key views and themes in relation to girls. I had also expected there to be marked differences in the attitudes towards girls between those who worked in single-sex and mixed agencies. In fact, subsequent field-work in Agencies One and Three did not reveal any distinctive differences.

Fieldwork

General questions
Background of social worker, probation officer, police officer, training, orientation?
Experience with or special training re: women and girls?
How long in present job?
Any special policies within office, etc. (no longer the case that women offenders have to be supervised by female probation officers (1972); what happens in practice?
Informal rules?
Any special facilities, e.g., women's group, girls' group, mother and baby group, support groups?
Practical supports more difficult to gain for women, e.g., accommodation? fostering?
Resources more scarce for women and girls?
What kinds of things taken into consideration when writing reports?
Social Inquiry Reports different for men and women, boys and girls?
General experiences males/females? Difficulties experienced with them?
Women more emotional? problems? adolescence, relationship problems greater for females? family problems greater? relationships more important to girls? to boys?
Contribution of physiological factors? periods, menopause, etc.?
Adolescence a more turbulent time for girls? psychological vulnerability?
Females more vulnerable to depression? Why?
Different needs re: affection? females naturally more affectionate?
Motivations underlying offending different source? different offences, e.g., shoplifting.
Characterize typical male offence/offender, female? Premeditation?
Which offence do you dislike most in a girl? which shocks you most in boys?
Why do you think boys TDA cars? girls not? girls/boys group offences, peer group pressure?
Unfeminine behaviour?
Dispositions? What would a girl have to do to gain recommendation for detention centre?

What alternative? Is a different response needed? Under what circumstances would you recommend a secure unit for a girl?
What does 'difficult to manage' mean? In moral danger?
Why are females perceived to be more vulnerable in this way?
How do boy/girl problems differ – anything distinctive about each?
Girls/boys easier to talk to? Is it the case in your experience that boys listen to reason and with girls that you have to *persuade* them? Girls manipulative? How?
Boys manipulative? In what ways?
Which do you enjoy working with most? advantages/disadvantages of working with boys and girls?
Females feel more guilty than boys when they have done wrong? Is this your experience? Is it the other way round in your experience? How do boys show feelings of remorse?
In popular conception females less criminal than males – views? Why do you think females are apparently so law-abiding?
Offending symptomatic of different things for males and females? If family problems why do males/females act out in different ways?
Components of femininity? Different management problems?
Different disturbance? Levels?

Case questions
Views on why and how the offender committed the offence? Ask social worker/probation officer, etc. to elaborate on the circumstances of the offence.
Characterization of client being referred to?
Aims and objectives in making particular recommendations? Timing of recommendations.
Question assessment, e.g.
   'personality disorder'
   'crazy in an indefinable way' (not amenable to psychiatric intervention)
   'beyond care and control'
   'manipulative'
   'difficult'
   'promiscuous'
(Having previously examined reports and comments which interviewee had made) How is —'s behaviour problematic?
Major concerns re: client/child?
Describe course of action to be taken? why?
Aims/objectives in supervision/probation order?
Main needs of girl at the time of her stay/dealings with the agency?
Status accorded to offenders' own understanding of the problem, expla-

nation for the offending?
Discrepancy between offender's account and that of practitioner.

Note

1. I mention these incidents as significant ones because the police officers revealed to me that they were surprised that I had not turned away. It transpired through discussion that civilians were 'okay' if they were willing to look at *all* the activities which the police find themselves engaged in. An incident which necessitated my standing as a witness regarding an accusation of corruption against a police officer in the JLO did much to boost my own standing with the police officers I was observing. I took it to mean 'acceptance' when the officers were open in expressing views about one another and about their senior officers, also when I was allowed to be party to certain 'irregularities' in their behaviour (for example, shopping when supposedly on duty, blackberrying when supposedly searching for absconders from a local community home).

References and select bibliography

Note

Where references are marked (BL) this means that material may be found in the British Library.

Abercrombie, N., Hill, S., and Turner, S. (1980) *The Dominant Ideology Thesi.*, London: George Allen and Unwin.
Ackland, J.W. (1982) *Girls in Care: A Case Study of Residential Treatment.* Aldershot: Gower.
Adams, P. (1979) 'A note on sexual division and sexual differences' *M/F.* no. 3, pp. 51–7.
Adamson, O., Brown, C., Harrison, J., and Price, J. (1976) 'Women's oppression under capitalism', *Revolutionary Communist,* no. 5, pp. 2–48.
Adler, F. (1975) *Sisters in Crime.* New York: McGraw Hill.
Adler, F. (1977) 'The interaction between women's emancipation and female criminality: a cross cultural perspective', *International Journal of Criminology and Penology,* vol. 5, pp. 101–12.
Agonito, R. (1977) *History of Ideas on Women.* New York: Paragon Books.
Althusser, L. (1972) 'Ideology and ideological state apparatuses', in B.R. Coser (ed.), *Education, Structure and Society.* Harmondsworth: Penguin.
Armstrong, G. (1977) 'Females under the law – protected but not unequal', *Crime and Delinquency,* vol. 14, no. 1, pp. 61–76.
Association of Headmasters, Headmistresses and Matrons of Approved Schools (Technical Sub-Committee) (1954) *Girls in Approved Schools,* Monograph No. 6 issued as a Supplement to the *Approved Schools Gazette,* no. 48 (April).
Atkinson, P. (1978) 'Fitness, feminism and schooling' in S. Delamont and L. Duffin (eds.), *The 19th Century Woman, Her Cultural and Physical World.* London: Croom Helm.
Atkinson, P. (1979) 'The problem with patriarchy', *Achilles Heel,* no. 2, pp. 18–22.
Austin, R.L. (1981) 'Liberation and female criminality in England and Wales', *British Journal of Criminology,* vol. 21, pp. 371–4.
Ball, J.C., and Logan, N. (1960) 'Early sexual behaviour of lower-class delinquent girls', *Journal of Criminal Law, Criminology and Police Science,* vol. 51, pp. 209–14.
Bambridge, F. (1979) 'Naughty little girls in intermediate treatment. Children at risk of being in trouble', Unpublished BA dissertation, University of Warwick.
Banks, J.A., and Banks, O. (1964) *Feminism and Family Planning in Victorian England.* Liverpool: Liverpool University Press.
Banks, O. (1981) *Faces of Feminism: A Study of Feminism as a Social Movement.* Oxford: Martin Robertson.
Barrett, M. (1980) *Women's Oppression Today.* London: Verso.
Becker, H.S. (1980) 'Notes on the concept of commitment', *American Journal of Sociology,* vol. 66, pp. 32–40.
Becker, H.S. (1963) *Outsiders.* New York: Free Press.
Becker, H.S., and Geer, B. (1960) 'Latent culture: a note on the theory of latent social roles', *Administrative Science Quarterly,* vol. 5, pp. 304–13.
Belson, W.A., and Hood, R. (1967) *The Research Potential of Case Records of*

171

Approved School Boys. London: Survey Research Centre.

Bines, H.C. (1978) An investigation of the ideas held by practitioners in regard to the assessment and subsequent treatment of juvenile delinquents. Unpublished MA dissertation, University of Sheffield.

Bittner, E. (1973) 'The concept of organisation', in G. Salaman and K.Thompson (eds.) *People and Organisations*. London: Longman.

Bland, L., Brunsdon, C., Hobson, D., and Winship. J. (1978) 'Women "inside and outside" the relations of production', in Women's Studies Group, Centre for Contemporary Cultural Studies, *Women Take Issue*. London: Hutchinson.

Blos, P. (1957) 'Preoedipal factors in the aetiology of female delinquency', *Psychoanalytic Studies of the Child*, vol. 12, pp. 229–49.

Blum, F.H. (1970) 'Getting individuals to give information to the outsider', in W.J. Filstead (ed.), *Qualitative Methodology*. Chicago: Markham.

Blumer, H. (1969) *Symbolic Interactionism*. Englewood Cliffs: Prentice Hall.

Bonger, W. (1916) *Criminality and Economic Conditions*. Boston: Little, Brown.

Bookbinder, G. (1982) 'The tender trap', *Community Care*, 30 September

Bottomley, A.K. (1979) *Criminology in Focus: Past Trends and Future Prospects*. Oxford: Martin Robertson.

Bottoms, A.E., and Pratt, J. (1985) 'Intermediate treatment for girls in England and Wales: a preliminary paper', conference paper, European University Institute, Florence.

Bouchier, D. (1978) *Idealism and Revolution. New Ideologies of Liberation in Britain and the United States*. London: Edward Arnold.

Bouchier, D. (1983) *The Feminist Challenge*. London: Macmillan.

Bowker, L.H. (ed.) (1978) *Women, Crime and the Criminal Justice System*. Lexington, Mass.: Lexington Books, D.C. Heath.

Box, S. (1981) *Deviance, Reality and Society*, 2nd edn, London: Holt, Rinehart and Winston.

Box, S., and Hale, C. (1983) 'Liberation and female criminality in England and Wales', *British Journal of Criminology*, vol. 23, pp. 35–49.

Bramham, P. (1980) *How Staff Rule: Structures of Authority in Two Community Schools*. Farnborough, Hants.: Saxon House.

Brittan, A., and Maynard, M. (1984) *Sexism, Racism and Oppression*. Oxford: Basil Blackwell.

Buckholdt, D., and Gubrium, J. (1979) *Caretakers: Treating Emotionally Disturbed Children*. Beverley Hills: Sage.

Bujra, J.A. (1978) 'Female solidarity and the sexual division of labour', in P. Caplan and J.M. Bujra (eds.), *Women United, Women Divided*. London: Tavistock.

Burniston, S., Mort, F., and Weedon, C. (1978) 'Psychoanalysis and the cultural acquisition of sexuality and subjectivity', in Women's Study Group, Centre for Contemporary Cultural Studies, *Women Take Issue*. London: Hutchinson.

Campbell, A. (1981) *Girl Delinquents*. Oxford: Basil Blackwell.

Carlebach, J. (1970) *Caring for Children in Trouble*. London: Routledge and Kegan Paul.

Carlen, P. (1987) 'Out of care, into custody: dimensions and deconstructions of the state's regulation of twenty-two working class women' in P. Carlen and A. Worrall (eds.) *Gender, Crime and Justice*. Milton Keynes: Open University Press.

Carlen, P., and Worrall, A. (1987) *Gender, Crime and Justice*, Milton Keynes: Open University Press.

Carpenter, M. (1853) *Juvenile Delinquents: Social Evils, Their Causes and Their Cure*. London: Cash.

Carpenter, M. (1863) 'On the treatment of female convicts', *Frasers Magazine*, vol. 67 no. 1, pp. 31–46.

Casburn, M. (1979) *Girls Will be Girls: Sexism and Juvenile Justice in a London Borough.* London: Women's Resource and Research Centre.

Catalino, A. (1972) 'Boys and girls in a co-educational training school are different aren't they?', *Canadian Journal of Criminology and Corrections*, vol. 14, no. 2, pp. 1–12.

Cawson, P. (1978) Community homes: a study of residential staff. DHSS Research Report, No. 2. London. HMSO.

Cawson, P. (1987) 'The sexist social worker? some gender issues in social work practice with adolescent girls', *Practice*, no. 1, pp. 39–52.

Central Council for Education and Training in Social Work (1974) 'Residential work is part of social work', Paper 3.

Chesney-Lind, M. (1973) 'Judicial enforcement of the female sex role: the family court and the female delinquent', *Issues in Criminology*, vol. 8, pp. 51–69.

Chesney-Lind, M. (1977) 'Judicial paternalism and the female status offender: training women to know their place, *Crime and Delinquency*, vol. 23, pp. 121–30.

Chesney-Lind, M. (1978) 'Chivalry re-examined: women and the criminal justice system', in L.H. Bowker (ed.), *Women, Crime and the Criminal Justice System.* Lexington, Mass.: Lexington Books.

Chetwynd, J. (1975) 'The effects of sex bias in psychological research', in J. Chetwynd (ed.), *The Role of Psychology in the Propagation of Female Stereotypes*, Proceedings of the British Psychological Symposium, pp. 3–5.

Chetwynd, J., and Hartnett, O. (1978) *The Sex Role System.* London: Routledge and Kegan Paul.

Chevalier, L. (1973) *Labouring Classes and Dangerous Classes*, uns. F. Jellinke. London: Routledge and Kegal Paul.

Children's Legal Centre (1983) 'Up to 36 hours in "solitary cell" ', *Childright*, no. 1 (October), p. 3.

Chodorow, N. (1978) *The Reproduction of Mothering: Psychoanalysis and the Sociology of Gender,* Berkeley: University of California Press.

Cicourel, A. (1964) *Method and Measurement in Sociology.* New York: Free Press.

Cicourel, A. (1976) *The Social Organization of Juvenile Justice.* London: Heinemann. (First published in USA, 1968.)

Cicourel, A., and Kitsuse, J. (1968) 'The social organization of the high school and deviant adolescent careers' in E. Rubington and M. Weinberg (eds.), *Deviance: The Interactionist Perspective.* New York: Wiley.

Clark, A. (1982) *Working Life of Women in the Seventeenth Century.* London: Routledge and Kegan Paul. (First published George Routledge, 1919.)

Clark, E.H. (1874) *Sex in Education: or a Fair Chance for Girls.* Boston: James R. Osgood.

Cohen, A.K. (1955) *Delinquent Boys: The Culture of the Gang.* Glencoe: Free Press.

Cohen, S., and Young, J. (eds.) (1973) *The Manufacture of News: Social Problems, Deviance and the Mass Media.* London: Constable.

Cohn, Y. (1970) 'Criteria for the probation officer's recommendation to the Juvenile Court Judge', in P.G. Garabedian and D.C. Gibbons (eds.), *Becoming Delinquent.* Chicago: Aldine.

Cooper, D. (1972) *The Death of the Family.* Harmondsworth: Penguin.

Corrigan, P., and Leonard, P. (1978) *Social Work Practice Under Capitalism: A Marxist Approach.* London: Macmillan.

Cotgrove, S. (1972) *The Science of Society.* London: George Allen and Unwin. (First published 1967.)

Counter Information Services (CIS) (1976) 'Crisis: women under attack', *Anti Report*, no. 15, London: CIS.

Cousins, M. (1980) 'Men's rea: a note on sexual difference, criminology and the law' in P. Carlen and M. Collinson (eds.), *Radical Issues in Criminology*. Oxford: Martin Robertson.

Coward, R. (1983) *Patriarchal Precedents: Sexuality and Social Relations*. London: Routledge and Kegan Paul.

Coward, R., and Ellis, J. (1977) *Language and Materialism*. London: Routledge and Kegan Paul.

Cowie, C., and Lees, S. (1981) 'Slags or drags', *Feminist Review*, no. 9 (October).

Cowie, J., Cowie, V., and Slater, E. (1968) *Delinquency in Girls*. London: Heinemann.

Crook, J.H. (1970) 'Introduction – social behaviour and ethology', in J.H. Crook (ed.), *Social Behaviour in Birds and Mammals*. London: Academic Press.

Dalla Costa, M., and James, S. (1972) *The Power of Women and the Subversion of the Community*. Bristol: Falling Wall Press.

Daly, M. (1979) *Gyn/Ecology: The Metaethics of Radical Feminism*. London: Women's Press.

Datesman, S., and Scarpitti, F. (eds.) (1980) *Women, Crime and Justice*. New York: Oxford University Press.

Datesman, S., and Scarpitti, F. (1980a) 'Unequal protection for males and females in the juvenile court', in S. Datesman and F. Scarpitti (eds.), *Women, Crime and Justice*. New York: Oxford University Press.

Datesman, S., Scarpitti, F.R., and Stephenson, R.M. (1975) 'Female delinquency: an application of self and opportunity theories', *Journal of Research in Crime and Delinquency*, vol. 12 no. 2, pp. 107–23.

Davies, L. (1979) 'Deadlier than the male? Girls' conformity and deviance in school', in J Barton and R. Meighan (eds.), *Schools, Pupils and Deviance*. Driffield: Nafferton.

de Beauvoir, S. (1979) *The Second Sex*. Harmondsworth: Penguin. (*Le Deuxième Sexe* first published 1949, English trans. first published Johnathan Cape, 1953.)

Deem, R. (1978) *Women and Schooling*. London: Routledge and Kegan Paul.

De Fleur, L.B. (1975) 'Biasing influences on drug arrest records', *American Sociological Review*, vol. 40, pp. 88–103.

Delamont, S., and Duffin, L. (eds.) (1978) *The Nineteenth Century Woman, Her Cultural and Physical World*. London: Croom Helm.

Denzin, N.K. (1970) *The Research Act in Sociology*. London: Butterworths.

Deutsch, H. (1944) *The Psychology of Women. A Psychoanalytic Interpretation*. New York: Grune and Stratton.

Donahue, E., and Todd, B. (1981) 'Tyn-Y-Pwill', in R. Adams, S. Allard, J. Baldwin and J. Thomas, *A Measure of Diversion: Case Studies in Intermediate Treatment*. Leicester: National Youth Bureau.

Donzelot, J. (1980) *The Policing of Families*. London: Hutchinson. (Originally published as *La Police des familles*, Éditions de Minuit, 1977.)

Douglas, J.D., (1971) *Understanding Everyday Life*. London: Routledge and Kegan Paul.

Downes, D.M. (1966) *The Delinquent Solution: A Study in Subcultural Theory*. London: Routledge and Kegan Paul.

Downes, D.M., and Rock, P. (eds.) (1979) *Deviant Interpretations: Problems in Criminological Theory*. Oxford Martin Robertson.

Dyhouse, C. (1981) *Girls Growing Up in Late Victorian and Edwardian England*. London: Routledge and Kegan Paul.

Eaton, M. (1986) *Justice for Women? Family, Court and Social Control*. Milton Keynes: Open University Press.

Edholm, F., Harris, O., and Young, K. (1977) 'Conceptualising women', *Critiques of Anthropology*, vol. 3 no. 9/10, pp. 101–30.

Edwards, A. (1981) 'Sex and area variations in delinquency rates in an English city', *British Journal of Criminology*, vol. 13, pp. 121–37.

Edwards, S. (1981) *Female Sexuality and the Law*. Oxford: Martin Robertson.

Ehrenreich, B., and English, D. (1979) *For Her Own Good. 150 Years of the Experts' Advice to Women*. London: Pluto Press.

Eichler, M. (1980) *The Double Standard: A Feminist Critique of Feminist Social Science*. London: Croom Helm.

Ellis, H. (1984) *Man and Woman*. London: Contemporary Science Series.

Ellis, R. (1980) 'The legal wrongs of battered women', in Z. Bankowski and G. Mungham (eds.), *Essays in Law and Society*. London: Routledge and Kegan Paul.

Emerson, R.M. (1969) *Judging Delinquents*. Chicago: Aldine.

Engels, F. (1972) *The Origin of the Family: Private Property and the State*. London: Lawrence and Wishart. (First published 1884.)

Erikson, K.T. (1966) *Wayward Puritans: A Study in the Sociology of Deviance*. New York: John Wiley.

Etzioni, A. (1964) *Modern Organizations*. Englewood Cliffs: Prentice-Hall.

Evans, R.J. (1977) *The Feminist Women's Emancipation Movement in Europe, America and Australasia, 1840–1920*. London: Croom Helm.

Eysenck, H.J. (1964) *Crime and Personality*. London: Routledge and Kegan Paul.

Farmer, M. (1979) *The Family*. London: Longman.

Farrington, D.P. (1983) 'Implications of biological findings for criminological research', in S.A. Mednick and T.E. Moffit (eds.), *The Biosocial bases of Anti-social Behaviour*. Netherlands: Kluwer-Nijhoff. Paper given at NATO Symposium, Greece, September 1982.

Farrington, D.P. (1984) 'The juvenile justice system in England and Wales', in M. Klein (ed.), *Western Systems of Juvenile Justice*. Beverley Hills: Sage.

Festinger, L. (1957) *A Theory of Cognitive Dissonance*. Evanston, Ill.: Row, Peterson.

Figes, E. (1978) *Patriarchal Attitudes*. London: Virago. (First published Faber and Faber, 1970.)

Filstead, W.J. (ed.) (1970) *Qualitative Methodology*. Chicago: Markham.

Firestone, S. (1979) *The Dialectic of Sex*. London: Women's Press. (First published Johnathan Cape, 1971.)

Foucault, M. (1972) *The Archaeology of Knowledge*, trns. A. Sheridan. London: Tavistock.

Freeman, D. (1983) *Margaret Mead and Samoa: The Making and Unmaking of an Anthropological Myth*. Cambridge, Mass.: Harvard University Press.

Garfinkel, H. (1967) *Studies in Ethnomethodology*. Englewood Cliffs: Prentice-Hall.

Gelsthorpe, L.R. (1984) 'Exploring accounts of female offenders and their treatment in theory, policy and practice: misconception and exaggeration'. Ph.D. Thesis, University of Cambridge.

Gelsthorpe, L.R., and Morris, J. (1987) *Children in Residential Care*. Report II., UK Project Report, Institute of Criminology, University of Cambridge.

Gibbens, T.C.N. (1957) 'Juvenile prostitution', *British Journal of Delinquency*, vol.

8 no. 1, pp. 3–12.

Gibbens, T.C.N. (1959) 'Supervision and probation of adolescent girls', *British Journal of Delinquency,* vol. 10, pp. 84–103.

Gibbens, T.C.N. (1971) 'Female offenders', *British Journal of Hospital Medicine,* vol. 6 (September).

Gibbens, T.C.N., and Prince, J (1962) *Shoplifting.* London: Institute for the Study and Treatment of Delinquency publication.

Giddens, A. (1979) *Central Problems in Social Theory.* London: Macmillan.

Gill, O. (1974) *Whitegates: An Approved School in Transition.* Liverpool: University Press.

Giller, H.J., and Morris, A.M. (1981) *Care and Discretion.* London: Burnett.

Goffman, E. (1961) *Asylums: Essays on the Social Situation of Mental and Other Inmates.* New York: Anchor.

Goodman, N., and Price, J. (1967) *Studies of Female Offenders.* Home Office studies in the causes of delinquency and the treatment of offenders, no. 11. London: HMSO.

Goodman, N., Maloney, E., and Davies, J. (1976) 'Borstal girls eight years after release', in *Further Studies of Female Offenders.* Home Office Research Studies no. 33. London: HMSO.

Gordon, L. (1976) *Woman's Body, Woman's Right: A Social History of Birth Control in America.* New York: Grossman.

Gouldner, A.W. (1968) 'The sociologist as partisan: sociology and the welfare state', *American Sociologist,* (May) pp. 103–16.

Gouldner, A.W. (1971) *The Coming Crisis of Western Sociology.* London: Heinemann.

Greenwald, H. (1958) *The Call Girl.* London: Elek Books.

Greenwood, V. (1981) 'The myths of female crime', in A.M. Morris with L.R. Gelsthorpe (eds.), *Women and Crime.* Cropwood Conference Series, no. 13. University of Cambridge: Institute of Criminology.

Gregory, J. (1987) *Sex, Race and the Law.* London: Sage.

Griffin. C. (1985) *Typical Girls?.* London: Routledge and Kegan Paul.

Guerry, A.M. (1854) *Statistique moral de L'Angleterre comparée avec la statistique morale de la France,* Paris: J. B. Baillière et Fils.

Hall, S., Critcher, C., Jefferson, T., Clarke, J, and Roberts, B. (1978) *Policing the Crisis. Mugging, the State, and Law and Order.* London: Macmillan.

Haller, J.S., and Haller, R.M. (1974) *The Physician and Sexuality in Victorian America.* Champaign, Ill.: University of Illinois Press. See R.R. Coleman on 'the education of women', p. 39.

Haraway, D. (1978) 'Animal sociology and a natural economy of the body politic, Part 1: a political physiology of dominance', *Signs,* no. 4, pp. 21–36.

Hardiker, P. (1975) *Ideologies in Social Inquiry Reports.* Final progress report to the Social Science Research Council. Leicester University, School of Social Work.

Hardiker, P. and Webb, D. (1979) 'Explaining deviant behaviour: the social context of "action" and "interaction" accounts in the probation service', *Sociology,* vol. 13 no. 1, pp. 1–17.

Hargreaves, D.H. (1967) *Social Relations in a Secondary School.* London: Routledge and Kegan Paul.

Hargreaves, D.H. (1971) An interactionist approach to deviance in school. Paper presented to British Sociological Association Conference, London.

Hargreaves, D.H. (1972) *Interpersonal Relations and Education.* London: Routledge and Kegan Paul.

Hargreaves, D.H. (1978) 'What ever happened to symbolic interactionism?', in L. Barton and R. Meighan (eds.), *Sociological Interpretations of Schooling and Classrooms: A Reappraisal.* Driffield: Nafferton Books.

Hargreaves, D.H., Hester, S.K., and Mellow, F.J. (1975) *Deviance in Classrooms.* London: Routledge and Kegan Paul.

Harris, A. (1977) 'Sex and theories of deviance: towards a functional theory of deviant typescripts', *American Sociological Review,* vol. 42, pp. 3–16.

Harris, R., and Webb, D. (1987) *Welfare, Power and Juvenile Justice.* London: Tavistock.

Hart, T. (1977) 'Girls are learning early on in life that violence pays ', in *Evening Standard,* 20 December.

Hartmann, H. (1981) 'The unhappy marriage of Marxism and feminism: towards a more progressive union', in L. Sargent (ed.), *Women and Revolution.* London: Pluto Press.

Hay, D. (1975) 'Property, authority and the criminal law', in D. Hay, P. Linebaugh, J.G. Rule, E.P. Thompson, and C. Winslow, *Albion's Fatal Tree,* Harmondsworth: Penguin.

Heidensohn, F. (1968) 'The deviance of women: a critique and an enquiry', *British Journal of Sociology,* vol. 19, pp. 160–75.

Heidensohn, F. (1970) 'Sex, crime and society' in G. A. Harrison and J. Perl (eds.), *Biosocial Aspects of Sex,* Oxford: Basil Blackwell.

Heidensohn, F. (1985) *Women and Crime,* London: Macmillan (Women in Society Series).

Hemming, J. (1967) *Problems of Adolescent Girls.* London: Heinemann, (First published 1960.)

Henry, J. (1963) *Culture Against Man.* New York: Random House.

Herskowitz, H.A. (1969) 'A psychodynamic view of sexual promiscuity' in O. Pollak and A.S. Friedman (eds.), *Family Dynamics and Female Delinquency.* Palo Alto: Science and Behaviour Books.

Hindelang, M.J. (1979) 'Sex differences in criminal activity', *Social Problems,* vol. 27, pp. 143–56.

Hirschi, T., and Selvin, H.C. (1967) *Delinquency Research: An Appraisal of Analytic Methods.* New York: Wiley.

Hoghughi, M. (1978) *Troubled and Troublesome: Coping with Severely Disordered Children.* London: Burnett.

Home Office. *Criminal Statistics, England and Wales* (Annual Reports). London: HMSO.

Home Office. Advisory Council on the Penal System (1968) *Detention of Girls in a Detention Centre.* Interim Report.

Home Office. Children's Department (1967) *Inspector's Panel on Girls' Approved Schools. Working Party* Report. London.

Hopkins, J. Ellice (1881) *Preventive Work: or The Care of Our Girls.* London: Hatchards (BL).

Hopkins, J. Ellice (1883) *The White Cross Army.* London: Hatchards. (BL)

Houghton, W. E. (1957) *The Victorian Frame of Mind.* New Haven, Conn.: Yale University Press.

Huber, J. (1973) 'Symbolic interaction as a pragmatic perspective: the bias of emergent theory', *American Sociological Review,* vol. 38, pp. 278–84.

Hudson, A. (1983) 'The welfare state and adolescent femininity', *Youth and Policy,* vol. 2 no. 1, pp. 5–13.

Hudson, A. (1985) 'Troublesome girls: towards alternative definitions and policies',

conference paper, European University Institute, Florence.
Hudson, B. (1981) 'Social workers and the discourse of femininity', unpublished paper, Univerisity of Lancaster: Department of Social Administration.
Hudson, B. (1982) 'Femininity and adolescence as mutually subversive discourses', unpublished paper. University of Lancaster: Department of Social Administration.
Hudson, B. (1984) 'Femininity and adolescence', in A. McRobbie and M. Nava (eds.), *Gender and Generation.* London: Macmillan.
Hudson, J. (1975) 'Admission to care', *Social Work Today,* 17 April.
Hudson, J. (1982) 'Observation posts', *Social Work Today,* 13 July.
Humphries, J. (1977) 'Class struggle and the persistence of the working class family', *Cambridge Journal of Economics,* vol. 1 no. 3, pp. 241–58.
Hutter, B., and Williams, G. (eds.) (1981) *Controlling Women: The Normal and the Deviant.* London: Croom Helm in association with Oxford University Women's Studies Committee.
Johnson, N.H. (1977) 'Special problems of the female offender', *Juvenile Justice,* vol. 28 no. 3, pp. 3–10.
Jones, J. Mervyn (1980) *Organisational Aspects of Police Behaviour.* Aldershot: Gower.
Jordanova, I. J. (1981) 'Mental illness, mental health: changing norms and expectations', in Cambridge Women's Studies Group (eds.), *Women in Society.* London: Virago.
Kantner, R. (1972) 'Symbolic interactionism and politics in systematic perspective', *Sociological Inquiry,* vol. 22 nos. 3–4, pp. 77–92.
Karabel, J., and Halsey, A. (1977) *Power and Ideology in Education.* New York: Oxford University Press.
Karslake, E. (1867) *Hansard's Parliamentary Debates,* (HC) vol. CLXXXVII: Col. 833 (May 20), London: Cornelius Buck.
King, P.J.R. (1984) 'Decision-makers and decision-making in the English criminal law, 1750–1800', *Historical Journal,* vol. 27 no. 1, pp. 25–58.
Kingdom, E. (1981) 'Sexist bias and law', in edited volume, *Politics and Power.* London: Routledge and Kegan Paul.
Kitsuse, J. I., and Cicourel, A.V. (1963) 'A note on the use of official statistics', *Social Problems,* vol. 11 no. 2, pp. 131–9.
Klein, D. (1973) 'The etiology of female crime: a review of the literature', *Issues in Criminology,* vol. 8, pp. 3–30.
Klein, D., and Kress, J. (1976) 'Any woman's blues: a critical overview of women, crime and the criminal justice system', *Crime and Social Justice,* vol. 5, pp. 34–49.
Konopka, G. (1966) *The Adolescent Girl in Conflict.* Englewood Cliffs: Prentice-Hall.
Kozuba-Kozubska, J., and Turrell, D. (1978) 'Problems of dealing with girls', *Prison Service Journal,* no. 29, pp. 4–6.
Kratcoski, P.C. (1974) 'Differential treatment of delinquent boys and girls in the Juvenile Court', *Child Welfare,* no. 53. pp. 16–22.
Kress, J. (1979) 'Bourgeois morality and the administration of criminal justice', *Crime and Social Justice,* no. 12, pp. 44–50.
Kuhn, A. (1978) 'Structures of patriarchy and capital in the family', A. Kuhn and A. M. Wolpe (eds.), *Feminism and Materialism. Women and Modes of Production.* London: Routledge and Kegan Paul.
Kuhn, A., and Wolpe, A.M. (1978) 'Feminism and Materialism', in A. Kuhn and A.M. Wolpe (eds.), *Feminism and Materialism. Women and Modes of Production.* London: Routledge and Kegan Paul.

Kuhn, M.H. (1962) 'The interview and the professional relationship', in A.M. Rose (ed.), *Human Behaviour and Social Processes*. London: Routledge and Kegan Paul.

Lacey, C. (1970) *Hightown Grammar*. Manchester: Manchester University Press.

Lacey, C. (1976) 'Problems of sociological fieldwork: a review of the methodology of "Hightown Grammar" ', in M. Shipman (ed.), *The Organization and Impact of Social Research*. London: Routledge and Kegan Paul.

Laing, R.D., and Esterson, A. (1970) *Society, Madness and the Family*. Harmondsworth: Penguin.

Larrain, J. (1979) *The Concept of Ideology*. London: Hutchinson.

Lawson, C. W., and Lockhart, D. (1985) 'The sex distribution of children in care', *Journal of Adolescence*, vol. 8, pp. 167–81.

Leonard, E.B. (1982) *Women, Crime and Society, A Critique of Criminological Theory*. New York and London: Longman.

L'Esperance, J. (1977) 'Doctors and women in nineteenth century society', in J. Woodward and D. Richards (eds.), *Health Care and Popular Medicine in 19th Century England*. London: Croom Helm.

Levin, Y., and Lindesmith, A. (1937) 'English ecology and criminology of the past century', *Journal of Criminology, Criminal Law and Police Science*. vol. 27, pp. 801–16.

Lichteim, G. (1967) *The Concept of Ideology and Other Essays*. New York: Random House.

Lipschitz, S. (1978) 'Women and Psychiatry', in J. Chetwynd and O. Hartnett (eds.), *The Sex Role System*, pp. 93–108. London: Routledge and Kegan Paul.

Lloyd, P.C. (1965) 'The Yoruba of Nigeria', in J.L. Gibbs (ed.), *Peoples of Africa*. New York: R. & W. Holt.

Lombroso, C., and Ferrero, W. (1895) *The Female Offender*. London: Fisher Unwin.

London Intermediate Treatment Association (LITA) (1983) *Eureka* (annual journal). London: LITA.

McCall, C. (1938) *They Always Come Back*. London: Methuen.

Maccoby, E.E. (ed.) (1966) *The Development of Sex Differences*. Stanford, Cal.: Stanford University Press.

MacCormack, C.P., and Strathern, M. (1980) *Nature, Culture and Gender*. Cambridge: Cambridge University Press.

McDonough, R., and Harrison, R. (1978) 'Patriarchy and relations of production', in A. Kuhn and A.M. Wolpe (eds.), *Feminism and Materialism. Women and Modes of Production*. London: Routledge and Kegan Paul.

McIntosh, M. (1974) 'The fifth demand', *Red Rag* (magazine for Women's Liberation) no. 7 pp. 4–5.

McIntosh, M. (1978) 'The state and the oppression of women', in A. Kuhn and A.M. Wolpe (eds), *Feminism and Materialism. Women and Modes of Production*. London: Routledge and Kegan Paul.

McIntosh, M. (1982) 'The family in socialist-feminist politics', in R. Brunt and C. Rowan (eds.), *Feminism, Culture and Politics*. London: Lawrence and Wishart.

MacIntyre, S. (1976) 'Who wants babies? The social construction of "instincts"', in D.L. Barker and S. Allen (eds.), *Sexual Divisions and Society: Process and Change*. London: Tavistock.

Mack, J.A. (1963) 'Police juvenile liaison schemes', *British Journal of Criminology*, vol. 3, pp. 361–75.

McRobbie, A. (1978) 'Working class girls and the culture of femininity', in Women's Studies Group, Centre for Contemporary Cultural Studies, *Women Take Issue*.

London: Hutchinson.

McRobbie, A. (1980) 'Settling accounts with subcultures: a feminist critique', *Screen Education*, vol. 34, pp. 37–49.

McRobbie, A., and McCabe, T. (eds.) (1981) *Feminism for Girls. The Adventure Story*. London: Routledge and Kegan Paul.

McWilliams-Tullberg, R. (1977) 'Women and degrees at Cambridge University, 1862–1897', in M. Vicinus (ed.), *A Widening Sphere: Changing roles of Victorian Women*. Bloomington: Indiana University Press.

Madge, J. (1965) *The Tools of Social Science*. London: Longmans, Green, (first published 1953.)

Manning, P.K. (1967) 'Problems in interpreting interview data', *Sociology and Social Research*, vol. 15, pp. 302–16.

Marcuse, H. (1965) 'Repressive tolerance', in H. Marcuse and R.P. Wolff (eds.), *A Critique of Pure Tolerance*. London: Beacon Press.

Marx, K. (1868) Letter to Kugelmann, 11 July, in K. Marx and F. Engels, *Selected Correspondence*, 1846–1895 (1934) London: Martin Lawrence (translated and edited by Dona Torr) p. 245.

Massie, J. (1758) 'A plan for the establishment of Charity Houses for exposed or deserted women and girls and for penitent prostitutes', London. (BL)

Mawby, R. (1977) 'Sexual discrimination and the law', *Probation Journal*, vol. 24 no. 2, pp. 38–43.

May, D. (1977) 'Delinquent girls before the courts', *Medicine, Science and the Law*, vol. 17, pp. 38–43.

Mayhew, H., and Binny, J. (1862) *The Criminal Prisons of London and Scenes of London Life*. London: Griffin, Bohn (Reprinted Frank Cass, 1968.)

Mayntz, R., Holm, K., and Hoebner, P. (1969) *Introduction to Empirical Sociology*. Harmondsworth: Penguin.

Mead, M. (1935) *Sex and Temperament in Three Primitive Societies*. New York: William Morris. (Published Penguin, 1963).

Menzies, I. (1960) 'Social systems as a defence against anxiety', *Human Relations*, vol. 13, pp. 95–121.

Mepham, J. (1972) 'The theory of ideology in capital', *Radical Philosophy*, no. 2., pp. 12–19.

Merton, R.K. (1957) *Social Theory and Social Structure*, rev. edn. Glencoe, Ill.: Free Press.

Millham, S., Bullock, R., and Cherrett, P. (1975) *After Grace – Teeth*. London: Chaucer.

Mills, C. Wright (1943) 'The professional ideology of social pathologists', *American Journal of Sociology*, vol. 49 no. 2, pp. 165–80.

Mitchell, H. (1974) *Psychoanalysis and Feminism*. London: Allen Lane.

Morgan, D. (1975) *Suffragists and Liberals: The Politics of Woman Suffrage in England*. Oxford: Basil Blackwell.

Morris, A. (1987) *Women, Crime and Criminal Justice*. Oxford: Basil Blackwell.

Morris, A.M., and Gelsthorpe, L.R. (1981) 'False clues and female crime', in A.M. Morris with L.R. Gelsthorpe (eds.), *Women and Crime*, Cropwood Conference series no. 13. University of Cambridge, Institute of Criminology.

Morris, R. (1964) 'Female delinquents and relational problems', *Social Forces*, vol. 43, pp. 82–9.

Morris, T. (1957) *The Criminal Area*, London: Routledge and Kegan Paul.

Moulds, E. (1980) 'Chivalry and paternalism: disparities of treatment in the criminal justice system', in S. Datesman and F. Scarpitti (eds.), *Women, Crime and Justice*.

New York: Oxford University Press.

Nagel, I., Cardascia, J., and Ross, C. (1980) 'Sex differences in the processing of criminal defendants' in D. Kelly Weisberg (ed.), *Women and the Law: an historical perspective*. Cambridge, Massachusetts: Schenkman. Paper presented to UCLA Symposium on International Sexism and Racism, April 1977.

Oakley, A. (1981) *Subject Women*. Oxford: Martin Robertson.

Oliver, I. T. (1978) *The Metropolitan Police Approach to the Prosecution of Juvenile Offenders*, London: Peel Press.

Parker, H. (1974) *View From the Boys*. Newton Abbot: David and Charles.

Parker, H., Casburn, M., and Turnbull, D. (1981) *Receiving Juvenile Justice*. Oxford: Basil Blackwell.

Parliamentary Papers, *Report of the Prison Commissioners*, 1956 (Cmnd. 322, 1957) p. 100; 1957 (Cmnd. 496, 1958)p. 79; 1960 (Cmnd. 1467, 1961) p. 56.

Parsloe, P. (1972) 'Cross-sex comparison in the probation and after-care service', *British Journal of Criminology*, vol. 12, pp. 269–79.

Parsons, T. (1960) *Structure and Process in Modern Societies*. Glencoe Ill.: Free Press.

Pearson, G. (1975) *The Deviant Imagination*. London: Macmillan.

Pearson, R. (1976) 'Women defendants in magistrates' courts', *British Journal of Law and Society*, vol. 3, pp. 265–73.

Perkins, T.E. (1978) 'Rethinking stereotypes', paper presented to British Sociological Association Conference (unpublished).

Petrie, C. (1986) *The Nowhere Girls*. Aldershot: Gower.

Phillipson, M. (1972) 'Phenomenological philosophy and sociology', in P. Filmer et al., (eds.), *New Directions in Sociological Theory*. London: Collier-Macmillan.

Piliavin, I., and Briar, S. (1964) 'Police encounters with juveniles', *American Journal of Sociology*, vol. 70, pp. 206–14.

Pinchbeck, I. (1969) *Women Workers and the Industrial Revolution: 1750–1850*. London: Frank Cass. (First published 1930.)

Pollak, O., and Friedman, A.S. (eds.) (1969) *Family Dynamics and Female Sexual Delinquency*. Palo Alto, Cal.: Science and Behaviour Books.

Pollock, J. (1978) 'Early theories of female criminality', in L.H. Bowker (ed.) *Women, Crime and the Criminal Justice System*. Ann Arbor: Michigan State University Press.

Price, R.R. (1977) 'The forgotten female offender', *Crime and Delinquency*, vol. 23, pp. 101–8.

Priestley, P., Fears, D., and Fuller, R. (1977) *Justice for Juveniles, the 1969 Children and Young Persons Act: a case for reform?* London: Routledge and Kegan Paul.

Procek, E. (1981) 'Psychiatry and the social control of women', in A.M. Morris and L.R. Gelsthorpe (eds.), *Women and Crime*. Cropwood Conference series no.13. University of Cambridge, Institute of Criminology.

Radzinowicz, L. (1966) *Ideology and Crime: A Study of Crime in its Social and Historical Context*. London: Heinemann.

Rafter, N.H., and Natalizia, E.M. (1981) 'Marxist feminism: implications for criminal justice', *Crime and Delinquency* (January), pp. 81–98.

Rasch. C. (1974) 'The female offender as an object of criminological research', *Criminal Justice and Behaviour*, vol. I, no. 4, pp. 301–20.

Reformatory and Refuge Union (1856–1906) (Annual Reports) *Fifty Years Record of Child Saving and Reformatory Work. Jubilee Report*. London. (BL)

Reige, M. (1972) 'Parental affection and juvenile delinquency in girls', *British Journal of Criminology*, vol. 12, pp. 55–73.

Reynolds, D., and Sullivan, M. (1980) 'Towards a new socialist sociology of education', in L. Barton *et al.* (eds.), *Schooling, Ideology and the Curriculum.* Lewes: Falmer Press.

Richardson, H.J. (1969) *Adolescent Girls in Approved Schools.* London: Routledge and Kegan Paul.

Roberts, J. (ed.) (1976) *Beyond Intellectual Sexism.* New York: David McKay.

Rock, P. (1973) *Deviant Behaviour.* London: Hutchinson.

Rock, P. (1977) Review of C. Smart (1976) *Women, Crime and Criminology, British Journal of Criminology,* vol. 17, pp. 392–5.

Rock, P. (1979) *The Making of Symbolic Interactionism.* London: Macmillan.

Rock, P. (1979) 'The sociology of crime, symbolic interactionism and some problematic qualities of radical criminology', in D. Downes and P. Rock (eds.), *Deviant Interpretations. Problems in Criminological Theory.* Oxford: Martin Robertson.

Rolph, C.H. (ed.) (1955) *Women of the Streets: a Sociological Study of the Common Prostitute.* London: Secker and Warburg.

Rosaldo, M.Z., and Lamphere, L. (eds.) (1974)*Women, Culture and Society,* Stanford, Cal.: Stanford University Press.

Rose, G. (1967) *Schools for Young Offenders.* London: Tavistock.

Rose, S.P.R., and Rose, H. (1973) 'Do not adjust your mind, there is a fault in reality – ideology in neural biology', *Cognition,* no. 2, pp. 479–502.

Rubin, G. (1975) 'The traffic in women, notes on the "political economy" of sex', in R. Reiter (ed.), *Towards an Anthropology of Women.* New York; Monthly Review Press.

Rubington, E., and Weinberg, M.S. (1968)*Deviance: The Interactionist Perspective.* London: Collier-Macmillan.

Sachs, A., and Wilson, J. Hoff (1978) *Sexism and the Law. A Study of Male Beliefs and Legal Bias in Britain and the United States.* Oxford: Martin Robertson.

Sacks, H. (1972) 'Notes on police assessment of moral character', in D. Sudnow (ed.) *Studies in Social Interaction.* New York: Free Press.

Sargent, L. (ed.) (1981) *Women and Revolution: The Unhappy Marriage of Marxism and Feminism.* London: Pluto Press.

Sayers, J. (1982) *Biological Politics.* London: Tavistock.

Schofield, P. (1965) *The Sexual Behaviour of Young People.* Harmondsworth: Penguin.

Schumpeter, J.A. (1955) *History of Economic Analysis.* London: George Allen and Unwin. (First published in 1954.)

Schutz, A. (1962) *Collected Papers,* vol. 1: *The Problems of Social Reality.* The Hague: Martinus Nijhoff.

Scott, M., and Lyman, S. (1968) 'Accounts', *American Sociological Review,* vol. 33, pp. 46–62.

Seccombe, W. (1974) 'The housewife and her labour under capitalism', *New Left Review,* no. 83, pp. 3–24.

Shacklady Smith, L. (1975) 'Female delinquency and social reaction', unpublished paper presented at the Women and Deviancy Conference (Spring), University of Essex.

Shacklady Smith, L. (1978) 'Sexist assumptions and female delinquency: an empirical investigation', in C. Smart and B. Smart (eds.), *Women, Sexuality and Social Control.* London: Routledge and Kegan Paul.

Sharp, R., and Green, A., with Lewis, J. (1975) *Education and Social Control.* London: Routledge and Kegan Paul.

Sharpe, S. (1976) *Just Like a Girl. How Girls Learn to be Women*, Harmondsworth: Penguin.

Shibutani, T. (1955) 'Reference groups as perspectives', *American Journal of Sociology*, vol. 60, pp. 562–9.

Silverman, D. (1970) *The Theory of Organisation*. London: Heinemann.

Silverman, D. (1974) 'Accounts of organisations – organisational "structures" and the accounting process', in J. McKinlay (ed.), *Processing People: Cases in Organisational Behaviour*. London: Holt, Rinehart and Winston.

Simon, R. (1975) *Sisters In Crime*. New York: McGraw Hill.

Smart, C. (1976) *Women, Crime and Criminology: A Feminist Critique*. London: Routledge and Kegan Paul.

Smart, C. (1977) 'Criminological theory: its ideology and implications concerning women', *British Journal of Sociology*, vol. 28, pp. 89–100.

Smart, C. (1981) 'Law and the control of women's sexuality: the case of the 1950s', in B. Hutter and G. Williams, *Controlling Women*. London: Croom Helm in association with Oxford University Women's Studies Committee.

Smart, C. (1983) 'Patriarchal relations and law: an examination of family law and sexual equality in the 1950s', in M. Evans and C. Ungerson (eds.), *Sexual Divisions: Patterns and Processes*. London: Tavistock.

Smart, C. (1984) *The Ties that Bind: Law, Marriage and the Reproduction of Patriarchal Relations:* London: Routledge and Kegan Paul.

Smith, D. (1973) 'Symbolic interactionism: definitions of the situation from H. Becker to J. Lofland', *Catalyst*, no. 7 (Winter), pp. 62–75.

Smith, G. (1973) 'Ideologies, beliefs and patterns of administration in the organisation of social work practice: a study with special reference to the concept of social need', Ph.D. thesis, University of Aberdeen (unpublished).

Smith, J.M. (1972) *Interviewing in Market and Social Research*. London: Routledge and Kegan Paul.

Society for Organising Charitable Relief (1888) *Guide to Schools, Homes and Refuges in England for the Benefit of Girls and Women*. London. (BL)

Stanley, L. (1981) 'The problem of women and leisure – an ideological construct and a radical feminist alternative', in Centre for Leisure Studies (ed.) *Leisure in the 80s*. University of Salford.

Stanley, L., and Wise, S. (1983) *Breaking Out: Feminist Consciousness and Feminist Research*, London: Routledge and Kegan Paul.

Stanworth, M. (1983) *Gender and Schooling. A Study of Sexual Divisions in the Classroom*. London: Hutchinson in association with the Explorations in Feminism Collective.

Stott, D.H. (1950) *Delinquency and Human Nature*. Dunfermline: Carnegie Trust.

Strauss, A., Schatzman, L., Bucher, B., Ehrlich, D., and Sabhin, M. (1964) *Psychiatric Ideologies and Institutions*. London: Collier-Macmillan.

Sumner, C.S. (1979) *Reading Ideologies*. London: Academic Press.

Sumner, M. (1980) 'Prostitution and images of women: a critique of the Victorian censure of prostitution', unpublished M.Sc. thesis, University of Wales.

Tappan, P.W. (1969) *Delinquent Girls in Court: A Study of the Wayward Minor Court of New York*. Montclair, New Jersey: Patterson Smith.

Taylor, I., Walton, P., and Young, J. (1973) *The New Criminology*. London: Routledge and Kegan Paul.

Taylor, I., Walton, P., and Young, J. (eds.) (1975) *Critical Criminology*. London: Routledge and Kegan Paul.

Taylor, J. (1975) Review article, 'Pre-capitalist modes of production', *Critique of*

Anthropology, no. 4/5, pp. 127–54.

Temin, C.E. (1973) 'Discriminatory sentencing of women offenders. The argument for ERA in a nutshell', *American Criminal Law Review* vol.11, (Winter), pp. 355–72.

Terry, R.M. (1970) 'Discrimination in the handling of juvenile offenders by social control agencies', in P.G. Garabedian and D.C. Gibbons (eds.), *Becoming Delinquent*. New York: Aldine Press.

Thorpe, D.H., Smith, D., Green, C.J., and Paley, J.H. (1980) *Out of Care: The Community Support of Juvenile Offenders*. London: George Allen and Unwin.

Turner, B. (1974) *Equality for Some*. London: Ward Lock.

Tutt, N. S. (1974) *Care or Custody*. London: Darton, Longman and Todd.

Tutt, N.S. (1977) 'The philosophy of observation and assessment' paper prepared for DHSS Seminar on Use and Development of O and A Centres for Children.

Vedder, G.B., and Somerville, D.B. (1970) *The Delinquent Girl*, Springfield, Illinois: Charles C. Thomas.

Velimesis, M. (1975) 'The female offender', *Crime and Delinquency Literature*, vol. 7 no. 1 (March), pp. 94–112.

Vicinus, M. (ed.) (1977) *A Widening Sphere: Changing Roles of Victorian Women*. Bloomington: Indiana University Press.

Volkart, E. (ed.) (1951) *Social Behaviour and Personality*. New York: Social Science Research Council.

Von Hayek, F.A. (ed.) (1942) J.S. Mill, *The Spirit of the Age*. Chicago University of Chicago.

Wadsworth, M. (1979) *Roots of Delinquency: Infancy, Adolescence and Crime*. Oxford: Martin Robertson.

Walker, A. (1962) 'Special problems of delinquents and maladjusted girls', *Howard Journal of Penology and Crime Prevention*, vol. xi, pp. 26–36.

Walker, N.D. (1965) *Crime and Punishment in Britain*. Edinburgh: University of Edinburgh Press.

Walker, N.D. (1966) 'A century of causal theory', in H. Klare and D. Haxby (eds.), *Frontiers of Criminology*. London: Pergamon.

Walker, N.D. (1973) *Crime and Punishment in Britain*. Edinburgh: University of Edinburgh Press.

Walker, N.D. (1974) 'Lost Causes in Criminology', in R.G. Hood (ed.), *Crime, Criminology and Public Policy*. London: Heinemann.

Walsh, J.L. (1977) 'Career styles and police behaviour', in D.H. Bayley (ed.), *Police and Society*. Beverley Hills: Sage.

Walter, J.A. (1977) 'A critique of sociological studies of approved schools', *British Journal of Criminology*, vol. 17, pp. 361–9.

Walter, J.A. (1978) *Sent Away: A Study of Young Offenders in Care*. Farnborough, Hants: Saxon House.

Warnock Report (1978) Committee of Enquiry into the Education of Handicapped Children and Young People. *Report*, (Cmnd. 7212), Special educational needs (chairman, H. Mary Warnock), Department of Education and Science, Scottish Education Department, Welsh Office. London: HMSO.

Warren, W. (1961) 'Behaviour disorders in girls', *Approved Schools Gazette*, vol. 55 no. 6, pp. 237–43.

Webb, D. (1984) 'More on gender and justice: girl offenders on supervision' *Sociology*, vol. 3, pp. 367–81.

Weber, M. (1947) *The Theory of Social and Economic Organisations*, trns. T. Parsons, New York: Free Press.

West, D.J. (1967) *The Young Offender.* Harmondsworth: Penguin.
West D.J., and Farrington, D.P. (1977) *The Delinquent Way of Life.* London: Heinemann.
White, S. (1972) 'The effect of social inquiry reports on sentencing decisions', *British Journal of Criminology,* vol. 12, pp. 230–49.
Wiles, P. (1971) 'Criminal statistics and sociological explanations', in W.G. Carson and P. Wiles (eds.), *Crime and Delinquency in Britain.* Oxford: Martin Robertson.
Wilkins, L.T. (1964) *Social Deviance: Social Policy, Action and Research.* London: Tavistock.
Williams, R. (1973) *Base and Superstructure in Marxist Cultural Theory.* London: New Left Books.
Willis, P. (1977) *Learning to Labour.* Farnborough, Hants. Saxon House.
Wilson, D. (1978) 'Sexual codes and conduct: a study of teenage girls', in C. Smart and B. Smart (eds.), *Women, Sexuality and Social Control.* London: Routledge and Kegan Paul.
Winship, J. (1978) 'A woman's world: woman – an ideology of femininity', in Women's Studies Group, Centre for Contemporary Cultural Studies, *Women Take Issue.* London: Hutchinson.
Wiseman, J.P. (1970) *Stations of the Lost: The Treatment of Skid Row Alcoholics.* Englewood Cliffs: Prentice-Hall.
Wittgenstein, L. (1971) *Tractatus Logico-Philosophicus.* London: Routledge and Kegan Paul.
Wolfgang, M.E., Savitz, L., and Johnston, N. (1979) *The Sociology of Crime and Delinquency,* 2nd edn. New York: John Wiley.
Wolpe, A.M. (1974) 'The official ideology of education for girls', in M. Flude and J. Ahier (eds.), *Educationality, School and Ideology.* London: Croom Helm.
Woodward, J., and Richards, D. (eds.) (1977) *Health Care and Popular Medicine in 19th Century England.* London: Croom Helm.
Wootton, B.F. (1959 *Social Science and Social Pathology.* London: George Allen and Unwin.
Worrall, A.J. (1981) 'Out of place: female offenders in court', *Probation Journal,* vol. 28 (September), pp. 90–3.
Wright, Sir A.E. (1913) *The Unexpurgated Case Against Woman Suffrage.* London: Constable.
Young, G.M. (1960) *Portrait of an Age,* 2nd edn. Oxford: Oxford University Press.
Young, J. (1971) 'The role of the police as amplifiers of deviancy, negotiators of reality and translators of fantasy: some consequences of our present system of drug control as seen in Notting Hill', in S. Cohen (ed.), *Images of Deviance.* Harmondsworth: Penguin.
Young, K., and Harris, O. (1976) 'The subordination of women in cross cultural perspectives', in Women's Publishing Collective (eds.), *Papers on Patriarchy.* Brighton: Women's Publishing Collective.
Young, M.F.D. (1971) *Knowledge and Control.* London: Collier Macmillan.
Young, R.M. (1977) 'Science as social relations', *Radical Science Journal,* vol. 5, pp. 65–131.
Zimmerman, D.H. (1974) 'Fact as a practical accomplishment', in R. Turner (ed.), *Ethnomethodology.* Harmondsworth: Penguin.

Index